Library of
Davidson College

AN ANTHOLOGY OF EIGHTEENTH-CENTURY SATIRE

Grub-Street

AN ANTHOLOGY OF EIGHTEENTH-CENTURY SATIRE

Grub-Street

Edited with an Introduction by
Peter Heaney

The Edwin Mellen Press
Lewiston/Queenston/Lampeter

Library of Congress Cataloging-in-Publication Data

An anthology of Eighteenth-Century satire : Grub-Street / edited with an introduction by Peter Heaney.
    p.   cm.
Includes bibliographical references and index.
ISBN 0-7734-9026-4
  1. English literature--18th century. 2. Satire, English.
3. Verse satire, English. 4. Popular culture--England--London--History--18th century. 5. London (England)--Social life and customs--18th century. I. Heaney, Peter.
PR1135.A58 1994
827'.508--dc20   94-26075
                                                                                                    CIP

A CIP catalog record for this book is available from the British Library.

Copyright © 1995 The Edwin Mellen Press

All rights reserved. For information contact

The Edwin Mellen Press	The Edwin Mellen Press
Box 450	Box 67
Lewiston, New York	Queenston, Ontario
USA 14092-0450	CANADA L0S 1L0

The Edwin Mellen Press, Ltd.
Lampeter, Dyfed, Wales
UNITED KINGDOM SA48 7DY

Printed in the United States of America

For My Parents

CONTENTS

	Acknowledgements	
	Introduction	1
Ned Ward	A Frolick to Horn-Fair	27
Daniel Defoe:	The Shortest-Way with the Dissenters or Proposals for the Establishment of the Church	37
Tom Brown	The Old Fumbler	49
	The Poet's Condition	50
	Farewell to Poor England	51
Jonathan Swift	A Digression concerning the Original, the Use and Improvement of Madness in a Commonwealth (from *A Tale of a Tub*)	55
John Arbuthnot	The History of John Bull, Or Law is a Bottomless Pit	69
Alexander Pope	A Full and True Account of A Horrid and Barbarous Revenge by Poison on the Body of Mr. Edmund Curll, Bookseller	81
	A Further Account of the Most Deplorable Condition of Mr. Edmund Curll, Bookseller	88
John Arbuthnot	The Memoirs of Martinus Scriblerus	˙95
Jonathan Swift	Advice to the Grub-street Verse-Writers	115
	A Satirical Elegy on the Death of a Late Famous General	116
Alexander Pope	The Dunciad (Book II)	119
Anon	Apollo's Maggot in his Cups	137
Richard Savage	An Author to Be Lett	157
Leonard Welsted	One Epistle to Mr. A. Pope	169
Jonathan Swift	A Modest Proposal for Preventing the Children of poor People in Ireland, from being a Burden to their Parents or Country	179
Colley Cibber	Ode for New-Years-Day	189
Anon	Ode humbly inscrib'd to the Poet Laureat	191
Colley Cibber	Ode for New-Year's-Day 1732	193

Anon	The Poet Laureat's Ode for New-Year's-Day burlesqu'd	195
John Arbuthnot	Epitaph on Francis Charteris	197
Anon	Epigram the Second: Of Merit Deserted	201
Anon	The Blatant-Beast	203
Anon	Sawney and Colley	213
	Bibliography	229
	Index	233

Acknowledgements

All the sources for items selected for this anthology are given due acknowledgement in the footnotes accompanying the texts. Some of these are modern editions; for example, I have consulted the editions of Swift's poems (edited by Herbert Davis, Oxford, 1967) and Pope's poems (edited by John Butt, RKP, 1992). For a number of pieces that have not become part of the literary canon (and are unlikely to do so), I have found especially valuable the Augustan Reprint Society's facsimile editions - notably some of the anonymous poems included in the Anthology, and *À Letter from Mr. Cibber to Mr. Pope.* Particular acknowledgement should also be made to Professor Pat Rogers for his *Grub Street: Studies in a Subculture* (Methuen, 1972). Thanks are due to the British Library and Staffordshire Library for their courtesy and assistance; also to Ian Watt, of Staffordshire University Computing Services Unit for his help and patience.

INTRODUCTION

Grub Street, in the early eighteenth century, was an actual location[1] in the seedier and seamier part of London. Here were crumbling tenements and the Fleet Ditch, an open sewer, from whose 'disemboguing streams/Rolls the large tribute of dead dogs to Thames'.[2] The derivation of the name is (probably) from 'grube', a ditch or drain. Earliest forms found are 'Grobstrat' and 'Grobbestrate', both twelfth century.[3] There is, therefore, an obvious connection between garbage, sewage, and the life-styles and literary practices of the eighteenth-century inhabitants of Grub Street (so the satirists insisted, anyway). Certainly Fleet Ditch is a significant topographical and symbolic feature in the writings of Pope and others. It was, according to one observer in 1722, 'a nauceious and abominable sink of nastiness' into which the tripe-dressers and sausage-makers flung their offal.[4] T.F. Reddaway's description of attempts made to clean up the Ditch is worth quoting at some length:

> In former times [up to the early sixteenth century] the Fleet river had been navigable up to Holborn Bridge, but as the years passed it had gradually deteriorated into a shallow and evil-smelling sewer. Navigation had ceased, and, in the middle of the seventeenth century, a not overparticular age, its condition had been described as 'very stinking and noisome'. Silt from the upper reaches, and mud and refuse from the growing streets in its valley

---

[1] See Pat Rogers's account in *Grub Street: Studies in a Subculture* (Methuen, 1972).
[2] *The Dunciad*, II, 271-2.
[3] R. Paulson, *Theme and Structure in Swift's Tale of a Tub* (Princeton, 1960, p.170); corroborated by the earlier work of H.B. Wheatley, *London Past and Present* (John Murray, 1891, 3 vols, ii. 166).
[4] D.M. George, *London Life in the Eighteenth Century* (Penguin, 1966, p. 94).)

had gradually choked it, with the result that, despite occasional cleansings, its condition more or less regularly troubled the minds of those in authority. During the reign of James I various projects had been put forward for clearing out accumulations down to the true floor of the channel, embanking its sides with brick,stone or timber, and then flushing it out at intervals from a reservoir constructed above Clerkenwell. The most detailed had envisaged grates on the upper waters to intercept debris and silt, a warden to remove carrion and bulky matter [such as Pope's 'dead dogs'] when the tide was out, and a vast grate at Bridewell to stop the Thames bringing up filth on the rising tide. Little seems to have come of them, and as the years passed an expanding population had added to the difficulties. The Commission of Sewers (in 1653)...clearly set out the evils which had arisen from this last cause. The river, they declared, from Hockley in the Hole to the Thames, was 'by many encroachments thereupon made by keeping of Hogs and Swine therein and elsewhere neer to it, the throwing in it of Offals and Garbage...become unpassable with boats [and a] very...great prejudice not only to the neighbourhood...but to the City of *London* and County of Middlesex.'[5]

This was the 'neighbourhood' which was the haunt of pimps and prostitutes; the home of booksellers, publishers, poets and a whole miscellany of writers. Fleet Street itself was adjacent to, and ran across, the Ditch; the 'houses of correction', Newgate and Bridewell were close by, as were Bedlam and Billingsgate (also now a part of the language in their own right). It would not be surprising, then, to discover poverty and squalor in this part of London; poverty, indeed, seems to inspire little sympathy from lofty commentators such as Dr Johnson, and wealthy brother-writers (like Pope) who lived in the more salubrious areas of the city. As Pat Rogers points out,[6] one of the changes Pope made to the final version of *The Dunciad* (1743) was to move the location of part of Book I from near Rag Fair to a place near to Bedlam. One reason was to make possible a further stab at Colley Cibber (see below for Pope v Cibber). Another, evidently, was to introduce poverty, metaphorically and literally - there was a point to be made. The point is in this passage from the poem:

> Close to those walls [Bedlam] where Folly holds her throne,
> And laughs to think Monroe would take her down,
> Where o'er the gates, by his fam'd father's hand
> Great Cibber's brazen, brainless brothers stand;
> One Cell there is, conceal'd from vulgar eye,

---

[5] T.F. Reddaway, Quoted by Pat Rogers, *Grub Street*, p. 147.
[6] Ibid pp. 56-7.

> The Cave of Poverty and Poetry.
> Keen, hollow winds howl thro' the bleak recess,
> Emblem of Music caus'd by Emptiness.
> Hence Bards, like Proteus long in vain ty'd down,
> Escape in Monsters, and amaze the town.
> Hence Miscellanies spring, the weekly boast
> Of Curl's chaste press, and Lintot's rubric post:
> Hence hymning Tyburn's elegiac lines,
> Hence Journals, Medleys, Merc'ries, Magazines:
> Sepulchral Lyes, our holy walls to grace,
> And New-year Odes, and all the Grub-street race (I. 29-44).

Locating this episode near Bedlam is more than a gratuitous insult to the Poet Laureate. It is placing Grub Street (which *was* close to Bedlam) amongst the insane, to start with. More, it is associating 'Dulness' (the Dunces' permanent condition) with poverty: 'Close to the walls' of Bedlam is the 'Cave of Poverty and Poetry'. It is from here that the creations of Grub Street - 'Monsters' of literary deformity - escape from the darkness of the cave and terrify the town. These monstrosities are 'Miscellanies'; newspapers like the *Medley* and the *Mercury*. All are born in the Cave of Poverty - they are the children of Poverty. Does Pope infer poverty of intellect only? A note to *The Dunciad Variorum* (the second edition of the poem, with notes, 1729), suggests otherwise. The 'scandalous rhimes, scurrilous weekly papers' and all the myriad other effusions from Grub Street can be imputed 'not so much to Malice or Servility as to Dulness; and not so much to Dulness as to Necessity'.[7] Necessity may be the mother of invention; but that was no excuse, so far as Pope was concerned, for the production of literary garbage. Samuel Johnson was a little more charitable towards the needy poet, when that poet was judged by Johnson to be a 'man of exalted sentiments' and 'extensive views'.[8] It was also, of course, a matter of class (not that Johnson would have made use of such terminology); Richard Savage, the subject of one of Johnson's *Lives*, evidently lived much as many another Grub-Street hack:

> He lodged as much by accident as he dined, and passed the night in mean houses, which are set open at night to casual wanderers, sometimes in

---

[7] *The Poems of Alexander Pope* (the Twickenham edition in one volume, ed. John Butt, Methuen, 1963, reprinted by Routledge, 1992, p. 353).
[8] His description of Richard Savage in his *Life of Savage*, 1744 (in *Johnson's Lives of the English Poets*, George Birkbeck Hill, Oxford, 1905, reprinted by Octagon Books, 1967, 3 vols, ii, p.399).

cellars, among the riot and filth of the meanest and most profligate of the rabble; and sometimes, when he had not money to support even the expences of these receptacles, walked about the street until he was weary, and lay down in the summer upon a bulk,[9] or in the winter, with his associates in poverty, among the ashes of a glass-house.[10]

Savage was tolerated by Johnson partly on account of his poetic pretensions, partly because he was of genteel stock. He was, moreover, almost a friend of Pope's, and invaluable as the bearer of inside information on the doings of Grub Street. (He thus escaped inclusion in *The Dunciad*.) His *Author to be Lett* (1729, q.v.), an account of the life and miseries of a half-starved scribbler, has too much authentic detail to be wholly fiction. But even he has little sympathy for the poverty of the hack-writers whose company he perforce kept in the meaner parts of London. Like Pope, he tends to associate material poverty with intellectual deprivation.

The rise of Grub Street can be traced to the lapsing of the Licensing Act in 1695. Where previously all publications had to be given the Government imprimatur, after 1695 the stopper was removed from the bottle. A flood of newspapers and periodicals was the result, and Grub Street was born. Its inhabitants - those who wrote for the infant publications - were a new breed of writer: their living was what they earned from their writing. They were, therefore, in the view of writers such as Swift and Pope, hired pens, mercenaries. It was no use John Oldmixon (one of Pope's victims in *The Dunciad*) protesting the purity of his motives: '[I have] never written a word in Vindication of any particular Person or Persons, nor of any measures, but what I thought tended to promote the publick Interest, Security, and Peace.'[11] He accepted payment for his efforts; he was therefore beneath the contempt of gentlemen-writers such as Swift and Pope - he was a hack.[12]

The *Oxford English Dictionary* defines Grub Street (quoting Samuel Johnson's Dictionary in testimony), thus: 'The name of a street near Moorfields in London (now Milton Street), "much inhabited by writers of small histories, dictionaries and temporary poems" (J.); hence used allusively for the tribe of mean and needy

---

[9] Defined by Johnson as 'a part of a building, jutting out'.
[10] From the *Life of Savage*, in *Lives of the Poets*, p. 398.
[11] *Memoirs of the Press, Historical and Political, For Thirty Years past, from 1710 to 1740* (London, 1742)
[12] 'Hack': short for 'hackney' (as in 'hackney carriage'). 'A literary drudge, who hires himself out to do any and every kind of literary work; hence, a poor writer, a mere scribbler' (*OED*).

authors, or literary hacks.' It was not until the seventeenth century that the name was used as a term of abuse. The first known reference of this kind was in 1630 by John Taylor, the 'Water-Poet' (cited, again, by the *OED*): 'When strait I might descry, The Quintessence of Grubstreet well distild.' In his *The Rehearsal Transpros'd* (1672), Andrew Marvell refers to a bishop: 'He, honest Man, was deep gone in Grubstreet and Polemical Divinity.' Similarly, in the same work, there is: 'Oh, these are your Nonconformist Tricks; Oh, you have learnt this of the Puritans in Grub Street.' Johnson's rather more precise use of the expression to denote literary unworthiness, however, is not found until the end of the seventeenth century. John Arbuthnot, of whom more will be said later, apostrophised (ironically) thus: 'O Grubstreet! thou fruitful Nursery of tow'ring Genius!'[13] For Swift, literary mainstay of the Harley-St John administration (1710-14), the enemy were 'those devils of Grubstreet rogues...always mauling lord treasurer, lord Bolingbroke [St John] and me. We have the dog under prosecution....'[14] Here we have, in essence, the position adopted by those who saw themselves as the Guardians of high culture: Grub Street was seen as a teeming ant-heap of illiterate scribblers. It was an extraordinary period in publishing and literary history - the early eighteenth century saw the arrival of the professional writer, in numbers. It was a prospect unpleasing to some.

Our contemporary use of 'Grub-Street' and 'hack' as terms of contempt is an uncritical adoption of Pope's view of his enemies as literary prostitutes and mercenaries. Pope depicted the denizens of Grub Street as

> A low-born, cell-bred, selfish, servile band,
> Prompt or to guard or stab, to saint or damn,
> Heav'n's Swiss, who fight for any God, or man.[15]

These were men (and women - a few) who were allied to the myriad booksellers, printers and publishers who mushroomed at the end of the seventeenth century. Notable amongst these were several of Pope's literary and political enemies; it would seem, however, that to be a bookseller was to be, ex-officio, a Dunce.[16] So,

---

[13] From the Preface to *Law is a Bottomless Pit*, the first part of his *History of John Bull*, 1712 (q.v.).
[14] *Journal to Stella*, October 28, 1712.
[15] *The Dunciad*, II, 356-8
[16] Pat Rogers, *Grub Street*, p. 206.

in *The Dunciad*, Pope has his publishers doing hilariously silly things, like diving in the Fleet Ditch in search of mud (to throw at their opponents, but also to publish in the newspapers). Here it is the Goddess of the Dunces who speaks:

> 'Here strip, my children! here at once leap in,
> Here prove who best can dash thro' thick and thin,
> And who the most in love of dirt excel,
> Or dark dexterity of groping well.
> Who flings most filth, and wide pollutes around
> The stream, be his the Weekly Journals bound...'[17]

It is a measure of Pope's contempt for the activities of his brother scribblers that he has the 'Weekly Journals' (the *Post-Boy*, the *Medley*, the *Flying-Post* etc.) as a joke prize for the winner of the mud-diving, filth-flinging contest. He did not regard them as his 'brothers', of course: their pursuit of filthy lucre by whatever (literary) means presented themselves was a debasement and a betrayal of literature. To have to earn one's living by writing was little short of shameful. So Swift laments that John Gay was not found office by Walpole's ministry in the 1720s: 'Tis a woeful Case to be under the necessity of writing a Play for Bread when perhaps a Mans Genius is not at that time disposed. I am sure it is an ill way of making a good Poet.'[18] When Swift was offered payment by the ministry of Robert Harley for services rendered (Swift was a one-man propaganda machine), he angrily declined it. His was not a pen to be bought.[19]

It was an anachronistic stance, however. Books were sold and writers were paid, though usually not much. Gay, despite his status as a 'gentleman-writer', made his living at least partly from his plays and poems. He, exceptionally, was made rich by the success of *The Beggar's Opera* in 1728.[20] Literature, moreover,

---

[17] *The Dunciad*, Book II (q.v., in the present volume), 274-280.

[18] Swift to Charles Ford, 13 February, 1724 (*The Correspondence of Jonathan Swift*, ed. Harold Williams, in 5 vols, Oxford, 1963-5, iii. 6).

[19] Not that Swift did not have hopes that his efforts for the Tory administration of 1710-14 would eventually bear fruit - his ambitions were for a bishopric in England. His reward, however, was the Deanery of St Patrick's, Dublin, and all the bitterness of what Swift saw as exile.

[20] Gay was paid over £700 for *The Beggar's Opera*; the sequel, *Polly*, though banned from the stage, brought in £1200 in book form (*DNB*). Others were less fortunate. In 1723, Curll paid four guineas for the sole rights to a treatise *In Praise of Drunkenness* (a literary gem discussed later in the Introduction), and ten guineas for one of his notorious 'Memoirs' - the victim on this occasion being Bishop Atterbury. (Information from Ralph Straus's 'Handlist' of books published by or for

Introduction

increasingly came to be seen as a commodity, to be bought and sold like any other commodity, in the practice of those publishers and booksellers,[21] who, to Pope, constituted Grub Street. (Some of these purveyors of literary merchandise used highly dubious methods to sell their wares, none more disreputable than the notorious Edmund Curll, of whom more will be said later). Pope, sufficiently successful to be contemptuous of their writing and publishing practices, was a frequent target; his revenge was to put them all in *The Dunciad*. His lofty stance as protector of the genteel occupation of the writer was not altogether honest, however. Subscriptions for his translations of Homer (the *Iliad*, completed in 1720, and the *Odyssey*, in 1726) made Pope a wealthy man.[22] It escaped Pope's notice that his commercial exploitation of literature was in effect no different from that of his Grub Street enemies. It was perhaps also a little ungenerous of him to include Bernard Lintot, the bookseller, amongst the contending dunces in *The Dunciad*: it was Lintot who helped Pope acquire his fortune from his translations.

Pope's onslaught on the hacks and dunces in *The Dunciad* was more than a paying-off of old scores - though it certainly was that. The poem is an overt political and aesthetic statement, an attack on the Whig hegemony led by Walpole. George I and George II are seen as the figureheads of the new Age of Dulness: 'Still Dunce the second reigns like Dunce the first.'[23] (George II is reported to have had no very high opinion of Pope either: 'who is this Pope that I hear so much about? I cannot discover what is his merit. Why will not my subjects write in prose?')[24] In so designating the two Georges as twin pillars of Dulness,[25] Pope was laying the foundations for his apocalyptic view of the impending demise of literature and civilisation. Both Georges were indeed notorious for their philistinism, and the monarch naturally set the tone for the court. In Book IV of *The*

Curll, in *The Unspeakable Curll*, first published in 1927 by Chapman and Hall, reprinted by Augustus M. Kelley, 1970, p. 273.)
21 The terms 'bookseller' and 'publisher' were almost synonymous in the early eighteenth century. 'Stationer' was another variant.
22 There were 575 subscribers for the *Iliad*, 610 for the *Odyssey*; these were not huge numbers - what mattered what the *quality* of the subscribers. Pope's two translations earned him £11,000. See Pat Rogers, 'The Writer and Society', pp. 50-53, *The Eighteenth Century* (Methuen, 1978).
23 *The Dunciad*, I, 6.
24 Sir James Prior, *Life of Edmund Malone...with Selections from his MSS Anecdotes* (1860). George had other literary opinions, too: 'I hear a great deal, too, of Shakespeare, but I cannot read him, he is such a *bombast* fellow' (same source).
25 Pope's term, in *The Dunciad*, for what he deemed to be the intellectual vapidity of Grub Street.

Dunciad, moreover, Prime Minister Walpole is put at the helm of this ghastly ship of state, steering it to cultural oblivion. But Pope's fear for the future of literature was also a reaction to the growth of the newspaper trade,[26] a rising tide of what Pope evidently saw as bourgeois rubbish. More particularly, it was the mercantile nature of the enterprise which offended Pope and his friends. And the entrepreneurial Whigs, under Walpole, represented a threat to the old, aristocratic order with which Pope, Swift and Gay associated themselves. As Brean Hammond argues, '[*The Dunciad*] and Scriblerian Satire generally, constructs as target a new type of writer...whose relations with the public are those of the market and whose art is merely a species of production quite on the level with any other: art as trade.'[27]

Grub Street (and all its doings) was therefore much more than a personal irritant, a thorn in the flesh of successful writers like Pope. Grub Street was the battleground of a fiercely fought war between the old literary and social order, and a new, uncompromising commercialism. It was a fairly bloody encounter, especially in Queen Anne's reign, but also in the Walpole-dominated decades that followed. The violence of the literary war was in many ways a reflection of the political turbulence of the early eighteenth century. (See below for further comment on the literary and publishing manifestations of this warfare.) Swift regretted the rage of party, while contributing to it; the growth of party loyalties was a significant feature of Queen Anne's reign,[28] as were the dangers attendant on political life. In addition to the immediate personal hazards (for example, Robert Harley, by then created Earl of Oxford - Lord Treasurer/Prime Minister - was stabbed and severely wounded[29] during a meeting of the Committee of Council in 1711), there was the continual threat posed by the Pretender. (After the death of Anne and the fall of the Tories in 1714, former Secretary of State Bolingbroke and Lord Treasurer Oxford were both impeached, accused of treasonous dealings with the Pretender. Bolingbroke escaped to France, Oxford spent two years in the Tower before being released.)

---

26 Fewer than 50,000 newspapers were sold per week in 1700; by 1760, the figure was around 200,000 (Rogers, op. cit., p. 42).
27 'Guard the Barrier Sure', in *Pope, New Contexts*, ed. D. Fairer (Harvester Wheatsheaf, 1990), p. 230.
28 See G. Holmes, *British Politics in the Age of Anne* (London, 1967), and B.W. Hill, *The Growth of Parliamentary Parties, 1689-1742* (London, 1976).
29 An account of this incident is given by Angus McInnes in *Robert Harley* (Gollanz, 1970), pp. 151-3.

Introduction

The Whigs were solidly behind the Hanoverian Succession; many Tories were rather more ambivalent, preferring to keep their options open, or actively seeking the return of the Stuart line. There was, of course, the Rebellion of 1715 to keep anxieties (and ambitions) alive. Not surprisingly, the political uncertainties of the time manifested themselves in violent party faction. This violence found expression in the organs of propaganda which mushroomed on both sides of the argument: the *Post-Boy*, the *Medley*, the *Political State of Great Britain*, the *Flying Post*, the *Examiner*, the *Observator* (and others), all appeared during Queen Anne's reign. Also, not surprisingly, the major writers of the period can be found lined up - more or less - behind the powerful figures and their parties on both sides of the political divide. For example, Swift, Pope, Arbuthnot, Gay (and other members of the Scriblerus Club - see below) gave support, in one form or another, to the Tories; Addison, Steele and Defoe were amongst those who allied themselves with the Whigs. Lesser mortals there were a-plenty who added their pennyworth, not necessarily from mercenary motives,[30] whatever Pope might insinuate to the contrary.

It is precisely this turbulence and unruliness which we, at our distance, find enlivening and entertaining in the literature of the period. (It has to be understood, however, that 'literature' must be allowed to embrace a range of writing and writers; there is much of interest and value in the work of the lesser fry.) Sometimes actual violence broke out when the injured party to a Grub-Street swindle decided that revenge could not be exacted in print. Tom Brown, Tom (some of whose verses appear in this volume) was a struggling poet and miscellaneous writer (his best known book was *Amusements, Serious and Comical*). His collision with Abel Roper, publisher of the *Post-Boy*, over an outrageous libel perpetrated against Brown, was high Grub-Street farce. Having suitably fortified himself with brandy, Brown descended on Roper's shop to deliver the deserved beating. Roper, the professional newspaper-man, immediately inserted an advertisement in the next issue of the *Post-Boy*: 'Last Tuesday happened a most terrible and bloody fight between Tom Brown and a bookseller, but the particulars not yet coming to our hands we refer you to the next [issue].'

---

[30] Philip Pinkus argues this point quite persuasively in *Grub Street stripped bare* (Constable and Co., 1968).

The 'particulars' came out in the next issue of the *Post-Boy* and also in a broadsheet:

A Full and True
ACCOUNT
of a
TERRIBLE & BLOODY FIGHT
BETWEEN
TOM. BROWN, THE POET,
And a BOOKSELLER.

On Tuesday last Tom Brown's passive valour being raised above its ordinary pitch by a large dose of brandy, and meditating a dire and bloody revenge against a bookseller that had spoke a few words to his disadvantage. In all haste he runs to a cane-shop for a oaken plant, but for want of twopence to purchase that dead-doing weapon, or so much credit as to be trusted for it, he was forced to leave it behind him.... However this disappointment of a weapon was no abatement to his fury. He immediately marches to the bookseller's shop. Charges him with slandering and dishonouring a person of his quality, and swaggers about the shop like a bully in a brandy cellar. The bookseller justifies himself, says, 'twas no injury to call a spade a spade nor Tom Brown a rake-hell, that had tricked him of three guineas, in palming a false copy upon him for a true one. These bitter words put Brown, and the bookseller to loggerheads helter-skelter. To Brown's immortal praise be it spoken, he gave the first blow, and strutted back with so much celerity and conduct, that the bookseller, who was immured behind the counter, was not able to reach him a Rowland for his Oliver. Whilst daring Tom made use of this stratagem, and fought at a distance, the fate of war inclined to the poet's side; but as the best formed designs are liable to accidents and mutabilities, so the bookseller by surprise, catching hold on the poet's sleeve with one hand, so battered his chops with the other, that quite turned the scales, and 'twas whether for a groat which would have the victory. A gentleman in the shop taking away the poet's sword, gave the bookseller the advantage of leaping over the counter; which amazed the poet perceiving, he scours off into the backshop, in hopes of a reinforcement. The enemy with all speed pursues him, and renews the engagement. Brown, like a gib-cat, fighting upon his back, and the itch, or his fears, rendering him unable to clench his fists, he fought open-handed, and clawed and scratched the bookseller's face, till the blood run down his fingers. This, with the loss of an old cravat, was all the damage the bookseller sustained in a bloody rencounter, that lasted thirteen minutes, and twenty seconds. Tom Brown, of the two, was the greater sufferer; for wanting eyes to ward off the blows, the bookseller so unmercifully belaboured the poet's lockram jaws, that put his phiz quite out of countenance, and his face was so swelled and begrimed with a mixture of blood, sweat, snot, and tears, that would have pierced a heart of stone, to see what a frightful figure he trooped off in. This is inserted in vindication of Tom Brown's honour, and to prove, though he is not fond of fighting without great advantage, he can claw and scratch like a tiger upon occasion; though some have been so bold to affirm, he does neither.[31]

Edmund Curll, the bookseller-publisher[32] was the embodiment of Grub Street. He was in business to sell books; he was a tradesman. So, in his 'Epilogue' to his *Compleat Key to The Dunciad*,[33] he concludes, characteristically: '...There are but Two Things to be consider'd in every HEROIC Poem; First, how to write it, Secondly, how to make it sell.'[34] With equally characteristic impudence, Curll elevates himself to the title of 'wit', and equal partner in the production of literature: 'How easily Two Wits agree/One finds the Poem; One the Key'. Ways of making books sell were his *first* consideration, however. His activities as publisher and bookseller were mostly unscrupulous, always interesting; he was *par excellence* the newly-emerged, no-holds-barred capitalist publisher of the first half of the eighteenth century. No writer was safe from his piratical plundering, no publishing trick was too low for him to stoop to in the name of profit. 'Curlicism' was the name coined by Defoe to describe Curll's knavery. It was the 'foul nature and purpose' of some of Curll's publications which caused Defoe, in a rage, to vent his feelings thus (in the *Weekly Journal*):

> There is but one Bookseller eminent among us for this Abomination, and from him the Crime takes the just Denomination of Curlicism. The Fellow is a contemptible Wretch a thousand ways: he is odious in his person, scandalous in his Fame; he is mark'd by Nature, for he has a bawdy Countenance, and a debauched Mien; his Tongue is an Echo of all the beastly Language his Shop is filled with and Filthiness drivels in the very Tone of his Voice.[35]

What had excited Defoe was the publication by Curll of a book entitled *Eunuchism Display'd. Describing all the different Sorts of Eunuchs* (1718). His

---

[31] Quoted by Pinkus, *Grub Street stripped bare*, pp. 22-3.
[32] For the full, uncensored story, see Ralph Straus's *The Unspeakable Curll.*.
[33] Printed for A. Dodd, 1728, p. 22.
[34] Curll even had ideas on the writing of epic poems. In the Epilogue to his *Compleat Key*, Curll tries his hand at a little epic-writing, in which he summarises the *Iliad* in thirty-six lines. In the following sample, we are informed that the 'Tale of Troy' tells
    How Troy held out Ten Years and more
    And all for one poor batter'd Whore;
    How all the Heroes had their Misses,
    But one sly Sinner call'd Ulysses.
[35] See Straus, p.79.

attack on Curll was merely incitement to even greater heights - Curll evidently believed that all publicity was good publicity. He immediately published a pamphlet entitled *Curlicism Display'd*, justifying his activities. While ostensibly defending his publishing practices, Curll brazenly used the opportunity to advertise the very book Defoe had most complained about. A publication which finally did land Curll in trouble was *Venus in the Cloister; or, The Nun in her Smock* (1724). An official complaint must have been made, and Curll was sufficiently alarmed to publish a defence: *The Humble Representation of Edmund Curll, Bookseller and Stationer of London, concerning Five Books, complained of to the Secretary of State*. Not only was this defence not particularly humble, but it also amounted to a further advertisement of the offending material. In addition to the story of the lightly-clad nun, Curll brought to public attention the *Treatise of Flogging, Ebriatatis Encomium* (*In Praise of Drunkenness*), *Three New Poems*, and *De Secretis Mulierum* (*Women's Secrets*). Of the poor nun, Curll said her story was a very moral one; the *Treatise of Flogging* was a learned, medical work, translated from the Latin; the treatise on drunkenness, he said, was a piece of irony; the poems objected to were modern renderings of Chaucer; and the fifth was a learned manual for married ladies, also translated from the Latin. Authority was not impressed, however, and Curll was taken into custody for five months before being released on bail. When his case finally came to trial, he was found guilty, but not sentenced. Curll therefore decided it expedient to issue a public apology that was also an announcement of his retirement from publishing. There was a blemish on this contrition, however, in the form of a further advertisement of two of the offending books, together with the announcement of a third of similar character:

> Having been found Guilty of publishing two Books, (1. A Treatise of the *Use* of Flogging, &c. 2. *Venus* in the *Cloister*; or the *Nun* in her *Smock*. This last not bearing my Name; but only a Copy of it was sold by me, as it might have been by any other Bookseller.) I most humbly ask Pardon for these Offences; but being resolved never more to offend in the like Manner, I give this Notice, that so soon as two Books now in the Press, are finish'd, (viz. 1. The Miscellaneous Works of that Memorable Patriot *Andrew Marvell* Esq.; in Prose and Verse. 2. The *Case* of *Seduction*; being the late Proceedings at Paris against the Rev. Abbé des Rues, for committing Rapes upon 133 Virgins. Written by himself.) I am resolved to retire from all Publick Business, with this Satisfaction, that whatever Human Frailties I may either unwarily, or wilfully, have committed, no Person can charge me

with the Guilt of any dishonourable Action; and I will therefore do myself
Justice gainst those who have libelled me upon this Occasion.
E. Curll.[36]

Curll's 'retirement' was nominal; the initial of his son, Henry, appeared instead of his own. Otherwise it was business as usual.

It must have greatly entertained the town to read the claim to 'honour' from one of its most energetically devious men of business. There were few tricks of the trade that escaped the eminent publisher. A favourite device was the use of famous names to sell the works of the distinctly less famous. Thus he gave the pseudonym of J. Gay (J. for 'Joseph' when the reader enquires more closely) to one of his tame poets[37] at a time when the other Gay was enjoying considerable success with his *Trivia* in 1716. Curll was quite brazen about this sleight of hand. In his *Compleat Key to the Dunciad* (published almost immediately after *The Dunciad* itself), Curll comments on this line, making no secret of his malpractice: 'The first Piece that ever bore the Name of Joseph Gay for its Author, was an excellent poem in Two Books intituled, The Hoop-Petticoat, By Francis Chute Esq..' Dr Arbuthnot, physician to Queen Anne and close friend of Pope, Gay and Swift, wrote to Swift that Curll was one of the new terrors of death: the reference was to Curll's publishing of instant, horribly potted biographies of the great and the good almost before the breath had left the body. Curll was also the master of the unauthorised publication. One such was a collection of poems he obtained (somehow or other), by Pope, Gay, and Lady Mary Wortley Montague, at the time a close friend of Pope's. It was a commercial opportunity not to be missed: *Court Poems* was duly published in 1716, attributed to 'a Lady of Quality', and with broad hints as to their authorship in a preface. It was, moreover, not the first time Curll had so offended against Pope.

Pope's revenge was dramatic, if also rather childish. He arranged a meeting with Curll at the Swan Tavern in Fleet Street, to which the publisher Bernard Lintot was also invited. Here is Curll's version of what followed:

My Brother *Lintot* drank his half Pint of *Old Hock,* Mr. *Pope* his half Pint of *Sack,* and I the same quantity of an *Emetic* Potion...but no threatenings past. Mr *Pope,* indeed said, that *Satires should not be Printed* (tho' he has

---

[36] For a full account of this episode, see Straus, pp. 98-121.
[37] Pope mentions this invention in *The Dunciad*:
Curl [sic] stretches after Gay, but Gay is gone:
He grasps an empty Joseph for a John (II, 127-8).

> now changed his mind) *I answered, they should not be wrote, for, if they were, they would be Printed. He replied, Mr.* Gay's *Interest at Court, would be greatly hurt by publishing these Pieces.* That was all that passed in our *Triumvirate.* We then parted, *Pope* and my Brother *Lintot* went together, to his Shop, and I went Home and *Vomited* heartily.[38]

This was the first stage of Pope's revenge against the publisher. The second was the publication of two pamphlets describing and considerably embroidering upon the incident. *A Full and True Account of a Horrid and Barbarous Revenge by Poison on the Body of Mr. Edmund Curll, Bookseller*, was the first, followed soon afterwards by *A Further Account of the Most Deplorable Condition of Mr. Edmund Curll, Bookseller*.[39] Thus began a running battle that enlivened and bespattered three decades of publishing history. It was by no means a one-sided contest. For example, a few weeks after the episode of the emetic, Curll was responsible for the publication of *Mr. Pope's Version of the First Psalm*.[40] This was a blasphemous and indelicate parody, obviously not intended for publication (such considerations seldom troubled Curll). Pope responded by inserting an advertisement in the *Post-Man*:

> Whereas there have been publish'd in my Name, certain scandalous Libels, which I hope no Persons of Candor would have thought me capable of, I am sorry to find my self obliged to declare, that no Genuine Pieces of mine have been printed by any but Mr. Tonson and Mr. Lintot. And in particular, as to that which is entitul'd, A Version of the first Psalm; I hereby promise a Reward of three Guineas to any who shall discover the Person or Persons concerned in the Publication of the said Libel, of which I am wholly ignorant.
>
> A. Pope[41]

Disingenuous of Mr Pope. Curll's accomplice in this little plot was a Mrs Burleigh, who answered Pope's advertisement with one of her own. This announced that the poem could be seen, in Pope's handwriting, by anyone who took the trouble to

---

[38] *The Curliad. A Hypercritic upon the Dunciad Variorum* (1729), pp. 20-21.
[39] The third, not published until 1720, was *A Strange But True Relation How Edmund Curll, of Fleet street, Stationer...was circumcis'd....* (probably the most indelicate of the three). The first two are reprinted in this volume.
[40] Written and published in 1716; see *Poems*, p. 300.
[41] For this quotation, and the story attached to it, I am indebted to Ralph Straus (*The Unspeakable Curll*, pp. 63-4).

visit her shop. There was no response to *this* advertisement. Pope might have bigger guns at his disposal, but he did not have things all his own way in the contest with Edmund Curll. There was the little matter of Pope's correspondence (mostly with Swift), which Curll obtained and gleefully printed (1735); there were also the monstrous *Memoirs* Curll published in 1745, after the poet's death. These bore the imposing title *Memoirs of the Life and Writings of Alexander Pope*, and ran to over seven hundred pages. However, on closer examination, the *Memoirs* are revealed to be a rag-bag of assorted odds and ends of material already published over the previous forty years. Curll sent his old enemy on his way with a literary tribute that would have graced the Goddess of Dulness's collection of booby-prizes (awarded to the heroic victors of the mock-Olympiad in Book II of *The Dunciad*).

The Dunciad, of course, was Pope's revenge upon the entire Grub Street tribe (and Curll, naturally, is given a leading role in the money-grubbing and muck-raking depicted in the poem). But *The Dunciad* is only a climactic moment in the warfare conducted by Pope, Swift and others against the Grub Street fraternity. Swift's anatomy of the 'numerous gross corruptions in Religion and Learning'[42] appeared in 1704 in *A Tale of A Tub*, two years before Curll established himself in the Strand. Large portions of the *Tale* are aimed at contemporary scholarship, philosophy and literary criticism. Thus 'a *true critic* in the perusal of a book, is like a *dog* at a feast, whose thoughts and stomach are wholly set upon what the guests *fling away*, and consequently is apt to *snarl* most when there are the fewest *bones*'.[43] While it is true that Swift was making a lofty stand on behalf of classical 'ancient' learning, against the arrogant effrontery of the 'modern' writers (his *Battle of the Books*, attached to the *Tale*, is a mock allegorical battle between the ancient and modern authors in St James's Library), there is a more immediate enemy at the gates. 'Grub-Street' writing - literary criticism in particular - was a dog which barked and snarled over whatever bones it could get its teeth and claws into. Both Swift and Pope (and others) exploited the culture they claimed to despise; their satire was directed at this upstart professionalism in literature, but also depended on it. Thus Swift, in *A Tale of a Tub*, makes virtuoso use of a series of Dunce

---

42 'The Author's Apology', *A Tale of a Tub* (The World's Classics, eds Angus Ross and David Woolley, 1986) p. 2.
43 'A Digression Concerning Critics', *Tale*, p. 49.

personae as his narrators. For example, in the *Digression on Madness*, the Hack-narrator earnestly argues that madness can be very useful to the nation. He demonstrates his thesis by declaring that the actions of great men, whether as warriors or statesmen, can be traced, in their motivation, to some abnormality, usually of the mind. (This *Digression* is included in the present volume.) Other narrators, denizens of Grub Street, are scarcely less frantically deluded in their worship of contemporary literary criticism (the dogs snarling over bones). Similarly, *The Dunciad* could be seen as celebration as well as excoriation; Pope invests his Dunce-world with an energy that is misplaced but also exhilarating.[44]

The Tory satirists' treatment of Grub Street was also at least partly ideological. Grub Street, 'modernism' and commercial vending of literature were all part of the same phenomenon: a dangerous slide towards a free press. Moreover, with the arrival of the Hanoverians in 1714, and the Whigs' ascent into government (for what must at the time have seemed like perpetuity),[45] an irreversible shift of power took place. Those who made money out of trade (as distinct from the landed gentry) were a rising force, and saw their interests best represented by the Whigs. Satire, in the hands of the Tory satirists was therefore a weapon of reaction, conservative rather than subversive. They were resisting the new mercantilism and the commercialised literature which came with it; they were also seeking to restore the certainties of a previous (aristocratic) age, mythologised in the writings of the ancient classics. Thus Pope chose to make a public declaration of his political position in his celebration, in *Windsor-Forest*, of the Stewart dynasty:

> Rich Industry sits smiling on the plains,
> And peace and plenty tell, a Stuart reigns.[46]

It was highly embarrassing to Pope (partly as a reminder of his relatively humble background) that his brother-in-law, Charles Rackett, was arrested for deer-stealing

---

[44] Howard Erskine-Hill goes even further. He suggests that Pope is fascinated by the world of Dullness: 'He constantly amplifies and explores, pressing deeper and deeper into fantasies of unreason, so that we are compelled to admit in them a kind of sublimity or beauty'. (*Pope: The Dunciad*, Edward Arnold, 1972, p. 33.) That does seem to be going a little far.

[45] Not even Margaret Thatcher's long reign can equal Robert Walpole's twenty-one years as Prime Minister (1721-42).

[46] *Windsor-Forest* was written in two stages (as Pope himself explains in a note to the poem). The first part was written in 1704, the second in 1713, but it was not published until 1713, at the height of speculation about the Queen's poor health, and the Succession. Pope could hardly have chosen a more highly-charged moment to declare his allegiance.

Introduction

in 1723. Perhaps especially embarrassing as the rustling took place in Windsor Forest.[47]

Cultural (and ideological) motives lay behind the invention of Martinus Scriblerus, another highly creative blow against new-fangled duncery (and its political manifestations from the party-hacks). Martinus Scriblerus was the name given to an imaginary dunce by the Scriblerus Club of Pope, Gay, Swift, John Arbuthnot, one of the Queen's physicians, and Thomas Parnell, a clergyman-poet. (Lord Treasurer Oxford himself was one of the Club's founder-members, moreover.) Many good things came out of this literary think-tank, including *Gulliver's Travels* (1726), *The Beggar's Opera* (1728), and, of course, *The Dunciad* (1728) - works by individual members of the group, inspired by suggestions from other members. In addition, there were works of actual collaboration, such as *The What D'Ye Call It* (1715), *Three Hours after Marriage* (1717), and *The Art of Sinking in Poetry* (1727). In particular, the Scriblerians had the long-standing ambition to produce the crowning monument to the Duncery of the Age in the *Memoirs of the Extraordinary Life, Works, and Discoveries of Martinus Scriblerus*.[48] Pope's original idea was to publish a monthly periodical entitled *The Works of the Unlearned*,[49] 'in which whatever Book that appears that deserves praise, shall be depreciated Ironically, and in the same manner that modern Critics take to undervalue Works of value, and to commend the high Productions of Grubstreet'.[50] The *Memoirs* has all the appearance of what it probably was - satire written by a committee (Part III of *Gulliver's Travels* gives a similar impression). It has some excellent moments, however, notably the double-mistress episode, almost certainly the work of Arbuthnot.[51] Martin falls in love with one of a pair of beautiful Siamese twins. When he marries her, after an elopement in which, perforce, both twins take part, he encounters legal as well as sexual problems. He

---

[47] See Pat Rogers, 'A Pope Family Scandal', in the *Times Literary Supplement*, 31 August, 1973, p. 1005. See also his *Eighteenth Century Encounters* (Harvester Press, 1985), and E.P. Thompson's *Whigs and Hunters* (Harmondsworth, rev. edn, 1977), for further accounts of 'Blacking' and the Black Acts of the 1720s.

[48] Not published, in the end, until 1741, for a variety of reasons (not least of which was the group's breaking up after 1714. It can now be read in the edition by C. Kerby-Miller (Russell and Russell, New York, 1966).

[49] Poking fun at the solemn pedantry of *The History of the Works of the Learned*, a monthly publication.

[50] Pope to Gay, October 23, 1713, *Correspondence of Alexander Pope*, ed. G. Sherburn (Oxford, 1956), I, 195.

[51] Charles Kerby-Miller's evidence to this effect is fairly conclusive.

is accused, by the 'Monster-master' (seeking to recover the twins for his freak-show) of rape, bigamy and incest: the twins, unfortunately, share the same sexual organs. It is, of course, a little indelicate (to the extent that the episode is omitted from the *Memoirs,* with only an obscure reference to its omission, by Arbuthnot's nineteenth-century editor and biographer).[52] Lawyers and the law provide Arbuthnot with some unmissable targets, though there is also incisive mockery of contemporary pseudo-scientific interest in monsters and raree-shows.[53] The episode provides its author with a useful vehicle for the expression of his (cheerful) misanthropy.

Arbuthnot had made his satirical mark some years before the Scriblerian collaboration. His contribution to the great debate about the Peace (1711-12) was his series of pamphlets relating the history of John Bull. Swift told Esther Johnson (Stella) to be sure to get a copy of the first pamphlet: 'You must buy the small 2 penny Pamphlet calld, *Law is a Bottomless Pit,* tis very prettily written, & there will be a second Part.'[54] *The History of John Bull* is a thinly-disguised fable supporting the Tory Government's peace negotiations, and deriding the efforts of its despised Allies in the war against France. John Bull is the sturdy, no-nonsense, roast-beef epitome of all that is British and best. Arbuthnot wrote a number of other lively pieces, in an off-hand sort of way. (He gave some of his best ideas to the others to adopt and develop.) 'The Fable of the Widow and Her Cat', has been ascribed to Swift, but the poem is mostly by Arbuthnot.[55] As an attack on the Duke of Marlborough - the Cat of the Fable - it lacks the venom of Swift's notorious 'Satirical Elegy on the Death of a Late Famous General' (1722). But its use of the cat-that-stole-the-cream metaphor is shrewdly suggestive of the venality of which the great man stood accused by his enemies.[56] 'Annus Mirabilis' (1722) is another

---

52 George Aitken, *The Life and Works of John Arbuthnot* (Russell and Russell, New York, 1892).
53 The Scriblerians probably had in mind the 'wild boy' brought up by a bear; the story seems to have caused quite a stir in the 1720s. A pamphlet printed in Arbuthnot's *Miscellanies* (London, 1746), though probably not by Arbuthnot, gives an account of the wild boy and his origins. It is dated 1726.
54 *Journal to Stella* (March 10, 1712), ed. Harold Williams (Oxford, 1948), II, 510.
55 'I was in the city today, and dined with my printer, and gave him a ballad made by several hands, I know not whom. I believe lord Treasurer [Oxford] had a finger in it; I added three stanzas; I suppose Dr. Arbuthnot had the greatest share.' Swift to Stella, Jan. 14, 1712 (*Journal*, II, 454). This was the day the ballad was published.
56 It was claimed, with some truth, that Marlborough built Blenheim Palace out of the proceeds of his French campaigns.

Scriblerian piece by Arbuthnot (*probably*! - it is signed 'M.S.'). What is 'remarkable' about the year is that the sexes are transformed and interchanged; not all the consequent changes are decent. It is an amusing piece, especially when seen in the context of Curll's rather more luridly titillating publications. (For example: 'Cupid's Bee-Hive, or the Sting of Love',[57] *Pancharis, Queen of Love; or Woman Unveil'd...containing the whole art of Kissing* - both published in 1721.)

All this energy, and this considerable output, was but a small drop in the ocean of what counted as literary publications in the first three decades of the eighteenth century. Grub Street ruled, hence Pope's anticipation of cultural apocalypse. Defoe (loftily consigned to the same fate as his lesser brethren by Pope - he too is pilloried in *The Dunciad*) was amongst the most prolific. For example, he wrote three issues per week of the *Review, The* single-handed, between 1704-13.[58] Defoe's background in one respect was not very different from Pope's; his father was a tradesman (a butcher - less genteel than a hatter, perhaps, but 'trade' nevertheless). Defoe's parents were Presbyterians, however, and Defoe himself remained faithful to the Dissenting cause, whatever other shifts of position he may have made. His career took a number of directions. He was an unsuccessful hosier in the 1680s, and no more successful brickmaker in the 1690s. By his own account,[59] he rode with the rebellious Monmouth forces in 1685 against the Catholic James II, and joined William III's army in 1688. This support for religious tolerance and the cause of Dissenting minorities got him into serious trouble with the Tory government in 1702. The cause was the publication of his pamphlet *The Shortest-Way with the Dissenters*, a response to the Tories' introduction of a Bill 'to Prevent Occasional Conformity'. (This was the practice whereby Dissenters were able to hold public office by 'conforming' nominally with the liturgy of the Church of England. By making such conformity illegal, the Tories could, at a stroke, have shunted many of their opponents into a permanent political siding.) Defoe's contribution was to suggest that the Tories should take draconian measures;

---

57 A Poem by Mr J[ohn] Addison.
58 5,610 pages, nearly all written by Defoe, who managed to combine his journalism with business ventures and, among other activities, the role of spy to Robert Harley (later Earl of Oxford and Prime Minister). His novels came later! (See Peter Earle, *The World of Defoe*, Weidenfeld and Nicholson, 1976.)
59 In *Applebee's Magazine*, 1725 (quoted by Peter Earle, *The World of Defoe*, Weidenfeld and Nicholson, 1976, p. 6).

the Dissenters were a nuisance, a cancer on the body politic which should be given immediate and drastic surgery. In tone as well as substance, the *Shortest-Way* resembles Dr Henry Sacheverell's sermon (June, 1702), in which he exhorted the Church 'to hang out the bloody flag of defiance against the Dissenters'.[60] Defoe's extremist position deceived some members of the government, initially. When they were undeceived, they were outraged at the attack on Tory policy, and a warrant was issued for Defoe's arrest. He went into hiding, but was caught a few months later and imprisoned. His sentence was savage: a heavy fine, three spells in the pillory (a bloody business, usually), and indefinite imprisonment. The London mob was on his side, however, and he was pelted with nothing more dangerous than flowers. (Although Pope has him in the stocks 'earless' and 'unabash'd', in Book II of *The Dunciad*, Defoe managed to retain his ears.) He was released, several months later, only after the intervention of Secretary of State Robert Harley, who realised Defoe's potential value. Defoe spent the next ten years as a paid government spy, reporting to Harley personally on a variety of sensitive issues on which Harley required information. The *Shortest-Way* bestowed a degree of notoriety on Defoe; his *Review* and *Mercator*, not to mention countless individual pamphlets, were part of his tireless campaign on behalf of commercial enterprise. Defoe was another writer who made his writing a profession (or attempted so to do): hence his place in Grub Street and dishonourable mention in *The Dunciad*.

One has to return to *The Dunciad*, however, for an insight into the violent animus that was an essential part of the phenomenon of Grub-Street. Pope carried on running battles with critics such as John Dennis and Lewis Theobald (editor of an edition of Shakespeare's plays). It is scarcely worth attempting to establish who was the first to cast a stone; Pope himself was certainly not blameless. However, the sheer volume and virulence of the many personal attacks made on him are a sign of the literary times; no explanation of his onslaught on the Dunces is complete without some reference to the very personal nature of the attacks on Pope. In particular, it was his physical deformity that attracted attention. Dennis took offence at slighting references to critics ('Bookful Blockheads') in Pope's *An Essay on Criticism* (1711) which may or may not have been aimed at him (Dennis's name is mentioned once only, and then in a manner that cannot be construed as insulting).

---

[60] See J. Sutherland, *Defoe* (Longman, 1970, p. 279).

Dennis immediately published a malicious, abusive pamphlet entitled *Reflections Critical and Satyrical, upon a Late Rhapsody, Call'd, An Essay upon Criticism.* Thus was set in motion a feud that lasted until Dennis's death in 1734. Like most of Pope's enemies, Dennis exploited the poet's deformity[61] without mercy: 'As there is no Creature so venomous, there is nothing so stupid and so impotent as a hunch-back'd Toad.'[62] And again: 'The Deformity of this Libeller, is visible, Present, Lasting, Unalterable, and Peculiar to himself. 'Tis the mark of God and nature upon him, to give us warning that we should hold no Society with him, as a Creature not of our Original, nor of our Species.'[63] In *Sawney, An Heroic Poem Occasion'd by the Dunciad*, Pope is given a 'Monster's Form,/Shap'd like a Bear, yet little as a Worm'.[64] The anonymous author of *Sawney and Colley*[65] declares that deformity is not suitable matter for satire, but is prepared to make an exception:

> A Hillock on the Breast or *Back*,
> Admits, I own, of no Attack;
> Unless, when hung out as a Blind
> To hide within a *hump-back'd* Mind.

The list of malicious detractors is endless. However, while there can be no justification for such relentless vindictiveness, an explanation is not difficult to find. As Brean Hammond suggests,[66] Pope's own satirical strikes at other writers can almost certainly be traced, in part, to his deformity. Pope bears an unmistakable resemblance to Homer's Thersites, whose 'Mountain-Shoulders half his Breast o'erspread', so described by Pope in his translation of the *Iliad* (Book II, 265). Pope's detractors gleefully leapt upon this gift;[67] there was a nice irony also about Thersites's scurrilous behaviour: 'With witty Malice, studious to defame,/Scorn all his Joy, and Laughter all his Aim' (259-60). One who had cause for complaint at

---

[61] At the age of twelve he was crippled by a tubercular infection of the spine, which left him permanently stunted in growth (4ft 6 in.), and with a hump-back.
[62] *Reflections...*, in *Works*, i. 415.
[63] *A True Character of Mr. Pope, and His Writings* (1716), in *The Critical Works of John Dennis*, ed. E.N. Hooker, Baltimore, 1939, 2 vols, ii. pp. 103-8.
[64] One Ralph James was responsible for this piece, published in 1728. 'Sawney' is short for Alexander; it is also colloquial for a tool, a simpleton (*OED*).
[65] First published in 1742, and reprinted in this volume.
[66] In *Pope: Harvester New Readings*, The Harvester Press, 1986, pp. 9-11.
[67] See, for example, Leonard Welsted's *The Blatant-Beast* (in this volume), which repeats 'Mountain Shoulders' verbatim.

Pope's 'witty Malice' was Colley Cibber, Colley, the actor-manager, and, from 1730, Poet Laureate. There were several skirmishes between the two (notably arising out of the Scriblerians' *Three Hours After Marriage*, which Cibber produced at Drury Lane in 1717). Cibber remained silent for many years, in the face of considerable provocation from Pope, who used Cibber as a comic touchstone, a symbol of a culturally degenerate age, in a number of poems.[68] The following epigram is fairly typical:

> In merry old England it once was a rule,
> The King had his Poet, and also his Fool:
> But now we're so frugal, I'd have you to know it,
> That C***r can serve both for Fool and for Poet.[69]

He broke his silence[70] in 1742, however - the publication of *The New Dunciad* was one insult too many. Cibber's response was *A Letter from Mr. Cibber to Mr. Pope*, which, for the most part, is a good-natured, somewhat rambling complaint-cum-self-justification. Any pretence at a rapprochement is abandoned, however, with an account Cibber dredges up of an alleged episode from Pope's distant past. This was in retaliation, Cibber maintained, for a line of Pope's in his *An Epistle to Dr. Arbuthnot* - 'And has not Colly still his Lord and Whore':

> He [Pope] must excuse me...if in what I am going to relate, I am reduced to make bold with a little private Conversation: But as he has shewn no Mercy to *Colley*, why should so unprovok'd an Agressor expect any for himself? And if the Truth hurts him, I can't help it. He may remember, then (or if he won't, I will) when *Button*'s Coffee-house was in vogue, and so long ago, as when he had not translated above two or three Books of *Homer*; there was a late young Nobleman (as much his *Lord* as mine) who had a good deal of wicked Humour, and who, though he was fond of having Wits in his Company, was not so restrained by his Conscience, but that he lov'd to laugh at any merry Mischief he could do them: This noble Wag, I say, in his usual *Gayeté de Cœur*, with another Gentleman still in Being, one Evening

---

[68] Not very exhaustive research uncovers four (unflattering or ribald) references to Cibber in Book III (and a paragraph in the 'Testimonies') of *The Dunciad Variorum*; Cibber appears twice in *An Epistle to Dr. Arbuthnot*, again in *The First Satire of the Second Book of Horace Imitated*, and on three further occasions in the *Imitations of Horace*.

[69] Footnote to Book III of *The Dunciad Variorum* (*Poems*, p. 422).

[70] Cibber may have carried on his side of the feud from the stage (by impersonation, and by inserting lines into his roles - he would have had ample opportunity so to do. (The suggestion is made in the Introduction to the Augustan Reprint Society's facsimile edition of the *Letter*, No 158, 1973.)

slily seduced the celebrated Mr. *Pope* as a Man of Wit, and myself as a Laugher, to a certain House of Carnal Recreation, near the *Hay-Market*; whereas his Lordship's Frolick propos'd was to slip his little *Homer*, as he call'd him, at a Girl of the Game, that he might see what sort of Figure a Man of his Size, Sobriety and Vigour (in Verse) would make, when the frail Fit of Love had got into him; in which he so far succeeded, that the smirking Damsel, who served us with Tea, happen'd to have charms sufficient to tempt the little-tiny Manhood of Mr. *Pope* into the next Room with her: at which you may imagine, his Lordship was in as much Joy, at what might happen within, as our small Friend could probably be in Possession of it: But, I (forgive me all ye mortified Mortals whom his fell Satyr has since fallen upon) observing he had staid as long as without hazard of his Health he might, I,

Prick'd to it by foolish Honesty and Love,[71]

as Shakespeare says, without Ceremony, threw open the Door upon him, where I found this little hasty hero, like a terrible *Tom Tit*, pertly perching upon the Mount of Love! But such was my Surprize, that I fairly laid hold of his Heels, and actually drew him down safe and sound from his Danger. My Lord, who staid tittering without, in hopes of the sweet Mischief he came for would have been compleated, upon my giving him an Account of the Action within, began to curse, and call me an hundred silly Puppies, for my impertinently spoiling the Sport; to which with great Gravity I reply'd: pray, my Lord, consider what I have done was, in regard to the Honour of our Nation! For would you have had so glorious a Work as that of Making *Homer* speak elegant English, cut short by laying up our little Gentleman of a Malady, which his thin Body might never have been cured of? No, my Lord! *Homer* would have been too serious a Sacrifice to our Evening Merriment. Now as his Homer has since been so happily compleated, who can say, that the World may not be obliged to the kindly Care of *Colley* that so great a Work ever came to Perfection?[72]

The *New Dunciad* was published before Cibber's *Letter*, in 1742; as a result of the *Letter*, Pope revised and published the fourth version of the poem, in 1743, with Cibber substituted as the Dunce-King hero. Despite a second *Letter* from Cibber, there can be no doubt who had the last word in this dispute. What is revealed by this lively exchange, however, is that the purity of Pope's concern at government-sponsored degradation of literature and culture was more than a little spotted.

---

[71] *Othello*, Act III, Scene 3, 418. This line is spoken by Iago, in the course of his ensnarement of the Moor. It seems scarcely credible that Cibber could have been unaware of the irony of the quotation, in his hands, at this moment. Could he?
[72] *A Letter From Mr. Cibber to Mr. Pope*, pp. 47-49.

That there were other motives underlying Pope's onslaught on Grub Street has already been suggested, above. He believed he was resisting what Brean Hammond has called 'literary commodification'.[73] He and the Scriblerians were attempting to close the cultural gates on the besieging barbarian hordes. Ironically, however, *The Dunciad* itself became a thriving centre of bourgeois literary activity. Following the publication of the poem in 1728, a veritable *Dunciad* industry blossomed and flourished. Not least (or last) among those feasting at the banquet laid on by Pope, was Curll himself, with *A Compleat Key to the Dunciad, The Popiad, The, The Female Dunciad, Codrus: or, The Dunciad Dissected*, and *The Curliad* (all from 1728, except the last, which was published in the following year, immediately after *The Dunciad Variorum*). Some measure of the level of activity stirred by Pope in 1728 (the year also of the Pope and Swift *Miscellanies*), is *A Compleat Collection of all the Verses, Essays, Letters and Advertisements Which Have been occasioned by the Publication of Three Volumes of Miscellanies by Pope and Company. The Dunciad* itself is savaged '...A scurrilous, obscene, gross Piece of Ribaldry' (p. xi), but more interesting is the catalogue of letters, mini-essays, epigrams, poems, etc., generated by the *Miscellanies* and *The Dunciad*: twenty-five separate items are listed, up to May 11, 1728. (Curll also helped himself to a pirated edition of *The Dunciad* in 1728.) Yet the very nature of Pope's Dunce-epic demonstrates that his relationship with his critics and enemies (synonyms, more or less), was clearly symbiotic: *The Dunciad* is as much a Grub-Street product as *Sawney and Colley* or *Apollo's Maggot in his Cups*. All those scribblers and booksellers long forgotten - Oldmixon, Concanen, Blackmore, Smedley, Curll (surely not wholly forgotten!) - are invested with a lunatic energy. Grub Street becomes an infernal, publishing Pandemonium, driven by demonic vendors of literary trash. Great Cibber himself, the Demon-king of Dunces, reigns over all, a Satanic, laureate-presence, representative on earth of the awesome pagan deity, the Goddess of Dulness. Vastly-swollen ego is given its head, as Cibber speaks from the throne:

'Hold - to the Minister I more incline;

---

[73] 'Guard the Barrier Sure', in *Pope: New Contexts*, ed. D. Fairer, Harvester Wheatsheaf, 1990, p. 238.

> To serve his cause, O Queen![74] is serving thine.
> And see! thy very Gazetteers give o'er,
> Ev'n Ralph repents, and Henley writes no more.
> What then remains? Ourself. Still remain
> Cibberian forehead, and Cibberian brain.
> This brazen Brightness, to the 'Squire so dear;
> This polish'd hardness, that reflects the peer;
> This arch Absurd, that wit and fool delights;
> This Mess,[75] toss'd up of Hockley-hole[76] and White's....'[77]

The Dunciad is a masterpiece, a mock-epic which derives its comic effects from the gross inflation of the petty and the trivial into bloated and monstrous gargoyles. Colley Cibber and Edmund Curll are only two of an entire army of grotesques paraded through the streets and squares of London, its seats of learning and centres of commerce, and the palaces of the rich and powerful. It is a poem teeming with life, bristling with energy. Ironically, it is the Dunces' energies - which Pope enhances with such hilarious extravagance - that he also seeks to stifle. The actual Grub Street, whatever else it lacked, was not deficient in energy. One should not, moreover, simply accept the Scriblerians' own evaluation of themselves in relation to Grub Street (as Pat Rogers appears to do when he asserts that it is Pope and Swift who 'point up the dreary pretensions and solemn vacuity of the hacks...Grub Street...[and] its shabby purlieus are irradiated by the gaiety of vision that belongs to Pope, Swift and his friends...').[78]

There exists, then, an umbilical cord between Pope and Grub Street. This link can be seen also in the pamphlets written as a record of the infamous 'vomit' discussed earlier. These started as trifling pieces, but (to quote Paul Hammond) 'were made classic and canonical by being reprinted in [Pope's] collected works; this is a development which, like *The Dunciad*, makes the destruction of culture the dominant subject of that culture's art'.[79] Pope's apocalyptic vision, as it is

---

[74] The Queen of Dulness, the 'Goddess' whose power is invoked, and who is the object of worship throughout the poem. Pope inserts also a passing jibe at Walpole, the prime 'minister' then in office.

[75] Partly 'dish' is intended, but with the further connotation of muddle and confusion also present.

[76] Not the most salubrious part of London; site of a bear-garden and celebrated in Gay's *The Beggar's Opera* as a haunt of prostitutes.

[77] The famous chocolate-house in St James's Street, London.

[78] *Grub Street*, p. 404.

[79] Introduction to *Selected Prose of Alexander Pope*, Cambridge University Press, 1987, p. 17.

expressed in Book IV of *The Dunciad*, foretells the destruction of aristocratic power and the high culture he so much admired: '*Art* after *Art* goes out, and all is Night.' 'Order', moreover, as understood by the Renaissance, is shown to have been subverted by the chaos of bourgeois culture:

> Lo! thy dread Empire, CHAOS! is restor'd;
> Light dies before thy uncreating word:
> Thy hand, great Anarch! lets the curtain fall,
> And Universal Darkness buries all.[80]

'Art' signifies the old traditional 'forms' of literature, which seemed to Pope to be disappearing under a cascade of new, non-genres. Swift and Pope themselves contributed to this generic fragmentation: *A Tale of a Tub* and *Gulliver's Travels*, Pope's assorted pamphlets, *The Art of Sinking in Poetry*, and other pieces in the *Miscellanies*, for example, do not readily categorise. In addition, the growth of an embryonic popular journalism, with its first uncertain steps towards a free press, was disturbing to men who still put their faith in an aristocratic social and political order. Above all, however, the Scriblerians put up satiric resistance to what Michael McKeon has described as social and generic instability,[81] the breaking down of the old social and cultural orders. The birth of the novel was the consequence of this instability; Pope and Swift were among the last of the old order, Defoe, wearing his novelist's hat, among the very first of the new.

A note on the text:

The texts by major authors included in this Anthology have been taken from modern, authoritative editions. Other texts, wherever possible, have made taken from the original pamphlets (often the *only* editions printed). I have preserved the character of the originals by tampering as little as possible with spelling, puntuation, etc., making changes only where there were obvious printing errors.

---

[80] The concluding lines of Book IV.
[81] In the Introduction to *The Origins of the English Novel, 1600-1740*, The Johns Hopkins University Press, 1987, p. 20.

A
FROLICK
to
Horn-Fair[1]

...When the happy morning came, and nothing but cuckold-makers, cuckoldom, cuckolds, and Horn-Fair,[2] were the common discourses of every sober citizen to his next neighbour, as soon as the shops were opened, I[3] getting up an hour before my time, had recourse to the barber's, that my face and periwig might not want the advantages of his nice management, but have all the effeminate improvement of powder, washball and perfume, that I might be as fragrant to my mistress's nostrils, as a Bermuda breeze, and smell as odoriferous as any sweet-bag. When I was thus washed, curled, and combed, like any lady's

---

[1] This is a piece (1699) by Ned Ward, to demonstrate his equal mastery of prose. By all accounts, he was one of the liveliest occupants of Grub Street. (See Philip Pinkus's account, in *Grub St. stripped bare*, Constable, 1968, pp. 170-228, from which this extract has been taken.) His style is not subtle (see *Apollo's Maggot*), but he has energy in abundance. *A Frolick to Horn-Fair* is an example of a genre discovered by Ward to be profitable - the 'trip'. Defoe's *Tour through the Whole Island of Great Britain*, 1724-6, is the masterpiece of the genre, Ward's a lively, coarse, and presumably fictional 'Frolick'. His first effort in this line was *A Trip to Jamaica* (1699), and, because that sold, he followed it with *A Trip to New England* (without having taken the trip - see Pinkus, p. 183). The 'Frolick' takes the reader on a jaunt to Deptford and Greenwich, during which the be-whigged and powdered narrator picks up a 'lady', who accompanies him down the river from Billingsgate to Deptford. It's an inconsequential but colourful narrative.

[2] Our hero's destination - the haunt, it would appear, of cuckold-makers, and even, possibly, of cuckolds. Horn-Fair remains as a place-name in Hornfair Road and Hornfair Park, Charlton, SE7. See also note 9, below, on the story of Cuckold's Point.

[3] Ward should be given the credit for having created the persona of a London spark, circa 1700; his minute (but also self-mocking) attention to toilette and dress somewhat exceed his concern for appropriate punctuation (grammar, even).

lapdog; and after I had spent as much time in dressing, as a merchant's wife on a Sunday before churchtime, I did at last judge by my glass I was a very complete figure to make an amour, though to a squeamish lady. My shoes were as black as Spanish balls could make 'em, and shone like a physician's ebony cane new rubbed upon a visit to an alderman. My stockings were gartered up as tight as a boot upon a last, and stuck as close to my calves as a bag to a boiled pudding. My garters being as hard girted as a fillet bound for bleeding, that I did more penance than a man half throttled to be pricked in the jugular. My knees hooped round with rolls, turned up with that exactness, that a wedding ring upon a citizen's wife's thumb, could no ways fit more precisely regular. My breeches stuck so close to the ignoblest of my flesh, that I durst not stride an inch beyond the given bounds of my tailor, without the danger of a rent; and when I came to a broad kennel[4] I was forced to wade through, because I could not venture to step over without damage. My coat was cut all-amode a Paree, with skirts not much longer than those of a waterman's jacket. My linen was made by an Inns-of-Court sempstress, and was digitized with her handle-bauble fingers, into as much formality as a lady's headdress. My wig, like the rest of the fools, was so woundily bepowdered, that whenever the wind sat in my face, it endangered the eyes of him that walked behind me. Which procured me as many curses in a day, as a good man has prayers for his charity. My hat was in the mathematical cock, with the brims tucked up to the crown, into an exact triangle. My gloves were right cordivant,[5] and stank so of Muscovy cat's turd, that persons subject to vapours started from me as I walked (like a beau from a chimney-sweeper) for fear of being suffocated. Thus equipped according to the nice rules of foppery and courtship, I went along, cursing the rudeness of the wind, that at every street's corner ruffled the curls of my wig into some disorder, being forced to give as many strokes to each bushy side as a milk woman does to a cow's teat at a meal, to reduce the straggling hairs into their proper places: till at last, with a panting heart, like a disspirited lover, I came to the place appointed; where, with as much

---

4   'The surface drain of a street; the gutter' (*OED*), an open sewer, in early eighteenth-century London.
5   'Obs., Cordwain; Spanish leather made originally at Cordova, of goat-skin, tanned and dressed, but afterwards frequently of split horse-hides; = Cordovan' (*OED*). His use of 'Muscovy' is a perversion of 'musk' - a perfume derived from the male musk-deer. 'It has a very powerful and enduring odour' (*OED*).

courage as I could summon together, I asked for my lady, who was not yet come. I thinking it my duty to wait, rather than hers, it made me careful to be something earlier than the time prefixed, to manifest my diligence, as well as the eager desires I had to her dear company. I bid 'em show me a room, and then called for a pint of canary, as the most amorous cordial I could think on, over which, I sat near half an hour, sometimes disheartening myself with the thoughts of being jilted, then comforting myself up with the assurance of her sincerity, from some little knowledge I had of her person. At last, to remove my doubts and jealousies, in steps my lady, dressed up with as much art, as if all the tirewomen in both Exchanges had been her chambermaids. But, to tell you the truth on't, finding her no more afraid of tumbling her pinners, than I was of rumpling my cravat, our greeting was so mutually kind and satisfactory, that it would have made the reader's heart go pit-a-pat to have seen our loving salutation. She begging pardon for her presumption, and desiring my good construction of the freedom she had taken. I answering her in a familiar dialect, that her company was the only happiness I had long coveted; and had not the conjugal obligations[6] she lay under frighted me from discovering my love, she long before now should have received sufficient testimonies of my inextinguishable affections; or had I in the least known the just reasons she had to withdraw her friendship, and alienate that beauty and delight remaining in her dear self from her marriage bed, no addresses and importunities should have been wanting from her humble servant, to have happily supplied those impotencies, which, according to the laws both divine and humane, she might modestly complain of....

Citizens and their mates, swarm now to the waterside, in order to take boat for the horn-headed rendezvous at Charlton: and nothing being heard beneath our window, but the wrangling of watermen about their fares, and the noisy mouthing acclamations of 'Greenwich, Greenwich Ho!' that had we been seated at the Hockly Hole Theatre,[7] when the blind bear had been let loose, our ears could not have been terrified with more discording outcries. Upon which we arose from our

---

[6] The lady evidently has a husband, whose 'impotencies' are the motive behind the trip to Cuckold's Point (see following lines).
[7] Hockley-in-the-Hole was the site of a bear-garden; bears, bulls, even leopards were baited for sport in the first decades of the eighteenth century. (See Pat Rogers, *Literature and Popular Culture in Eighteenth Century England*, The Harvester Press, 1985, p. 13.)

seats, and moved to the window, to divert ourselves a little with seeing the bachelor cuckold-makers and the citizens' wives; also city cuckolds, and their maiden-looking mistresses, stow themselves as close in a boat together, as they do in a Cheapside balcony, at my Lord Mayor's Show, to gaze like a drove of bullocks, between one another's horns, at the triumphs of the city....

Having thus pretty well secured our bodies from the coldness of the water [by a flask of wine] we took boat at Billingsgate[8] stairs, and away for Cuckold's Point;[9] but we were no sooner put off from the shore, but we were got into such an innumerable fleet of oars, skullers, barges, cock-boats, bum-boats,[10] pinnaces and yawls; some going, some coming, and all attacking each other with such volleys of hard words, that I thought Billingsgate market had been kept upon the Thames, and all the fish whores in the town, had been scolding for a plate, given 'em by some rich oyster woman, to encourage the industry of the tongue; calling my poor lady and I, so often by the opprobrious names of whore and rogue, that for my part, I thought they were witches, and had known what we had been doing; tossing ladlefuls of water into one another's boats, till the passengers were many

---

[8] Their point of departure is only a little down river from the outlet of the notorious Fleet Ditch, the site of Pope's mud-diving, filth-flinging contest in Book II of *The Dunciad*: the Dunces descend
        To where Fleet-ditch with disemboguing streams
        Rolls the large tribute of dead dogs to Thames...(ll, 271-2).
Dead dogs and much else, as our hero discovers.

[9] Not one of Ward's inventions, though it sounds like it. Defoe mentions Cuckold's Point twice in his *Tour* (Everyman, 1962, vol. i, p.169, and p.320). Although no longer to be found on the map, Cuckold's Point was on the Surrey side of the river, a little below where Rotherhithe Church once stood. According to H. B.. Wheatley, *London Past and Present* (John Murray, 3 vols, 1891), the spot was once marked by a tall pole with a pair of horns on the top. Legend has it that King John, no less, wearied with hunting and seeking refreshment, called at a miller's house at Charlton. The miller was not at home, but his beautiful young wife was. When the miller arrived home, he drew his conclusions and a large knife, at which the king hastily made himself known. To appease the miller, the king told him to claim a long strip of land, from Charlton to a point near Rotherhithe. Conditions were attached however: the miller had to walk that distance every year on that day - October 18 - wearing a pair of buck's horns on his head. Horn Fair was kept up, every October 18, until 1872 by the village of Charlton in Kent. (See H. B.. Wheatley, op. cit., vol. 1, pp. 481-482.)

[10] 'Scavenger's boat, employed to remove 'filth' from ships lying in the Thames, as prescribed by the Trinity House Bye Laws of 1685. These 'dirt-boats' also used to bring vegetables etc for sale on board the ships' (*OED*). G. M.. Trevelyan gives a similar account of traffic on the Thames: 'In London the river was the most crowded of the highways. Passengers were perpetually threading the heavy commercial traffic, to the accompaniment of volleys of traditional abuse exchanged between boatmen and bargees' (*England Under Queen Anne*, Longman, 3 vols, vol. i. p. 80). A boat such as our hero's, loaded with fops and their 'ladies' (and bound for the notorious Cuckold's Point!), would no doubt be fair game for the less genteel elements also using the Thames.

of 'em as wet as a turbulent woman just taken out of the ducking-stool. At last an unlucky rogue, with Bridewell-looks and a ladle in his hand, fishes up a floating Sir-reverence[11] in his wooden vehicle, and gives it an unfortunate toss upon my lady's bubbies. She crying out to me her protector, to do the office of a scavenger, and take away the beastliness, she being herself so very squeamish, that she could no more endure to touch it with her fingers, than a monkey does a mouse, it being lodged in the cavity, between her breasts and her stays, she could not shake it off, but I was forced to lend a hand to remove the poisonous pellet from her snowy temptations, giving on't a toss into another boat, with the like success, wounding an old cuckoldy waterman just in the forehead, and so bedunged his brow antlers, that I make no question but they spread and flourished, being thus manured like the horns of an ox after well greasing, which put the grisly churl (who I'll warrant, by his grey hairs, had at least served nine prenticeships to the Thames) into such a wonderful passion, that he began to roar out his aquatic scurrility at us, with as much indignation and revenge, as a she-mumper[12] when bilked of her crib, or an alley-scold when called barren bitch, by her neighbour, clawing the unsavoury birdlime off his face, snapping on't, as a barber does suds from the ends of his fingers; saluting my mistress, and I, in the height of his fury, after the following manner. 'You shitten-skulled son of a t—d, that has spat your brains in my face, who was begotten in buggery, born in a house of office,[13] and delivered at the fundament, fit for nothing but to be cast into a goldfinder's ditch, there lie till you're rotten, and then be sold out to gardeners, for a hot bed, to raise pumpkins to feed the Devil withall. And as for you, you brandy-faced, bottle-nosed, bawdy, brimstone whore, every time you conjobble together, may he beget your belly full of live crabs and crawfish, that as you strive to pluck 'em out, they may hang by the sides of your toquoque, and make you squeak nine times louder than a woman frighted into labour a month before her reckoning.' This, and such sort of waterbred language, he pelted at our ears, till we were out of hearing: being both as glad when we had out-rowed his impudence, as a man that has outrun a bailiff;

---

[11] The reader, with a little prompting, should be able to guess what this is. The more obvious meaning of the phrase is 'saving your reverence', or 'with all respect to'.
[12] Mumper: 'A beggar, mendicant'; one who sponges on others - *thieves' cant* (*OED*).
[13] Privy.

for if ever anybody was under an ill tongue, we thought ourselves at that time in the same condition.

Every boat that came by had a pelt at my poor mistress and I, who being but two, besides watermen, were most lamentably mauled by other boats, who being better manned, were quite too many for us, and rattled us into silence with a broadside of Billingsgate language, which was thrown on all sides so thick upon us, that we found it but a vain attempt to endeavour to be heard amidst this shower of ill words. We jogged gently on, as fast as our neighbouring enemies would give us leave, who lay ahead of us, upon our bow, broadside, quarters, and stern, that we could not turn our heads any way out of tongueshot, but either rogue, or whore, pimp, cuckold, or tailor, hit us a box of the ear, that almost deafened us. 'Dear heart,' says my mistress, 'I wonder the magistrates of the city do not take some care to prevent these sad abuses upon the water; for 'tis a shameful thing that civil people should be called thus out of their names.' 'Prithee,' said I, 'never mind 'em; for if my Lord M— were here himself, they'd be as ready to call him cuckold as they would anybody else; and he would not know which way to help himself, but must put it up as we do. There's no remedy.'

After we had spent about half an hour upon the water in this misery, we arrived at our intended port, Cuckold's Point, where we landed in a crowd, with as much difficulty as a man crosses the Change at two o'clock, or squeezes into Paul's choir on a Sunday, whilst they are singing of an anthem. Having discharged our watermen, we went into the house, where the troop of merry cuckolds used to rendezvous armed with shovel, spade, or pickaxe; their heads adorned with horned helmets; and from thence to march, in order, for Horn-Fair, levelling the way as they go, according to the command of their leaders, that their wives might come after with their gallants, without spoiling their laced shoes, or draggling their holiday petticoats....

When we had warmed and refreshed our chilled carcasses, we set forward for Deptford, and having heard great commendation of that serviceable projection, the New Dock, I had a great desire to take a view of that by the way, and so shaped my course accordingly. After we had passed by a long range of little cottages, at the doors of which sat abundance of Dutch-buttocked lasses, with sea handkerchiefs about their pouting bubbies, which were swelled with much handling, so far beyond their natural proportion, that their breast and their bellies, like Mother Shipton's[14] nose and chin, met one with the other; some knitting, some spinning, and others picking okum;[15] but all, as I suppose, ready enough to quit their several exercises and betake themselves to a pleasanter pastime, if anybody will hire 'em....

From hence we proceeded till we came to Deptford, where I think the first house in the town, like many others, is accounted a convenience for his Majesty's Waterrats, when residing upon land, to cool their tails in; when we came a little further into the town, we might easily discern, by the build of the houses, what amphibious sort of creatures chiefly inhabited this part of the kingdom; their dens were chiefly wood, all of one form, as if they were obliged by Act of Parliament, to all build after the same model; here a pretty woman or two at a door, there another or two at a window, all looking as melancholy as old maids and widows, for want of male conversation; gazing upon each man that passed 'em, with as much earnestness and desire, as ever our great grandmother did upon the forbidden fruit. The ladies that chiefly inhabit these cabins, were the wives of mariners, whose husbands were some gone to the East Indies, and some to the West, some Northward, some Southward, leaving their disconsolate spouses to make trial of their virtue, and live upon public credit till their return, who if it were not for the benevolence of a well-disposed neighbouring knight, and a few more charitable worthy gentlemen, they might, though married, grow sullen, like the Negro women,[16] for want of husbands, and pine away because nature is not supplied with due accommodation. Many shops we observed open in the streets, but a brandy-bottle, and a quartern, a butcher mending of a canvas doublet, a few apples in a cabbage-net, a peelful of Deptford cheesecakes, an old waistcoat, a thrum cap, and a pair of yarn mittens, were the chief shows that they made of their commodities, every house being distinguished by either the sign of the Ship, the Anchor, the Three Mariners, Boatswain and Call, or something relating to the sea: for as I suppose, if they should hang up any other, the salt water novices would be

---

[14] The celebrated witch-prophet, whose cave at Knaresborough still draws many visitors.
[15] Or oakum: 'Loose fibre, obtained by untwisting and picking old rope; used in caulking ships' seams, in stopping up leaks; the picking of it formerly the employment of convicts and inmates of workhouses' (*OED*).
[16] Presumably a reference to the (thriving) slave trade.

as much puzzled to know what the figure represented, as the Irishman was when he called the Globe the golden casement, and the unicorn the white horse with a barber's pole in his forehead....

We walked on till we came to the upper end of the town, where stood some very pretty houses, whose gates, for ostentation's sake, were made with bars, that each passenger might delight his eyes, with an external prospect of these their most creditable and beautiful habitations: in this row stood a most famous hospital,[17] erected for the entertainment of thirty-one decayed masters of vessels, or their widows, depending on the Trinity House; the masters of which, having the care thereof; to the relief and support of which charitable design, every ship at her clearing, pays according to her burden so much money. Our curiosity led us to take a turn into it, which we found very pleasant and commodious, as to the building and situation; but when I enquired into the allowance, it was so very small, that it might rather be called Pinch-Gut-College,[18] than a hospital for poor pensioners; who with much difficulty gaining admittance into these starving confines, have no more allowed 'em, to find meat, drink, washing, fire, clothes, and all the necessaries of life, than twelve shillings per month; and four months in the year are set at five weeks, to take in the odd month; most that are there having paid more money towards it, before they came into it, than ever their allowance would amount to, if they were to live fifty years in the hospital; to which many legacies have been left, but the number of pensioners never increased, nor their pensions advanced; so that how it is sunk, or embezzled, or to what use converted, nobody knows, but those persons who have the discretionary power, as 'tis supposed, of laying it up safe in their own pockets. An East India captain, some few years since, dying, bequeathed thirteen hundred pounds to this hospital; out of which money, it never received any other apparent advantage, than the statue of the benefactor set up in the garden, for the pensioners to feast their eyes, instead

---

[17] The narrative takes a rather more serious turn from this point. Ward's mask slips, the self-consciously over-dressed philanderer disappears, and there emerges a man with a social conscience, angry at the exploitation of an ancient foundation for needy retired mariners. The bawdy 'trip' becomes, by the end of the extract, a fierce polemic.

[18] The Royal Hospital for distressed sailors at Greenwich, founded in 1694 by Mary II on the site of the Tudor palace at Greenwich (Philippa Glanville, *London in Maps*, The Connoisseur, London, 1972). Defoe, writing some twenty years later than Brown, is rather more complimentary. After enthusing about the fortunate lot of the pensioners at the Chelsea Hospital, he adds: 'The same may be said of the invalid sea men at the hospital of Greenwich' (*Tour*, vol. ii, p.11).

of their bellies, withall. The members of this society of tarpaulin paupers, are only during the pleasure of the masters of the Trinity, and are liable to be turned out, upon very slender misbehaviours. There is another such hospital by the church, originally founded by Queen Elizabeth, but for twenty-one poor masters, or their widows; and except in number, is equal in every particular, with the former; so that by all the observations I could make, in so short a passage through the town, I could not but think it very well deserved this following character: the town's without necessaries, they've butchers without meat, alehouses without drink, houses without furniture, and shops without trade; captains without commissions, wives without husbands, whores without smocks, a church without religion, and hospitals without charity....[19]

---

[19] There is a little more of this 'trip', but enough is probably enough.

The Shortest-Way with the Dissenters: or Proposals for the Establishment of the Church[1]

Sir *Roger L'Estrange*[2] tells us a Story in his Collection of Fables, of the Cock and the Horses. The Cock was gotten to Roost in the Stable, among the Horses, and there being no Racks, or other Conveniences for him, it seems, he was forc'd to roost upon the Ground; the Horses jostling about for room, and putting the Cock in danger of his Life, he gives them this grave Advice; *Pray Gentlefolks let us stand still, for fear we should tread upon one another.*

---

[1] The reader who has not read this pamphlet before should avoid any hints and tips from footnotes and attempt to determine where, as they say, Defoe is coming from. Irony is a subtle weapon; is Defoe using it here, or not? For those determined to have further information before proceeding: the *Shortest-Way* was written and published in December, 1702. Defoe's pamphlet was written in response to a move by the Tories in November 1702 to end the practice of 'occasional conformity' (with Church of England liturgical practice), by means of which Dissenters were able to qualify for state office. Defoe correctly saw the Bill 'to Prevent Occasional Conformity' as a threat to the Dissenters and therefore the Whigs, many of whom were Dissenters. The *Shortest-Way* caused an instant sensation. Defoe's apparently innocent, extremist-Tory proposal (it is a humble forebear of Swift's more celebrated *Modest Proposal*, q.v.) was initially taken at face value. When the Tories in power realised they had been hoaxed, they were outraged. Defoe was arrested after five months of lying low; the warrant for his arrest was issued on 3 January, 1703, the pamphlet was burned by the common hangman, on the order of the Commons, on 25 February, and Defoe was finally apprehended in May, 1703. He spent several months in jail, until Robert Harley, the Secretary of State, contrived his release, with a view to making use of Defoe's talents (see Introduction). The text is that of the original pamphlet, as re-printed in *Selected Writings of Daniel Defoe*, ed. J.T. Boulton, C.U.P., 1965.

[2] 1616-1704, English journalist and pamphleteer, born in Hunstanton. He narrowly escaped hanging as a Royalist spy for a plot to seize Lynn in Norfolk, in 1644, and was imprisoned in Newgate, from where he escaped after four years. He was pardoned by Cromwell in 1653 (*Chambers Biographical Dictionary*, 1990). He became licenser of the press after the Restoration, the official 'snooping government censor' (Pat Rogers, *Grub Street*, p. 278).

THERE are some People in the World, who now they are *unpearcht*, and reduc'd to an Equality with other People, and under strong and very just Apprehensions of being further treated as they deserve, begin with *Aesop's* Cock, to Preach up Peace and Union, and the Christian Duties of Moderation, forgetting, that when they had the Power in their Hands, those Graces were Strangers in their Gates.

It is now near Fourteen Years, that the Glory and Peace of the purest and most flourishing Church in the World has been Eclips'd, Buffetted, and Disturb'd, by a sort of Men, who God in his Providence has suffer'd to insult over her, and bring her down; these have been the Days of her Humiliation and Tribulation: She has born with an invincible Patience the Reproach of the Wicked, and God has at last heard her Prayers, and deliver'd her from the Oppression of the Stranger.

And now they find their Day is over, their Power gone, and the Throne of this Nation possest by a Royal, *English*, True, and ever Constant Member of, and Friend to the Church of *England*. Now they find that they are in danger of the Church of *England's just* Resentments; now they cry out *Peace*, *Union*, *Forbearance*, and *Charity*, as if the Church had not too long harbour'd her Enemies under her Wing, and nourish'd the viperous Brood, till they hiss and fly in the Face of the Mother that cherish'd them.

No Gentlemen, the Time of Mercy is past, your *Day of Grace is over*; you shou'd have practis'd Peace, and Moderation, and Charity, if you expected any your selves.

We have heard none of this Lesson for Fourteen Years past: We have been huff'd and bully'd with your Act of Tolleration;[3] you have told us that you are the *Church establish'd* by *Law* as well as others; have set up your Canting-Synagogues at our Church-Doors, and the Church and her Members have been loaded with Reproaches, with Oaths, Associations, Abjurations, and what not; where has been the Mercy, the Forbearance, the Charity you have shewn to tender *Consciences of the Church* of *England that* cou'd not take Oaths *as fast as you made 'em;* that having sworn Allegiance to their lawful and rightful King, cou'd not dispence with

---

[3] The Act of 1689, which declared that penal statutes against Dissenters should not be enforced - the practice of non-conformity (to Church of England liturgy) thus became possible.

that Oath,[4] *their King being still alive* and swear to your new *Hodge-podge of a Dutch-Government*. These ha' been turn'd out of their livings and they and their Families left to starve; their Estates double Tax'd, to carry on a War they had no *Hand in* and you *got nothing* by: What Account can you give of the Multitudes you have forc'd to comply, against their Consciences, with your new *sophistical Politicks*, who like the new Converts in *France*, Sin because they can't Starve. And now the Tables are turn'd upon you, you *must not be Persecuted, 'tis not a Christian Spirit*.

You have *Butcher'd* one King, *Depos'd* another King, and made a *mock King* of a Third; and yet you cou'd have the Face to expect to be employ'd and trusted by the Fourth; any body that did not know the Temper of you wou'd stand amaz'd at the Impudence, as well as Folly, to think of it.

Your Management of your *Dutch Monarch* whom you reduc'd to a meer *King of Cl[ub]s*, is enough to give any future Princes such an Idea of your Principles, as to warn them sufficiently from coming into your Clutches; and God be thank'd, the Queen is out of your Hands, knows you, and will have a care of you.

There is no doubt but the supreme Authority of a Nation has in its self a Power, *and a Right to that Power*, to execute the Laws upon any Part of that Nation it governs. The execution of the known Laws of the Land, and that with but a weak and gentle Hand neither, was all that the phanatical Party of this Land have ever call'd Persecution; this they have magnified to a height, that the Sufferings of the *Hugonots* in *France* were not to be compar'd with — Now to execute the known Laws of a Nation upon those who transgress them having first been voluntarily consenting to the making those Laws, can never be call'd Persecution, but Justice. But Justice is always Violence to the Party offending, for every Man is Innocent in his own Eyes. The first execution of the Laws against the Dissenters in *England* was in the Days of King *James* the First; and what did it amount to, truly, the worst they suffer'd, was at their own request, to let them go to *New-England*,[5] and erect a new Collony, and give them great Privileges, Grants, and suitable Powers, keep them under the Protection, and defend them against all Invaders, and receive no Taxes or Revenue from them. This was the cruelty of the Church of *England*, fatal

---

[4] This is a reference to the 'non-jurors, who refused to swear allegiance to William and Mary, insisting that James II was the rightful king.
[5] The Pilgrim Fathers set sail for New England, aboard the *Mayflower*, on 6 September, 1620.

Lenity! 'Twas the ruin of that excellent Prince, King *Charles* the First. Had King *James* sent all the Puritans in *England* away to the *West-Indies*, we had been a national unmix'd Church; the Church of *England* had been kept undivided and entire.

To requite the Lenity of the Father, they take up Arms against the Son; Conquer, Pursue, Take, Imprison, and at last put to Death the anointed of God, and Destroy the very Being and Nature of Government, setting up a sordid Impostor,[6] who had neither Title to Govern, nor Understanding to Manage, but supplied that want with Power, bloody and desperate Councils and Craft, without Conscience.

Had not King *James* the First witheld the full execution of the Laws; had he given them strict Justice, he had clear'd the Nation of them, and the Consequences had been plain; his *Son had never been murther'd by them*, nor the Monarchy overwhelm'd; 'twas *too much Mercy* shewn them, was the ruin of his Posterity, and the ruin of the Nation's Peace. One would think the Dissenters should not have the Face to believe that we are to be wheedl'd and canted into Peace and Toleration, when they know that they have once requited us with a civil War, and once with an intollerable and unrighteous Persecution for our former Civillity.

Nay, to encourage us to be Easy with them, 'tis apparent, that they never had the Upper-hand of the Church, but they treated her with all the Severity, with all the Reproach and Contempt as was possible: What Peace, and what Mercy did they shew the Loyal Gentry of the Church of *England:satirised by Defoes* in the time of their Triumphant Common-wealth? How did they put all the Gentry of *England* to ransom, whether they were actually in Arms for the King or not, making People compound for their Estates, and starve their Families? How did they treat the Clergy of the Church of *England,* sequester'd the Ministers, devour'd the Patrimony of the Church, and divided the Spoil, by sharing the Church-Lands among their Soldiers, and turning her Clergy out to starve; just such Measure as they have mete, shou'd be measur'd to them again.

Charity and Love is the known Doctrine of the Church of *England,* and 'tis plain she has put it in practice towards the Dissenters, even beyond what they ought, till she has been wanting to her self, and in effect, unkind to her own Sons; particularly, in the too much Lenity of King *James* the First, mentioned before, had

---

[6] Oliver Cromwell, Lord Protector from 1653 to 1658.

he so rooted the Puritans from the Face of the Land, which he had an opportunity, early to ha' done, they had not the Power to vex the Church, as since they have done.

IN the Days of King *Charles* the Second, how did the Church reward their bloody Doings with Lenity and Mercy, *except the barbarous Regicides of the pretended Court of Justice*; not a Soul suffer'd for all the Blood in an unnatural War: King *Charles* came in all Mercy and Love, cherish'd them, preferr'd them, employ'd them, witheld the rigour of the Law, and oftentimes, even against the Advice of his Parliament, gave them liberty of Conscience; and how did they requite him with the villainous Contrivance to Depose and Murther him and his Successor at the *Rye-Plot*..[7]

KING James, as if Mercy was the inherent Quality of the Family, began his Reign with unusual Favour to them: Nor could their joining with the Duke of *Monmouth*[8] against him, move him to do himself Justice upon them; but that mistaken Prince thought to win them by Gentleness and Love, proclaim'd universal Liberty to them, and rather discountenanc'd the Church of *England* than them; how they requited him all the World knows.

THE late Reign is too fresh in the Memory of all the World to need a Comment; how under Pretence of joining with the Church in redressing some Grievances, they pusht things to that extremity, in conjunction with some mistaken Gentlemen, as to Depose the late King,[9] as if the Grievance of the Nation cou'd not ha' been redress'd but by the absolute ruin of the Prince: Here's an Instance of their Temper, their Peace, and Charity. To what height they carried themselves during the Reign

---

[7] The Rye-House plot was an attempt to assassinate the King and his brother, the Duke of York (future James II), in 1683. The incident gave Charles the excuse to increase the religious persecution of dissenters.

[8] James, Duke of Monmouth (1649-85); the rebellion of the 'Protestant Duke' was suppressed and Monmouth beheaded. Defoe claimed 'to have been in arms under the Duke of Monmouth', in *The Complete English Tradesman*, 1738 (quoted by Peter Earle in *The World of Daniel Defoe*, Weidenfeld and Nicholson, 1976, p. 6).

[9] If suspicions had not already been aroused about the *real* political stance of the writer of the pamphlet, the lavish encomiums on James II should have done; only the most rabid jacobite would have found a word of sympathy for that most foolish and blinkered of monarchs.

of a King of their own; how they crope[10] into all Places of Trust and Profit; how they insinuated into the Favour of the King and were at first preferr'd to the highest Places in the Nation; how they engrost the Ministry, and *above all, how pitifully they Manag'd,* is too plain to need any Remarks.

BUT particularly, their Mercy and Charity, the Spirit of Union, they tell us so much of, has been remarkable in *Scotland,* if any Man wou'd see the Spirit of a Dissenter, let him look into *Scotland*; there they made an entire Conquest of the Church, trampled down the sacred Orders, and supprest the Episcopal Government, with an absolute, and as they suppose, irretrievable Victory, tho', 'tis possible, *they may find themselves mistaken:* Now 'twou'd be a very proper Question to ask their *Impudent Advocate, the Observator,*[11] Pray how much Mercy and Favour did the Members of the Episcopal Church find in *Scotland,* from the *Scotch* Presbyterian-Government; and I shall undertake for the Church of *England,* that the Dissenters shall still receive as much here, tho' they deserve but little.

In a small Treatise *of the Sufferings of the Episcopal Clergy in Scotland,*[12] 'twill appear, what Usage they met with, how they not only lost their Livings, but in several Places, were plunder'd and abus'd in their Persons; the Ministers cou'd not conform, turn'd out, with numerous Families, and no Maintenance, and hardly Charity enough left to relieve them with a bit of Bread; and the Cruelties of the Party are innumerable, and not to be attempted in this short Piece.

And now to prevent the distant Cloud which they perceiv'd to hang over their Heads from *England;* with a true Presbyterian Policy, they put in for *a union of Nations,* that *England* might unite their Church with the Kirk of *Scotland,* and their Presbyterian Members sit in our House of Commons, and their Assembly of *Scotch* canting Long-Cloaks in our Convocation; what might ha' been, if our Phanatick, Whiggish States-men had continu'd, God only knows; but we hope we are out of fear of that now.

---

[10] Defoe's cavalier treatment of punctuation will already have been observed. Here he is not inventing, but making use of an obsolete past participle of 'creep' (known to the *OED*).

[11] A Whig periodical, which later (1710-11) directed most of its energies into opposition to Swift's *Examiner.*

[12] An anonymous pamphlet, published in 1691: *A late letter, giving a full account of the Sufferings of the Episcopal Clergy in Scotland* (J.T. Boulton's note, op. cit., p. 268).

'Tis alledg'd by some of the Faction, and they began to Bully us with it; that if we won't unite with them, they will not settle the Crown with us again but when her Majesty dies, will chuse a King for themselves.

If they won't, we must make them, and 'tis not the first time we have let them know that we are able: The Crowns of these Kingdoms have not so far disowned the right of Succession, but they may retrieve it again, and if *Scotland* thinks to come off from a Successive to an Elective State of Government, *England* has not promised not to assist the right Heir, and put them into possession, without any regard to their ridiculous Settlements.

THESE are the Gentlemen, these their ways of treating the Church, both at home and abroad. Now let us examine the Reasons they pretend to give why we shou'd be favourable to them, why we should continue and tollerate them among us.

First, THEY are very Numerous, they say, they are a great Part of the Nation, and we cannot suppress them.

To this may be answer'd 1. THEY are not so Numerous as the Protestants in *France,* and yet the *French* King effectually clear'd the Nation of them at once, and we don't find he misses them at home.[13]

But I am not of the Opinion they are so Numerous as is pretended; their Party is more Numerous than their Persons, and those mistaken People of the Church, who are misled and deluded by their wheedling Artifices, to join with them, make their Party the greater; but those will open their Eyes, when the Government shall set heartily about the work, and come off from them, as some Animals, which they say, always desert a House when 'tis likely to fall.

2dly. The more Numerous, the more Dangerous, and therefore the more need to suppress them; and God has suffer'd us to bear them as Goads in our sides for not utterly extinguishing them long ago.

3dly. If we are to allow them, only because we cannot suppress them, then it ought to be tryed whether we can or no; and I am of Opinion 'tis easy to be done, and cou'd prescribe Ways and Means, if it were proper, but I doubt not the

---

[13] Bloody persecution of the French Protestants by Louis XIV in the 1680s and 1690s led to the mass emigration of the Huguenots to England and Holland

Government will find effectual Methods for the rooting the Contagion from the Face of this Land.

ANOTHER Argument they use, which is this, That 'tis a time of War, we have need to unite against the common Enemy.

WE answer, this common Enemy had been no Enemy, if they had not made him so; he was quiet, in peace, and no way disturb'd, or encroach'd upon us, and we know no reason we had to quarrel with him.

But further, We make no question but we are able to deal with this common Enemy without their help; but why must we unite with them because of the Enemy, will they go over to the Enemy, if we do not prevent it by a union with them — We are very well contented they shou'd; and make no question we shall be ready to deal with them and the common Enemy too, and better without them than with them.

Besides, if we have a common Enemy, there is the more need to be secure against our private Enemies; if there is one common Enemy, we have the less need to have an Enemy in our Bowels.

'Twas a great Argument some People used against suppressing the Old-Money, that 'twas a time of War, and 'twas too great a Risque for the Nation to run, if we shou'd not master it, we shou'd be undone; and yet the Sequel prov'd the Hazard was not so great, but it might be mastered; and the Success was answerable. The suppressing the Dissenters is not a harder Work, nor a Work of less necessity to the Publick; we can never enjoy a settled uninterrupted Union and Tranquility in this Nation, till the Spirit of Whiggisme, Faction, and Schism is melted down like the Old-Money.[14]

To talk of the Difficulty, is to Frighten our selves with Chimæras and Notions of a Powerful Party, which are indeed a Party without Power; Difficulties often appear greater at a distance, than when they are search'd into with Judgment, and distinguish'd from the Vapours and Shadows that attend them.

We are not to be frightned with it; this Age is wiser than that, by all our own Experience, and *their's too*; King *Charles* the First, had early suppress this Party, if he had took more deliberate Measures. In short, 'tis not worth arguing to talk of

---

[14] The practice of clipping silver coins was finally tackled in 1695; after May, 1696, clipped coins were no longer legal tender, and were melted down.

The Shortest-Way with the Dissenters

their Arms, their *Monmouths*, and *Shaftsburys*, and *Argiles*[15] are gone, their *Dutch-Sanctuary* is at an end, Heaven has made way for their Destruction, and if we do not close with the Divine occasion, we are to blame our selves, and may remember that we had once an opportunity to serve the Church of *England*, by extirpating her implacable Enemies, and having let slip the Minute that Heaven presented, may experimentally Complain, *Post est Occasio Calvo*.[16]

Here are some popular Objections[17] in the way.

> As first, THE Queen has promis'd them, to continue them in their tollerated Liberty; and has told us she will be a religious Observer of her Word.

WHAT her Majesty will do we cannot help, but what, as the Head of the Church, she ought to do, is another Case: Her Majesty has promised to Protect and Defend the Church of *England,* and if she cannot effectually do that without the Destruction of the Dissenters, she must of course dispence with one Promise to comply with another. But to answer *this Cavil more effectually*: Her Majesty did never promise to maintain the Tolleration, to the Destruction of the Church; but it is upon supposition that it may be compatible with the well being and safety of the Church, which she had declar'd she would take especial Care of: Now if these two Interests clash, 'tis plain her Majesties Intentions are to Uphold, Protect, Defend, and Establish the Church, and this we conceive is impossible.

> Perhaps it may be said, THAT the Church is in no immediate danger from the Dissenters, and therefore 'tis time enough: But this is a weak Answer.

For first, IF a Danger be real, the Distance of it is no Argument against, but rather a Spur to quicken us to prevention, lest it be too late hereafter.

And 2dly, Here is the Opportunity, and the only one perhaps that ever the Church had to secure her self, and destroy her Enemies.

---

[15] Supporters of the Duke of Monmouth.

[16] 'The opportune moment has passed.' 'Calva' would be better Latin.

[17] Here the mask slips perceptibly, as Defoe puts forward some potent justifications for religious (and therefore political) tolerance. His extremist Tory persona knocks each one of these justifications on the head with a violence bordering on dementia.

The Representatives of the Nation have now an Opportunity, the Time is come which all good Men ha' wish'd for, that the Gentlemen of *England* may serve the Church of *England*; now they are protected and encouraged by a Church of *England* Queen.

What will ye do for your Sister in the Day that she shall be spoken for.

If ever you will establish the best Christian Church in the World.

If ever you will suppress the Spirit of Enthusiasm.[18]

If ever you will free the Nation from the viperous Brood that have so long suck'd the Blood of their Mother.

If you will leave your Posterity free from Faction and Rebellion, this is the time.

This is the time to pull up this heretical Weed of Sedition, that has so long disturb'd the Peace of our Church, and poisoned the good Corn.

BUT, says another Hot and Cold Objector, this is renewing Fire and Faggot, reviving the Act *De Heret. Comburendo*:[19] This will be Cruelty in its Nature and Barbarous to all the World.

I answer, 'TIS Cruelty to kill a Snake or a Toad in cold Blood, but the Poyson of their Nature makes it a Charity to our Neighbours, to destroy those Creatures, not for any personal Injury receiv'd, but for prevention; not for the Evil they have done, but the Evil they may do.

Serpents, Toads, Vipers, &c. are noxious to the Body, and poison the sensative Life, these poyson the Soul, corrupt our Posterity, ensnare our Children, destroy the Vitals of our Happyness, our future Felicity, and contaminate the whole Mass.

---

[18] 'Enthusiasts' (meaning 'fanatics') was an insulting name given to Protestant Dissenters. In Swift's *A Tale of a Tub*, the Dissenter, Jack (one of the three brothers of the 'Tale'), has strange habits: 'When he had some Roguish Trick to play, he would down with his Knees, up with his Eyes, and fall to Prayers, tho' in the midst of the Kennel [gutter - open sewer]. Then it was that those who understood his Pranks, would be sure to get out of his Way; And whenever Curiosity attracted Strangers to Laugh, or to Listen; he would, of a sudden, with one Hand out with his *Gear*, and piss full in their Eyes, and with the other, all to-bespatter them with Mud' (*A Tale of a Tub and other Satires*, ed. Kathleen Williams, pp. 124-5). In a note, the narrator of the *Tale* remarks that this passage represents 'The Villanies and Cruelties committed by Enthusiasts and Fanaticks among us, [which] were all performed under the Disguise of Religion and long Prayers'.

[19] 'On the burning of heretics.'

Shall any Law be given to such wild Creatures: Some Beasts are for Sport, and the Huntsmen give them advantages of Ground; but some are knock'd on the Head by all possible ways of Violence and Surprize.

I do not prescribe Fire and Faggot, but as *Scipio* said of *Carthage*, *D[e]lenda est Carthago*;[20] they are to be rooted out of this Nation, if ever we will live in Peace, serve God, or enjoy our own: As for the Manner, I leave it to those Hands who have a right to execute God's Justice on the Nation's and the Church's Enemies.

BUT if we must be frighted from this Justice, under the specious Pretences, and odious Sense of Cruelty, nothing will be effected: 'Twill be more Barbarous, and Cruel to our own Children, and dear Posterity, when they shall reproach their Fathers, as we do ours, and tell us, 'You had an Opportunity to root out this cursed Race from the World, under the Favour and Protection of a true *English* Queen; and out of your foolish Pity you spared them, because, forsooth, you would not be Cruel, and now our Church is supprest and persecuted, our Religion trampl'd under Foot, our Estates plundred, our Persons imprisoned and dragg'd to Jails, Gibbets, and Scaffolds; your sparing this *Amalakite*[21] Race is our Destruction, your Mercy to them proves Cruelty to your poor Posterity.'

HOW just will such Reflections be, when our Posterity shall fall under the merciless Clutches of this uncharitable Generation, when our Church shall be swallow'd up in Schism, Faction, Enthusiasme, and Confusion; when our Government shall be devolv'd upon Foreigners, and our Monarchy dwindled into a Republick.

'Twou'd be more rational for us, if we must spare this Generation, to summon our own to a general Massacre, and as we have brought them into the World Free, send them out so, and not betray them to Destruction by our supine negligence, and then cry *it is Mercy*.

---

[20] 'Carthage must be destroyed.'

[21] Ancient nomadic tribe, or collection of tribes, described in the Old Testament as relentless enemies of Israel, even though they were closely related to one of the twelve tribes of Israel. Their name derives from Amalek who is celebrated in Arabian tradition but not identified. The Amalakites harassed the Hebrews in their exodus from Egypt, attacking them near Mt Sinai, where they were defeated by Joshua. Their final defeat came in the time of Hezekiah; they were the subject of a perpetual curse (*Encyclopaedia Britannica*).

Moses was a merciful meek Man, and yet with what Fury did he run thro' the Camp, and cut the Throats of Three and thirty thousand[22] of his dear *Israelites* that were fallen into Idolatry; what was the reason? 'twas Mercy to the rest, to make these be Examples, to prevent the Destruction of the whole Army.

How many Millions of future Souls we save from Infection and Delusion, if the present Race of poison'd Spirits were purg'd from the Face of the Land....

And may God Almighty put it into the Hearts of all the Friends of Truth , to lift up a Standard against Pride and Antichrist that the Posterity of the Sons of Error be rooted out from the Face of this Land for ever—

FINIS

---

[22] J.T. Boulton (op. cit., p. 268) points out that this figure is almost certainly an exaggeration (*Exodus*, XXXII, 28, has 3,000; *Numbers*, XXV, 9, has 24, 000). It obviously serves Defoe's purpose, however, to convey root-and-branch extirpation.

THE OLD FUMBLER.[1] A SONG:
Set by Mr. Hen. Purcell.

Smug, rich and fantastic old fumbler was known,

That wedded a juicy brisk girl of the town,

Her face like an angel, fair, plump, and a maid,

Her lute well in tune too, could he but have played;

But lost was his skill let him do what he can,

She finds him in bed a weak silly old man,

He coughs in her ear, 'tis in vain to come on,

Forgive me, my dear, I'm a silly old man.

She laid his dry hand on her snowy soft breast,

And from those white hills gave a glimpse of the best;

But ah! what is age when our youth's but a span,

She found him an infant instead of a man:

Ah! Pardon, he'd cry, that I'm weary so soon,

---

[1] Tom Brown (1663-1704) was no unlettered Dunce. He studied at Christ Church College, Oxford, where he produced for Dr Fell, his tutor, the extempore adaptation of a Martial epigram for which he is (or perhaps is not) chiefly remembered:
> 'I do not love thee, Doctor Fell,
> The reason why I cannot tell;
> But this alone I know full well,
> I do not love thee, Doctor Fell.'

(Quoted by Philip Pinkus, *Grub Street stripped bare*, p. 118.)
'The Old Fumbler', it has to be conceded, is scarcely high culture. It *is* Grub Street culture, however (or part of it): whatever sells is good. One should also note that it is *the* Henry Purcell who deigned to set this grubby little piece to music.

You have let down my bass, I'm no longer in tune,
Lay by the dear instrument, prithee lie still,
I can play but one lesson and that I play ill.

THE POET'S CONDITION[2]

Without formal petition
Thus stands my condition:
I am closely blocked up in a garret,
Where I scribble and smoke,
And sadly invoke
The powerful assistance of claret.
Four children and a wife,
'Tis hard on my life,
Beside myself and a muse,
To be all clothed and fed,
Now the times are so dead,
By my scribbling of doggerel and news.
And what I shall do,
I'm a wretch if I know,
So hard is the fate of a poet;
I must either turn rogue,
Or, what's as bad, pedagogue,
And so drudge like a thing that has no wit.

My levee's[3] all duns,[4]
Attended by bums,[5]

---

[2] Not immortal verse either. This one is interesting, though, like the one that follows, for what it reveals of the life of an inhabitant of Grub Street in the early eighteenth century. All the expected ingredients are present: the garret, hungry children, pursuit by creditors - suggesting that the mythical Grub Street was no myth.

[3] 'A reception of visitors on rising from bed; a morning assembly held by a prince or person of distinction' (OED). Even doggerel is permitted a little irony.

[4] These are the creditors, listed further down.

[5] Short (and contemptuous) for 'bumbailiffs'; it was their task to arrest debtors.

And my landlady too she's a teaser,
At least four times a day
She warns me away,
And what can a man do to please her?
Here's the victualler and vintner,
The cook and the printer,
With their myrmidons[6] hovering about, sir:
The tailor and draper,
With the cur that sells paper,
That, in short, I dare not stir out, sir,
But my books sure may go,
My master Ovid's did so,
And tell how doleful the case is;
If it don't move your pity,
To make short of my ditty,
'Twill serve you to wipe your arses.[7]

FAREWELL TO POOR ENGLAND[8]

Farewell false friends, farewell ill wine,
Farewell all women with design;
Farewell all pocky cheating punks,[9]
Farewell lotteries, farewell banks;
And England, I'm leaving thee,
May say, farewell to poverty:
Adieu, where e're I go, I'm sure to find,
Nothing so ill, as that I leave behind.

---

[6] Achilles' sinister bodyguard in Shakespeare's version of *Troilus and Cressida*.
[7] A familiar Grub Street jest (cp. *Apollo's Maggot In his Cups, Sawney and Colley*, etc.), with here an added bitterness.
[8] Written in 1704, just before he died. This is a sad little piece; like the preceding one, it affords an insight into the life of a man who has spent his life struggling to make a living as a writer.
[9] Prostitutes.

Farewell nation without sense,
Farewell exchequer without pence;
Farewell Army with bare feet;
Farewell navy without meat;
Farewell wrighting[10] fighting beauxs,
And farewell useless plenipoes.
Adieu, &c.

Farewell you *Good Old Cause*,[11] promoters,
Farewell bribed artillery voters;
Farewell to all attainting bills,
And record which for witness kills;
Farewell to laymen's villainy,
And farewell church-men's perjury;[12] Adieu, &c.

Instead of one king, farewell nine,
And all who associating sign;
Farewell you gulled unthinking fops,
Poor broken merchants empty shops;
Farewell packed[13] judges, culled for blood,[14]
With eight years war for England's good; Adieu, &c.

---

[10] Only makes sense if the obsolete form of 'writing' is intended; in the next line, 'plenipoes' are plenipotentiaries, a prince's viceroys. Brown appears to despair of the war (not brought to a conclusion until the Treaty of Utrecht, 1713).

[11] The slogan of the proponents of a free commonwealth. Milton used the phrase in his *Ready and Easy Way to establish a Free Commonwealth* (published in 1660, two months before the restoration of Charles II: 'What government comes nearer to [the] precept of Christ than a free commonwealth; wherein they who are the greatest are perpetual servants and drudges to the public at their own cost and charges, neglect their own affairs, yet are not elevated above their brethren....But if people be so affected as to prostitute religion and liberty to the vain and groundless apprehension that nothing but kingship can restore trade...our condition is not sound but rotten, both in religion and all civil prudence....What I have spoken is the language of that which is not called amiss, "the Good Old Cause".' (This extract is taken from *The Good Old Cause*, *The English Revolution of 1640-1660*, eds C. Hill and E. Dell, Augustus M. Kelley, rev. ed., 1969, pp. 462-3.)

[12] The foregoing is a litany of corruption; Brown starts with those bribed to vote to continue the war, and ends with dishonest churchmen. He is evidently (or wishes to appear to be) a disillusioned observer of the socio-political scene.

[13] 'Selected or manipulated to serve party ends' (*OED*).

[14] Chosen because of their class origin, but also to enforce bloody laws and their penalties.

The Old Fumbler

>Farewell you judges, who dispense,
>With perjured cut-throat evidence;
>Farewell thou haughty little mouse,
>With those that choose thee for the house;
>Farewell long—and spiteful looks,
>With Reverend Oates,[15] and all his books Adieu, &c.
>
>Adieu once more, Britannia fare thee well,
>And if all this wont mend thee,
>May the D - triumph in your spoil,
>May beggary run throughout your isle,
>And no one think it worth his while
>To take up to defend thee.[16]

---

[15] This is a reference to the Titus Oates (1649-1705) of the infamous Popish Plot of 1678: 'English conspirator and perjurer, son of an anabaptist preacher. He attended Cambridge University, took orders, and held curacies and a naval chaplaincy, from all of which he was expelled for infamous practices' (*Chambers Biographical Dictionary*, 1990).

[16] For all his cynicism, there is a vein of the 'good old cause' runs through Brown's writing, as it does through the work of many of his Grub Street brethren. (Though by no means all - there were plenty who willingly sold their pens to whoever was in power. Defoe, for one, stands charged with (at least partly) turning his coat.)

A TALE of a TUB[1]

SECT. IX.

A Digression concerning the Original, the Use and Improvement of Madness *in a Commonwealth.*

NOR shall it any ways detract from the just Reputation of this famous Sect,[2] that its Rise and Institution are owing to such an Author as I have described *Jack* [3] to be; A Person whose Intellectuals were overturned, and his Brain shaken out of its Natural Position; which we commonly suppose to be a Distemper, and call by the Name of *Madness or Phrenzy.* For, if we take a Survey of the greatest Actions that have been performed in the World, under the Influence of Single Men; which are, *The Establishment of New Empires by Conquest: The Advance and Progress of New Schemes in Philosophy; and the contriving, as well as the propagating of New Religions:* We shall find the Authors of them all, to have been Persons, whose

---

[1] *A Tale of a Tub* was first published in 1704, and with additional items, in 1710. It is a satire on corruption in religion and learning, in a form which itself parodied much contemporary publishing practice. (Before the 'Tale' gets under way, there is a *Dedication, The Bookseller to the Reader, The Epistle Dedicatory, The Preface* and *The Introduction.*) The *Tale* is presented as a typical Grub-Street production: a rag-bag of garrulous, pompous, short-sighted and long-winded but vacuous verbiage. Digressions litter the reader's path through the story of the three brothers (the actual 'Tale'); included here is an extraordinary piece of Grub-Street nonsense, purporting (in all solemnity) to examine the value of madness to the nation. Swift, as elsewhere in the *Tale,* employs the *persona* of Grub-Street hack; in this case, the voice is that of a particularly gullible, dim-witted observer of the socio-historical scene. (The text is taken from *A Tale of a Tub and Other Satires,* ed. Kathleen Williams, Dent, 1975.)

[2] The 'Æolists' - subject of an earlier Digression. Their philosophy (expounded at great length by another of Swift's hacks), declares 'the Original of all Things to be *Wind*'; therefore, 'the wise Æolists affirm the Gift of BELCHING to be the noblest Act of a rational Creature' (Section VIII).

[3] One of the three brothers who are the subject of the 'Tale'.

natural Reason hath admitted great Revolutions from their Dyet, their Education, the Prevalency of some certain Temper, together with the particular Influence of Air and Climate. Besides, there is something Individual in human Minds, that easily kindles at the accidental Approach and Collision of certain Circumstances, which tho' of paltry and mean Appearance, do often flame out into the greatest Emergencies of Life. For great Turns are not always given by strong Hands, but by lucky Adaption, and at proper Seasons; and it is of no import, where the Fire was kindled, if the Vapor has once got up into the Brain. For the *upper Region* of Man, is furnished like the *middle Region* of the Air; The Materials are formed from Causes of the widest Difference, yet produce at last the same Substance and Effect. Mists arise from the Earth, Steams from Dunghils, Exhalations from the Sea, and Smoak from Fire; yet all Clouds are the same in Composition, as well as Consequences: and the Fumes issuing from a Jakes, will furnish as comely and useful a Vapor, as Incense from an Altar.[4] Thus far, I suppose, will easily be granted me; and then it will follow, that as the Face of Nature never produces Rain, but when it is overcast and disturbed, so Human Understanding, seated in the Brain, must be troubled and overspread by Vapours, ascending from the lower Faculties, to water the Invention, and render it fruitful. Now, altho' these Vapours (as it hath been already said) are of as various Original, as those of the Skies, yet the Crop they produce, differs both in Kind and Degree, meerly according to the Soil. I will produce two Instances to prove and Explain what I am now advancing.

A certain Great Prince[5] raised a mighty Army, filled his Coffers with infinite Treasures, provided an invincible Fleet, and all this, without giving the least Part of his Design to his greatest Ministers, or his nearest Favourites. Immediately the whole World was alarmed; the neighbouring Crowns, in trembling Expectation, towards what Point the Storm would burst; the small Politicians, every where forming profound Conjectures. Some believed he had laid a Scheme for Universal Monarchy: Others, after much Insight, determined the Matter to be a Project for pulling down the *Pope* and setting up the *Reformed* Religion, which had once been

---

[4] If the reader has not already become alerted to the outrageous logic of the narrator (the hacks who are given the narration of the *Tale* are not men of great intellect), this comparison between 'the Fumes from a Jakes' and 'Incense from an Altar' surely must do so.
[5] '*This was* Harry *the Great of* France ' (footnote to the original text). Henri IV (1553-1610), King of France from 1589 until his assassination at the hands of a Catholic religious fanatic (see next note).

A Digression on Madness

his own. Some, again, of a deeper Sagacity, sent him into *Asia* to subdue the *Turk* and recover Palestine. In the midst of all these Projects and Preparations; a certain *State-Surgeon*,[6] gathering the Nature of the Disease by these Symptoms, attempted the Cure, at one Blow performed the Operation, broke the Bag, and out flew the *Vapour*; nor did any thing want to render it a compleat Remedy, only, that Prince unfortunately happened to Die in the Performance. Now, is the Reader exceeding curious to learn, from whence this *Vapour* took its Rise, which had so long set the Nations at a Gaze? What secret Wheel, what hidden Spring could put into Motion so wonderful an Engine? It was afterwards discovered, that the Movement of this whole Machine had been directed by an absent *Female,* whose Eyes had raised a Protuberancy, and before Emission, she was removed into an Enemy's Country. What should an unhappy Prince do in such ticklish Circumstances as these? He tried in vain the Poet's never-failing Receipt of *Corpora quaeque*;[7] For,

> *Idque petit corpus mens unde est saucia amore;*
> *Unde feritur, eo tendit gestitq; coire.* Lucr.[8]

HAVING to no purpose used all peaceable Endeavours, the collected part of the *Semen,* raised and enflamed, became adust, converted to Choler, turned head upon the spinal Duct, and ascended to the Brain. The very same Principle that influences a *Bully* to break the Windows of a Whore, who has jilted him, naturally stirs up a Great Prince to raise mighty Armies, and dream of nothing but Sieges, Battles, and Victories.
>   ————*Teterrima belli*
> *Causa*————————[9]

---

[6] 'Ravillac, *who stabb'd* Henry *the Great in his Coach*' (note to text). François Ravaillac (1578-1610), was the French schoolmaster and religious fanatic who assassinated Henri IV. His punishment was to be torn apart by horses (*DNB*).

[7] Any bodies.

[8] 'And the body seeks that object by which the mind is wounded in love. He tends to that by which he is struck and desires to unite with it': Lucretius, *De Rerum Natura* (note by Angus Ross and David Woolley, in the World's Classics edition of *A Tale of a Tub*, Oxford University Press, 1986, p. 215).

[9] So 'the most dreadful cause of war' (lust for a woman) is no different from the motive behind the actions of the thwarted lout (in the view of the narrator). Swift's irony has an unsettling effect - his persona/narrator from time to time puts his finger on uncomfortable truths. Our problem, as readers, is to determine where Swift for a moment joins company with his naïve, self-opinionated hack.

THE other Instance is, what I have read somewhere, in a very antient Author, of a mighty King,[10] who for the space of above thirty Years, amused himself to take and lose Towns; beat Armies, and be beaten; drive Princes out of their Dominions; fright Children from their Bread and Butter; burn, lay waste, plunder, dragoon, massacre Subject and Stranger, Friend and Foe, Male and Female. 'Tis recorded, that the Philosophers of each Country were in grave Dispute, upon Causes Natural, Moral, and Political, to find out where they should assign an original Solution of this *Phenomenon*. At last the *Vapour* or *Spirit* which animated the Hero's Brain, being in perpetual Circulation, seized upon that Region of the Human Body, so renown'd for furnishing the *Zibeta Occidentalis*,[11] and gathering these into a Tumor, left the rest of the World for that Time in Peace. Of such mighty Consequence it is, where those Exhalations fix; and of so little, from whence they proceed. The same Spirits which in their superior Progress would conquer a Kingdom, descending upon the *Anus*, conclude in a *Fistula*.

LET us next examine the great Introducers of new Schemes in Philosophy,[12] and search till we can find, from what Faculty of the Soul the Disposition arises in mortal Man, of taking it into his Head, to advance new Systems with such an eager Zeal, in things agreed on all hands impossible to be known: from what Seeds this Disposition springs, and to what Quality of human Nature these Grand Innovators have been indebted for their Number of Disciples. Because, it is plain, that several of the chief among them, both *Antient* and *Modern*, were usually mistaken by their Adversaries, and indeed, by all, except their own Followers, to have been Persons Crazed, or out of their Wits, having generally proceeded in the common Course of their Words and Actions, by a Method very different from the vulgar Dictates of *unrefined* Reason: agreeing for the most Part in their several Models, with their

---

[10] The king this time is Louis XIV, whose mighty conquests are attributed, here, to a cyst on his anus.

[11] 'Western perfume' (civet). A learned note from the narrator reads: 'Paracelsus, *who was so famous for Chymistry, try'd an Experiment upon human Excrement, to make a Perfume of it, which when he had brought to Perfection, he called* Zibeta Occidentalis, *or* Western-Civit, *the back parts of Man...being the* West'. The reader should be able to deduce the rest.

[12] The next stage in the development of the premise that madness has great potential value. Nobody, however pre-eminent, in whatever field, is safe from the enthusiastically amateurish probings of this intellectual giant. So, in the discussion that follows, we are treated to discourse on Epicurus, Diogenes et al - they, too, qualify for Bedlam.

A Digression on Madness

present undoubted Successors in the *Academy of Modern Bedlam*[13] (whose Merits and Principles I shall farther examine in due Place.) Of this Kind were *Epicurus, Diogenes, Apollonius, Lucretius, Paracelsus, Des Cartes* and others, who, if they were now in the World, tied fast, and separate from their Followers, would in this our undistinguishing Age, incur manifest Danger of *Phlebotomy* and *Whips* and *Chains* and *dark Chambers,* and *Straw.* For, what Man in the natural State, or Course of Thinking, did ever conceive it in his Power, to reduce the Notions of all Mankind, exactly to the same Length, and Breadth, and Heighth of his own? Yet this is the first humble and civil Design of all Innovators in the Empire of Reason. *Epicurus* modestly hoped, that one Time or other, a certain Fortuitous Concourse of all Mens Opinions, after perpetual Justlings, the Sharp with the Smooth, the Light and the Heavy, the Round and the Square, would by certain *Clinamina*[14] unite in the Notions of *Atoms* and *Void* as these did in the Originals of all Things. *Cartesius* reckoned to see before he died, the Sentiments of all Philosophers, like so many lesser Stars in his *Romantick* System, rapt and drawn within his own *Vortex.* Now, I would gladly be informed, how it is possible to account for such Imaginations as these in particular Men, without Recourse to my *Phænomenon of Vapours*, ascending from the lower Faculties to over-shadow the Brain, and thence distilling into Conceptions, for which the Narrowness of our Mother-Tongue has not yet assigned any other Name, besides that of *Madness* or *Phrenzy*. Let us therefore now conjecture how it comes to pass, that none of these great Prescribers, do ever fail providing themselves and their Notions, with a Number of implicite Disciples. And, I think, the Reason is easie to be assigned: For, there is a peculiar *String* in the Harmony of Human Understanding, which in several individuals is exactly of the same Tuning. This, if you can dexterously screw up to its right Key, and then strike gently upon it; Whenever you have the Good Fortune to light among those of the same Pitch, they will by a secret necessary Sympathy, strike exactly at the same time. And in this one Circumstance, lies all the Skill or Luck of the Matter; for if you chance to jar the String among those who are either above or below your own Height, instead of subscribing to your Doctrine, they will tie you fast, call you

---

[13] Bethlehem Hospital, or Bedlam, a mental hospital for 150 patients, moved to a new building in 1675, near to where the Royal Society held its gatherings.

[14] Clinamen - 'the inclination or turning aside of a thing' (C.T. Lewis and C. Short, *A Latin Dictionary*). Our Dunce is showing off again.

Mad, and feed you with Bread and Water. It is therefore a Point of the nicest Conduct to distinguish and adapt this noble Talent, with respect to the Differences of Persons and of Times. *Cicero* understood this very well, when writing to a Friend in *England* with a Caution, among other Matters, to beware of being cheated by our *Hackney-Coachmen* (who, it seems, in those days, were as arrant Rascals as they are now) has these remarkable Words. *Est quod gaudeas te in ista loca venisse, ubi aliquid sapere viderere.*[15] For, to speak a bold Truth, it is a fatal Miscarriage, so ill to order Affairs, as to pass for a *Fool* in one Company, when in another you might be treated as a *Philosopher*. Which I desire *some certain Gentlemen of my Acquaintance* to lay up in their Hearts, as a very seasonable *Innuendo*.

THIS, indeed, was the Fatal Mistake of that worthy Gentleman, my most ingenious Friend, Mr. *Wotton:*[16] A Person, in appearance ordain'd for great Designs, as well as Performances; whether you will consider his *Notions* or his *Looks*. Surely, no Man ever advanced into the Publick, with fitter Qualifications of Body and Mind, for the Propagation of a new Religion. Oh, had those happy Talents misapplied to vain Philosophy; been turned into their proper Channels of *Dreams* and *Visions*, where *Distortion* of Mind and Countenance, are of such Sovereign Use; the base detracting World would not then have dared to report, that something is amiss, that his Brain hath undergone an unlucky Shake; which even his Brother *Modernists* themselves, like Ungrates, do whisper so loud, that it reaches up to the very *Garrat* I am writing in.

LASTLY, Whosoever pleases to look into the Fountains of *Enthusiasm*, from whence, in all Ages, have eternally proceeded such fatning Streams, will find the Spring Head to have been as *troubled* and *muddy* as the Current; Of such great Emolument, is a Tincture of this *Vapour* which the World calls *Madness*, that without its Help, the World would not only be deprived of those two great Blessings, *Conquests* and *Systems*, but even all Mankind would unhappily be reduced to the same Belief in Things Invisible. Now, the former *Postulatum* being held, that it is of no Import from what Originals this *Vapour* proceeds, but either in

---

[15] 'It is a matter for rejoicing to arrive in a place where you may pass yourself off as a knowledgeable man.' What matters (to our Dunce-philosopher) is the *appearance* of wisdom....

[16] William Wotton (1666-1727), who has a leading, if ignominious role in Swift's *The Battle of the Books*.

A Digression on Madness

what *Angles* it strikes and spreads over the Understanding, or upon what *Species* of Brain it ascends; It will be a very delicate Point, to cut the Feather,[17] and divide the several Reasons to a Nice and Curious Reader, how this numerical Difference in the Brain, can produce Effects of so vast a Difference from the same *Vapour* as to be the sole Point of Individuation between Alexander *the Great, Jack of Leyden,* and Monsieur *Des Cartes*. The present Argument is the most abstracted that ever I engaged in, it strains my Faculties to their highest Stretch; and I desire the Reader to attend with utmost Perpensity; For, I now proceed to unravel this knotty Point.[18]

THERE is in Mankind a certain * * * * *
* * * * * * * * * * *
* * * * * * * * * * *
* * * * * * * * * *Hic multa*
* * * * * * * * * *desiderantur*
* * * * * * * * * * *
* *
* * * And this I take to be a clear Solution of the Matter.

HAVING therefore so narrowly past thro' this intricate Difficulty, the Reader will, I am sure, agree with me in the Conclusion; that if the *Moderns* mean by *Madness* only a Disturbance or Transposition of the Brain, by Force of certain *Vapours* issuing up from the lower Faculties; Then has this *Madness* been the Parent of all those mighty Revolutions, that have happening in *Empire*, in *Philosophy*, and in *Religion*. For, the Brain, in its natural Position and State of Serenity, disposeth its Owner to pass his Life in the common Forms, without any Thought of subduing Multitudes to his own Power, his *Reasons* or his *Visions*; and the more he shapes his Understanding by the Pattern of Human Learning, the less he is inclined to form Parties after his particular Notions; because that instructs him in his private Infirmities, as well as in the stubborn Ignorance of the People. But when a Man's Fancy gets *astride* on his Reason, when Imagination is at Cuffs with the Senses, and common Understanding, as well as common Sense, is Kickt out of Doors; the first Proselyte[19] he makes, is Himself, and when that is once

---

[17] To split hairs, quibble over a detail.
[18] As the note amongst the asterisks remarks - much is missing (it's one way of coping with a particularly knotty part of the argument).
[19] 'One who has come over from one opinion, belief, creed, party to another; a convert' (*OED*).

compass'd, the Difficulty is not so great in bringing over others; A strong Delusion always operating from without as vigorously as from *within*. For, Cant and Vision are to the Ear and the Eye, the same that Tickling is to the Touch.[20] Those Entertainments and Pleasures we most value in Life, are such as *Dupe* and play the Wag with the Senses. For, if we take an Examination of what is generally understood by *Happiness*, as it has Respect, either to the Understanding or the Senses, we shall find all its Properties and Adjuncts will herd under this short Definition: That, *it is a perpetual Possession of being well Deceived*. And first, with Relation to Mind or Understanding; 'tis manifest, what mighty Advantages Fiction has over Truth; and the Reason is just at our Elbow, because Imagination[21] can build nobler Scenes, and produce more wonderful Revolutions than Fortune or Nature will be at Expence to furnish. Nor is Mankind so much to blame in his Choice, thus determining him, if we consider that the Debate meerly lies between *Things past,* and *Things conceived*; and so the Question is only this; Whether Things that have Place in the *Imagination* may not as properly be said to *Exist*, as those that are seated in the *Memory*; which may be justly held in the Affirmative, and very much to the Advantage of the former, since This is acknowledged to be the *Womb* of Things, and the other allowed to be no more than the *Grave*. Again, if we take this Definition of Happiness, and examine it with Reference to the Senses, it will be acknowledged wonderfully adapt. How sad and insipid do all Objects accost us that are not convey'd in the Vehicle of *Delusion*? How shrunk is every Thing, as it appears in the Glass of Nature? So, that if it were not for the Assistance of Artificial *Mediums*, false Lights, refracted Angles, Varnish, and Tinsel; there would be a mighty Level in the Felicity and Enjoyments of Mortal Men. If this were seriously considered by the World, as I have a certain Reason to suspect it hardly will; Men would no longer reckon among their high Points of Wisdom the Art of exposing weak Sides, and publishing Infirmities; an Employment in my Opinion,

---

[20] That is, pleasurable titillation. It is difficult to keep a firm grip on one's own sanity as the narrator goes into lunatic overdrive. It is worth remembering that the persona (dunce philosopher) really does believe there is value in the 'Fancy' and 'Imagination' running riot, abandoning 'Reason' and 'common Sense': that way madness lies.

[21] It is also worth remembering that imagination was not at this time held in the high critical esteem it was to achieve later in the century (when it became the defining feature of Romantic poetry).

neither better nor worse than that of *Unmasking*, which I think, has never been allowed fair Usage either in the *World* or the *Play-House*.

IN the Proportion that Credulity is a more peaceful Possession of the Mind, than Curiosity,[22] so far preferable is that Wisdom which converses about the Surface, to that pretended Philosophy which enters into the Depth of Things, and then comes gravely back with Informations and Discoveries, that in the inside they are good for nothing. The two Senses, to which all Objects first address themselves, are the Sight and the Touch. These never examine farther than the Colour, the Shape, the Size, and whatever other Qualities dwell, or are drawn by Art on the Outward of Bodies; and then comes Reason officiously with Tools for cutting, and opening, and mangling, and piercing, offering to demonstrate, that they are not of the same consistence quite thro'. Now, I take all this to be the last Degree of subverting Nature; one of whose Eternal Laws it is, to put her best Furniture forward. And therefore, in order to save the Charges of all such expensive Anatomy for the Time to come, I do here think fit to inform the Reader, that in such Conclusions as these, Reason is certainly in the Right, and that in most Corporeal Beings, which have fallen under my Cognizance, the outside hath been infinitely preferable to the *In*:: Whereof I have been farther convinced from some late Experiments. Last week I saw a Woman *flay'd*, and you will hardly believe, how much it altered her Person for the worse. Yesterday I ordered the Carcass of a *Beau* to be stript in my Presence; when we were all amazed to find so many unsuspected Faults under one Suit of Cloaths: Then I laid open his *Brain*, his *Heart*, and his *Spleen*; But I plainly perceived at every Operation, that the farther we proceeded, we found the Defects encrease upon us in Number and Bulk: from all which, I justly formed this Conclusion to my self; That whatever Philosopher or Projector can find out an Art to sodder[23] and patch up the Flaws and Imperfections of Nature, will deserve much better of Mankind, and teach us a more useful Science, than that so much in present Esteem, of widening and exposing them (like him who held *Anatomy* to be the ultimate End of *Physick*). And he, whose Fortunes and Dispositions have placed

---

[22] By this time, the reader should have a fairly clear view of where the Hack-narrator is coming from. He prefers not to peer too closely into things, and believes that true happiness consists of averting one's gaze from the world as it really is. With that in mind, the reader is invited to trace a path through the extraordinary attitudes displayed in the next devastating paragraph.

[23] Obsolete or dialect for 'solder' (*OED*).

him in a convenient Station to enjoy the Fruits of this noble Art; He that can with *Epicurus* content his Ideas with the *Films* and *Images* that fly off upon his Senses from the *Superficies* of Things; Such a Man truly wise, creams off Nature, leaving the Sower and the Dregs, for Philosophy and Reason to lap up. This is the sublime and refined Point of Felicity, called, *the Possession of being well deceived*; The Serene Peaceful State of being a Fool among Knaves.

BUT to return to *Madness*. It is certain, that according to the System I have above deduced; every *Species* thereof proceeds from a Redundancy of *Vapour*; therefore, as some kinds of *Phrenzy* give double Strength to the Sinews, so there are of other *Species* which add Vigor, and Life, and Spirit to the Brain: Now, it usually happens, that these active Spirits, getting Possession of the Brain, resemble those that haunt other waste and empty Dwellings, which for want of Business, either vanish, and carry away a Piece of the House, or else stay at home and fling it all out of the Windows. By which are mystically display'd the two principal Branches of *Madness,* and which some Philosophers not considering so well as I, have mistook to be different in their Causes, over-hastily assigning the first to Deficiency, and the other to Redundance.

I think it therefore manifest, from what I have here advanced, that the main Point of Skill and Address, is to furnish Employment for this Redundancy of *Vapour,* and prudently to adjust the Seasons of it; by which means it may certainly become of Cardinal and Catholick Emolument in a Commonwealth. Thus one Man chusing a proper Juncture, leaps into a Gulph, from thence proceeds a Hero, and is called the Saver of his Country;[24] Another atchieves the same Enterprise, but unluckily timing it, has left the Brand of *Madness*, fixt as a Reproach upon his Memory; Upon so nice a Distinction are we taught to repeat the Name of *Curtius* with Reverence and Love; that of *Empedocles*, with Hatred and Contempt. Thus, also it is usually conceived that the Elder *Brutus*[25] only personated the *Fool* and

---

[24] Mettus Curtius (4th century BC), a noble Roman youth who is said to have leapt on horseback into a chasm that opened in the Forum; the soothsayers had declared that it could only be filled by throwing into it the most precious treasure of Rome. The Greek philosopher Empedocles (5th century BC), with whom he is here compared, was thought to have jumped into the crater of Mt Etna to demonstrate his divinity (*Chambers Biographical Dictionary*). Our sagacious Dunce concludes it's a question of being in the right place at the right time.

[25] Lucius Junius Brutus (6th century BC), legendary hero who founded the Roman republic. He feigned madness (hence his name - 'Brutus' means 'stupid') to escape execution at the hands of the Tarquins.

A Digression on Madness

Madman, for the Good of the Publick: but this was nothing else, than a Redundancy of the same *Vapor* long misapplied, called by the *Latins, Ingenium par negotiis*:[26] Or, (to translate it as nearly as I can) a sort of *Phrenzy*, never in its right Element, till you take it up in Business of the State.

UPON all which, and many other Reasons of equal Weight, though not equally curious; I do here gladly embrace an Opportunity I have long sought for, of Recommending it as a very noble Undertaking, to Sir *Edward Seymour*, Sir *Christopher Musgrave*, Sir *John Bowls, John How*, Esq;[27] and other Patriots concerned, that they would move for Leave to bring in a Bill, for appointing Commissioners to Inspect into *Bedlam*, and the Parts adjacent; who shall be empowered to *send for Persons, Papers, and Records*: to examine into the Merits and Qualifications of every Student and Professor; to observe with utmost Exactness their several Dispositions and Behaviour; by which means, duly distinguishing and adapting their Talents, they might produce admirable Instruments for the several Offices in a State, * * * * * *[28] *Civil* and *Military*; proceeding in such Methods as I shall here humbly propose. And, I hope the Gentle Reader will give some Allowance to my great Solicitudes in this important Affair, upon Account of that high Esteem I have ever born that honourable Society, whereof I had some Time the Happiness to be an unworthy Member.

IS any Student tearing his Straw in piece-meal, Swearing and Blaspheming, biting his Grate, foaming at the Mouth, and emptying his Piss-pot in the Spectator's Faces? Let the Right Worshipful, the *Commissioners of Inspection*, give him a Regiment of Dragoons, and send him into *Flanders* among the *Rest*.[29] Is another eternally talking, sputtering, gaping, bawling, in a Sound without Period or Article? What wonderful Talents are here mislaid! Let him be furnished immediately with a green Bag and Papers, and *three Pence* in his Pocket, and away with Him to *Westminster-Hall*. You will find a Third, gravely taking the Dimensions of his kennel; A Person of Foresight and Insight, tho' kept quite in the Dark; for why, like *Moses, Ecce cornuta erat ejus facies*.[30] He walks duly in one Pace, intreats your

---

[26] A genius for business.
[27] All leading Tory MPs.
[28] 'Ecclesiastical' - note in the text.
[29] The joke is that our Hack-narrator *means* all these crack-pot recommendations. Whatever irony is at work here, he is certainly not aware of it.
[30] Behold, his face was shining.

Penny with due Gravity and Ceremony; talks much of hard Times, and Taxes, and the *Whore of Babylon*; Bars up the woodden Window of his Cell constantly at eight a Clock: Dreams of *Fire* and *Shop-lifters* and *Court -Customers* and *Priviledg'd Places*. Now, what a Figure would all these Acquirements amount to, if the Owner were sent into the City among his Brethren! Behold a Fourth, in much and deep Conversation with himself, biting his Thumbs at proper Junctures; His Countenance chequered with Business and Design; sometimes walking very fast, with his Eyes nailed to a Paper that he holds in his Hands: A great Saver of Time, somewhat thick of Hearing, very short of Sight, but more of Memory. A Man ever in Haste, a great Hatcher and Breeder of Business, and excellent at the Famous Art of *whispering Nothing*. A huge Idolater of monosyllables and Procrastination; so ready to *Give* his Word to every Body, that he never *keeps* it. One that has forgot the common *Meaning* of Words, but an admirable Retainer of the *Sound*. Extreamly subject to the *Looseness,* for his *Occasions* are perpetually *calling him away*. If you approach his Grate in his familiar Intervals; *Sir,* says he, *Give me a Penny and I'll sing you a Song: But give me the Penny first*. (Hence comes the common Saying, and commoner Practice of parting with Money for a *Song*.) What a compleat System of *Court-Skill* is here described in every Branch of it, and all utterly lost with wrong Application? Accost the Hole of another Kennel, first stopping your Nose, you will behold a surley, gloomy, nasty, slovenly Mortal, raking in his own Dung, and dabling in his Urine. The best Part of his Diet, is the Reversion of his own Ordure, which exspiring into Steams, whirls perpetually about, and at last reinfunds. His Complexion is of a dirty Yellow, with a thin scattered Beard, exactly agreeable to that of his Dyet upon its first Declination; like other Insects, who having their Birth and Education in an Excrement, from thence borrow their Colour and their Smell. The Student of this Apartment is very sparing of his Words, but somewhat over-liberal of his Breath; He holds his Hand out ready to receive your Penny, and immediately upon Receipt, withdraws to his former Occupations. Now, is it not amazing to think, the Society of *Warwick-Lane*[31] should have no more Concern, for the Recovery of so useful a Member, who, if one may judge from these Appearances, would become the greatest Ornament to that Illustrious Body? Another Student struts up fiercely to your Teeth, puffing with his Lips, half

---

[31] The Royal Society of Physicians was to be found in Warwick Lane at this time.

A Digression on Madness

squeezing out his Eyes, and very graciously holds you out his Hand to kiss. The *Keeper* desires you not to be afraid of this Professor, for he will do you no Hurt: To him alone is allowed the Liberty of the Anti-Chamber, and the *Orator*[32] of the Place gives you to understand, that this solemn Person is a *Taylor* run mad with Pride. This considerable Student is adorned with many other Qualities, upon which, at present, I shall not farther enlarge. - - - - - - - [33] *Heark in your Ear* - - - - - - - I am strangely mistaken, if all his Address, his Motions and his Airs, would not then be very natural, and in their proper Element.

I shall not descend so minutely, as to insist upon the vast Number of *Beaux Fidlers*, *Poets*, and *Politicians*, that the World might recover by such a Reformation; But what is more material, besides the clear Gain redounding to the Commonwealth, by so large an Acquisition of Persons to employ, whose Talents and Acquirements, if I may be so bold to affirm it, are now buried, or at least misapplied: It would be a mighty Advantage accruing to the Publick from this Enquiry, that all these would very much excel, and arrive at great Perfection in their several Kinds; which, I think, is manifest from what I have already shewn; and shall inforce by this one plain Instance; That even, I my self, the Author of these momentous Truths, am a Person, whose Imaginations are hard-mouth'd, and exceedingly disposed to run away with his *Reason*,[34] which I have observed from long Experience, to be a very light Rider, and easily shook off; upon which Account, my Friends will never trust me alone, without a solemn Promise, to vent my Speculations in this, or the like manner, for the universal Benefit of Human kind; which, perhaps, the gentle, courteous, and candid Reader, brimful of that *Modern* Charity and Tenderness, usually annexed to his *Office*, will be very hardly persuaded to believe.

---

[32] The guide.
[33] *I cannot conjecture what the Author means here, or how this Chasm could be fill'd, tho' it is capable of more than one Interpretation* (note below the text).
[34] At last, we have it from the Hack's own mouth - he, too, is more than a little mad (and, therefore, of considerable value to the 'commonwealth').

THE HISTORY OF JOHN *BULL*
OR
LAW IS A BOTTOMLESS PIT[1]
CHAPTER IV
HOW *BULL* AND *FROG* WENT TO LAW WITH LORD *STRUTT* ABOUT THE PREMISSES,[2] AND WERE JOINED BY THE REST OF THE TRADESMEN

---

[1] The initial pamphlet, about which Swift was so enthusiastic (see Introduction), was called *Law is a Bottomless Pit*, and was the first of a series attacking the conduct of the war with France and her allies. The first was published in March 1712; the second, *John Bull in His Senses*, was on sale two weeks later, and was followed by four more in the next four months. It was a very popular series, running to several editions in London alone. The 'law-suit' in question was the war, which dragged on through most of Queen Anne's reign. England (not Great Britain until 1707), came late into the war, which was essentially the rest of Europe resisting French hegemony. By the time of Queen Anne's last ministry, which came into office with the Tories' election victory of 1710, most of the Allies' war aims had been achieved. It was the task of the secretary of state, Henry St John (soon to be Viscount Bolingbroke), to secure a peace; he was helped by some powerful propaganda from Swift. Between November 1710, and June 1711, Swift wrote, single-handed, thirty-two numbers of the *Examiner*, a Tory organ. His pamphlet *The Conduct of the Allies* (November, 1711), swept all opposition before it. Arbuthnot's *John Bull* pamphlets were another contribution to the peace movement. (For a definitive account of the War of the Spanish Succession, see G. M.. Trevelyan, *England Under Queen Anne*.) John Bull, the hearty, bluff, honest Englishman, is Arbuthnot's invention; he stands for England, and Lewis Baboon is the King of France (Louis XIV), Lord Strutt the late King of Spain. Mrs Bull (John's first wife) is the Whig administration which vigorously promoted the war, and was defeated in the election of 1710; Nic Frog is the Dutch. In Arbuthnot's pamphlet, John Bull is a tradesman, a draper, and the dispute he has is with the less than honest competition. In particular, he is incensed that Lewis Baboon is poaching trade by obtaining contracts from Lord Strutt (i.e. Louis XIV had long been attempting to put a French puppet on the throne of Spain, to the horror of the rest of Europe - hence the War of the Spanish Succession). Further explanation when needed! The extract here is taken from the first edition of the first pamphlet, *Law is a Bottomless-Pit*, reprinted in *The History of John Bull*, edited by Alan W. Bower and Robert A Erickson (Oxford, 1976).

[2] Just to reinforce a necessary point - the English joined forces with the Dutch to wage war on Spain and France (1702) as a result of Louis XIV's establishment of his grandson on the throne of Spain as Philip V. It was this unholy alliance between the two kingdoms that was unacceptable to England and Holland. The Whig ministry (Mrs Bull) pursued the war with great energy; Arbuthnot, writing after ten years of their enthusiastic war-making, now turns the war into a comic chronicle of petty domestic wrangling and unneighbourly discord.

All endeavours of Accommodation between Lord *Strutt* and his Drapers prov'd vain, Jealousies increas'd, and indeed it was rumour'd abroad that Lord *Strutt* had bespoke his new Liveries of old *Lewis Baboon*. This coming to Mrs. *Bull*'s Ears, when *John Bull* came Home, he found all his Family in an uproar. Mrs. *Bull*, you must know, was very apt to be Cholerick. *You sot*, says she, *you loyter about AleHouses and Taverns, spend your time at Billiards, Nine-pins, or Puppet-shows, or flaunt about the Streets in your new gilt Chariot, never minding me nor your numerous Family. Don't you hear how Lord* Strutt *has bespoke his Liveries at* Lewis Baboon's *Shop? Don't you see how that old Fox steals away your Customers, and turns you out of your Business every day, and you sit like an idle Drone with your hands in your Pockets? Fie upon't! up Man, rouse thy self; I'll sell to my Shift before I'll be so used by that Knave.* You must think Mrs. *Bull* had been pretty well tun'd up by *Frog*, who chim'd in with her learn'd Harangue. No further delay now, but to Counsel learned in the Law they go, who unanimously assur'd 'em both of the Justice and infallible Success of their Law-Suit.

I told you before, that old *Lewis Baboon* was a sort of a *Jack of all Trades*, which made the rest of the Tradesmen jealous, as well as *Bull* and *Frog*; they hearing of the quarrel were glad of an Opportunity of joining against old *Lewis Baboon*, provided that *Bull* and *Frog* would bear the Charges of the Suit; even lying *Ned*, the Chimney-sweeper, and *Tom*, the Dustman,[3] put in their Claims; and the Cause was put into the Hands of *Humphry Hocus* the Attorney.

A Declaration was drawn up to shew 'That *Bull* and *Frog* had undoubted Right by Prescription to be Drapers to the Lord *Strutts*; that there were several old Contracts to that purpose; that *Lewis Baboon* had taken up the Trade of Clothier and Draper, without serving his Time or purchasing his Freedom; that he sold Goods, that were not Marketable, without the Stamp; that he himself was more fit for a Bully than a Tradesman, and went about through all the Country Fairs challenging People to fight Prizes, Wrestling and Cudgel-Play;' and abundance more to this purpose.

---

[3] The Allies (the Duke of Savoy and the King of Portugal) - not accorded any great respect! Swift's *Conduct of the Allies* (1711) argues for a peace to be made with or without the Allies. St John, indeed, more or less dictated the terms of the peace settlement to the Allies (see Trevelyan, *England Under Queen Anne*, vol. iii, Preface, p. viii).

CHAPTER V.
THE TRUE CHARACTER OF JOHN *BULL*, NIC. *FROG*, AND *HOCUS*[4]

For the better understanding the following History, the Reader ought to know, That *Bull*, in the main, was an honest plain-dealing Fellow, Cholerick, Bold, and of a very unconstant Temper; he dreaded not Old *Lewis* either at Back-Sword, single Faulcion,[5] or Cudgel-play; but then he was very apt to quarrel with his best Friends, especially if they pretended to govern him: If you flatter'd him, you might lead him like a Child. John's Temper depended very much upon the Air; his Spirits rose and fell with the Weather-glass. *John* was quick, and understood his Business very well; but no Man alive was more careless in looking into his Accounts, or more cheated by Partners, Apprentices, and Servants. This was occasioned by his being a Boon-Companion, loving his Bottle and his Diversion; for, to say Truth, no Man kept a better House than *John*, nor spent his Money more generously. By plain and fair dealing, *John* had acquir'd some Plumbs, and might have kept them, had it not been for his unhappy Law-Suit.

Nic. Frog was a cunning sly Whoreson, quite the reverse of *John* in Many Particulars; Covetous, Frugal; minded domestick Affairs; would pine his Belly to save his Pocket, never lost Farthing by careless Servants, or bad Debtors: He did not care much for any sort of Diversions, except Tricks of *High German* Artists, and *Leger de main*: no Man exceeded *Nic.* in these, yet it must be owned that *Nic.* was a fair Dealer, and in that way acquir'd immense Riches.

Hocus was an old cunning Attorney;[6] what he wanted of Skill in Law, was made up by a Clerk[7] which he kept, that was the prettiest Fellow in the World; he lov'd Money, was smooth-tongu'd, gave good Words, and seldom lost his Temper; he was not worse than an Infidel, for he provided plentifully for his Family; but he

---

[4] Humphrey Hocus: the Duke of Marlborough, commander of the Allied army who masterminded the great victories of Blenheim, Ramillies, Oudenarde and Malplaquet. His enemies (see, for example, Swift's 'Epitaph') maintained, with some truth, that the Duke exploited the war to enrich himself; hence the grandeur of Blenheim Palace.

[5] 'A broad sword more or less curved with the edge on the convex side' (*OED*).

[6] That is, skilful man of war (see note 4, above). There was no doubting his generalship (Trevelyan calls him a 'genius').

[7] 'Probably Prince Eugene...Marlborough's military partner in most of the major battles of the war. Eugene was known for great bravery and exemplary skill as a tactician; as to his appearance, reports varied' (note by Bower and Erickson, op. cit., p. 134). One of the Tory satirists' devices was to suggest that Marlborough's successes should really be credited to Eugene.

lov'd himself better than them all: He had a Termagant[8] Wife, and as the Neighbours said, was plaguy Hen-peck'd; he was seldom observed, as some Attornies will practice, to give his own personal Evidence in Causes; he rather chose to do it *per test. conduct.*[9] in a Word, the Man was very well for an Attorney.

CHAPTER VI
OF THE VARIOUS SUCCESS OF THE LAW-SUIT

Law is a Bottomless-Pit; it is a Cormorant, a Harpy that devours every thing; *John Bull* was flattered by the Lawyers, that his Suit would not last above a Year or two at most; that before that time he would be in quiet possession of his Business: yet ten long Years did *Hocus* steer his Cause through all the *Meanders* of the Law, and all the Courts. No Skill, no Address was wanting; and, to say truth, John did not starve his Cause; there wanted not *Yellow-boys*[10] to fee Counsel, hire Witnesses, and bribe Juries: Lord *Strutt* was generally Cast, never had one Verdict in his favour; and *John* was promis'd that the next, and the next, would be the final Determination; but alas! that final Determination and happy Conclusion was like an inchanted Island, the nearer *John* came to it, the further it went from him: new Tryals upon new Points still arose; new Doubts, new Matters to be cleared; in short, Lawyers seldom part with so good a Cause, till they have got the Oyster, and their Clients the Shell. *John*'s ready Mony, Book-Debts, Bonds, Mortgages, all went into the Lawyers' Pockets; then *John* began to borrow Money upon *Bank-Stock* and *East-India* Bonds; now and then a Farm went to Pot; at last it was thought a good Expedient to set up Esquire South's[11] Title, to prove the Will forg'd, and dispossess *Philip* Lord *Strutt* at once. Here again was a new field for the Lawyers, and the Cause grew more intricate than ever. *John* grew madder and madder; where-ever he met any of Lord *Strutt*'s Servants, he tore off their Cloaths: Now and then you would see them come home naked, without

---

[8] Sarah, Duchess of Marlborough, was noted for her violent temper, which the Tory satirists were not slow to exploit. She was, for many years, Queen Anne's close friend and confidant.

[9] 'Per testimonium conductorum', is the guess hazarded by Bower and Erickson (op. cit., p. 136). Arbuthnot is hinting at a lack of courage in the great man.

[10] Gold.

[11] Louis XIV's grandson, the king of Spain. The will referred to is that of Charles II of Spain, who bequeathed his throne to Louis XIV's grandson, and turmoil to Europe.

The History of John Bull

Shoes, Stockings, and Linnen. As for old *Lewis Baboon*, he was reduc'd to his last Shift,[12] tho' he had as many as any other: His Children were reduced from rich Silks to *Doily*[13] stuffs, his Servants in Rags, and bare-footed, instead of good Victuals, they now lived upon Neck-Beef, and Bullock's-Liver; in short, no Body got much by the Matter, but the Men of Law.

CHAPTER VII.
HOW *JOHN BULL* WAS SO MIGHTILY PLEASED WITH HIS SUCCESS, THAT HE WAS GOING TO LEAVE OFF HIS TRADE, AND TURN LAWYER.[14]

It is wisely observed by a great Philosopher, That Habit is a second Nature: This was verify'd in the case of *John Bull*, who, from an honest and plain Tradesman, had got such a haunt about the Courts of Justice, and such a Jargon of Law-Words, that he concluded himself as able a Lawyer as any that pleaded at the Bar, or sat on the Bench. He was overheard one Day talking to himself after this manner, 'How capriciously does Fate or Chance dispose of Mankind? How seldom is that Business allotted to a Man, for which he is fitted by Nature? It is plain, I was intended for a Man of Law: How did my Guardians mistake my Genius in placing me, like a mean Slave, behind a Counter? Bless me! What immense Estates[15] these Fellows raise by the Law! Besides, it is the Profession of a Gentleman: What a Pleasure it is to be victorious in a Cause? To swagger at the Bar? What a Fool am I to drudge any more in this Woollen Trade? for a Lawyer I was born, and a Lawyer I will be; one is never too Old to learn.' All this while *John* had con'd over such a Catalogue of hard Words, as were enough to conjure up the Devil; these he used to bubble indifferently in all Companies, especially at Coffee-houses; so that his Neighbour Tradesmen began to shun his Company as a Man that was crack'd. Instead of the Affairs at *Blackwell-Hall*,[16] and Price of

---

[12] The French economy was badly damaged by the war.
[13] Doily was a draper who introduced a cheap material that was named after him.
[14] Herein lies the political message Arbuthnot and his fellow pamphleteers were peddling: England was becoming too embroiled in the war (for which she was footing the bill) - no good would come of it.
[15] Marlborough was rewarded by Queen Anne with the estate of Woodstock. James Brydges, later Duke of Chandos, enriched himself while Paymaster of the army. (See G. Davies, 'The Seamy Side of Marlborough's War', *HLQ*, xv, 1952, 21-4.)
[16] 'Bakewell or Blackwell Hall was a market-place used weekly for the sale of woollen goods, in Basinghall Street' (note by George Aitken, *The Life and Works of John Arbuthnot.*, Russell and Russell, New York, 1892, p. 206).

Broad-cloath, Wool and Bayses, he talk'd of nothing but *Actions upon the Case, Returns, Capias, Alias capias, Demurrers, Venire facias, Replevins, Superseda's, Certiorari's, Writs of Error, Actions of Trover and Conversion, Trespasses, Precipes & Dedimus*: This was matter of Jest to the learned in Law; however, *Hocus*, and the rest of the Tribe, encouraged *John* in his Fancy, assuring him, That he had a great Genius for Law; that they question'd not but in Time he might raise Money enough by it to reimburse him all his Charges; That, if he study'd, he would undoubtedly arrive to the Dignity of a Lord Chief Justice; as for the Advice of honest Friends and Neighbours, *John* despis'd it; he look'd upon them as Fellows of a low Genius, poor groveling Mechanicks; *John* reckon'd it more Honour to have got one favourable Verdict, than to have sold a bale of Broad-cloath. As for *Nic. Frog*, to say the Truth, he was more prudent;[17] for, tho' he followed his Law-Suit closely, he neglected not his ordinary Business, but was both in Court and in his Shop at the proper Hours.

CHAPTER VIII.
HOW *JOHN* DISCOVERED THAT *HOCUS* HAD AN INTRIGUE WITH HIS WIFE; AND WHAT FOLLOWED THEREUPON

John had not run on a madding so long, had it not been for an extravagant Bitch of a Wife, whom *Hocus* perceiving *John* to be fond of, was resolv'd to win over to his side. It is a true saying, *That the last Man of the Parish that knows of his Cuckoldom is himself.* It was observed by all the Neighbourhood that *Hocus* had Dealings with *John's* Wife[18] that were not so much for his Honour; but this was perceived by *John* a little too late. She was a luxurious Jade, lov'd splendid Equipages, Plays, Treats and Balls, differing very much from the sober Manners of her Ancestors, and by no means fit for a Tradesman's Wife. *Hocus* fed her Extravagancy (what was still more shameful) with *John's* own Money. Every body said that *Hocus* had a Month's mind[19] to her Body; be that as it will, it is matter of Fact, that upon all occasions she run out extravagantly on the Praise of

---

[17] Arbuthnot insinuates, as do others, that England's share of the cost of the war was disproportionate.

[18] Marlborough was intimately connected with the Whig ministry that fell in 1710; he had, earlier in Anne's reign, played a key role in what was seen as the Marlborough-Godolphin ministry, before the Whig Junto asserted their control of the ministry.

[19] 'An inclination to' (*OED*).

Hocus. When *John* us'd to be finding fault with his Bills, she us'd to reproach him as ungrateful to his greatest Benefactor; One that had taken so much pains in his Law-Suit, and retrieved his Family from the Oppression of Old *Lewis Baboon*. A good swinging Sum of *John*'s readiest Cash, went towards building of *Hocus*'s Country-House.[20] This Affair between *Hocus* and Mrs. *Bull* was now so open that all the World were scandaliz'd at it; *John* was not so Clod-pated, but at last he took the Hint. The Parson of the Parish[21] preaching one Day a little sharply against Adultery, Mrs. *Bull* told her Husband, that he was a very uncivil Fellow to use such coarse Language before People of Condition, That *Hocus* was of the same mind; and that they would join to have him turn'd out of his Living for using personal Reflections. 'How do you mean,' says *John*, 'by personal Reflections? I hope in God, Wife, he did not reflect upon you?' 'No thank God, my Reputation is too well established in the World to receive any hurt from such a foul-mouth'd Scoundrel as he; his Doctrine tends only to make Husbands Tyrants, and Wives Slaves; must we be shut up, and Husbands left to their Liberty? Very pretty indeed; a Wife must never go abroad with a Platonick[22] to see a Play or a Ball, she must never stir without her Husband; nor walk in *Spring-Garden*[23] with a Cousin. I do say, Husband, and I will stand by it, That without the innocent Freedoms of Life, Matrimony would be a most intolerable State; and that a Wife's Vertue, ought to be the result of her own Reason, and not of her Husband's Government; for my part, I would scorn a Husband that would be Jealous, if he saw a Fellow a-bed with me.' All this while *John*'s Blood boil'd in his Veins, he

---

[20] Bleinheim Palace. It was in 1704 that the Queen gave the Royal manor of Woodstock (and all that went with it) to the Churchill family in perpetuity. See also note 4, above.

[21] There was a famous row in 1709, triggered by a sermon preached by Dr Henry Sacheverell in 1709. Choosing November 5 as a suitable date to detonate his bombshell, Sacheverell delivered an extreme statement of the doctrine of non-resistance (in all circumstances), to the monarch. When the sermon was then printed and circulated as a pamphlet, it was seen by the Whigs (and moderate Tories) as provocation - an attack on the Revolution and Settlement of 1688, and the Hanoverian Succession. The Whigs overreacted by having Sacheverell impeached and tried; rioting by extremist gangs followed (see the continuation of Arbuthnot's narrative), and the ultimate upshot was the fall of the Whig ministry. Having lost the confidence of the electorate (and the Queen), they also lost the election of 1710. (See Trevelyan, op. cit., vol. iii, pp. 47-60.)

[22] An interesting label for the non-cuckolding lover. Its usage here is cited by the *OED* to exemplify its definition.

[23] Either the 'Old Spring Garden', a public park at Charing Cross...the scene of midnight masquerades, which were the cause of much scandal (*Spectator*, 9 March, 1711), or 'Spring Gardens' at Vauxhall, where females of doubtful virtue tended to congregate (Bower and Erickson, pp. 142-3).

was now confirm'd in all his Suspicions; Jade, Bitch, and Whore were the best Words, that *John* gave her. Things went from better to worse, till Mrs. *Bull* aim'd a Knife at *John*, though *John* threw a Bottle at her Head very brutally indeed: After this there was nothing but Confusion: Bottles, Glasses, Spoons, Plates, Knives, Forks, and Dishes flew about like Dust; the result of which was, that Mrs. *Bull* receiv'd a Bruise in her Right-side, of which she dy'd half a Year after: The Bruise imposthumated, and afterwards turned to a stinking Ulcer, which made every body shie to come near her she smelt so; yet she wanted not the help of Many able Physicians, who attended very diligently, and did what Men of Skill could do, but all to no purpose, for her Condition was now quite desperate, all regular Physicians, and her nearest Relations, having giv'n her over.

CHAPTER IX.
HOW SOME QUACKS UNDERTOOK TO CURE MRS. *BULL* OF HER ULCER.

There is nothing so impossible in Nature, but Mountebanks will undertake; nothing so incredible, but they will affirm: Mrs. *Bull*'s Condition was look'd upon as desperate by all the Men of Art; then Signior *Cavallo*[24] judg'd it was high Time for him to interpose, he bragg'd he had an infallible Ointment and Plaister, which, being applied to the Sore, would Cure it in a few days; at the same time they would give her a Pill that would purge off all her bad Humours, sweeten her Blood, and rectifie her disturb'd Imagination. In spite of all Applications the Patient grew worse, every Day she stank so, no Body durst come within a Stone's throw of her, except Signior *Cavallo* and his Wife, whom he sent every Day to Dress her, she having a very gentle soft Hand. All this while Signior apprehended no Danger. If one ask'd him how Mrs. *Bull* did? Better and better, says Signior *Cavallo*; the Parts heal, and her Constitution mends; if she submits to my Government, she will be abroad in a little time. Nay, it is reported that he wrote to her Friends in the Country, that she would dance a Jig next *October* in *Westminster-Hall*, and that her Illness had been chiefly owing to bad Physicians. At last, Signior was sent for in great haste, his Patient growing worse and worse; when he came, he affirmed that it was a gross Mistake, that she was never in a

---

[24] Charles Seymour, Duke of Somerset and Master of the Horse, a prominent Whig. Aitken identifies 'Cavallo' thus (p. 208), but omits him from the text, here and subsequently.

fairer way: Bring hither the Salve, says he, and give her a plentiful Draught of my Cordial. As he was applying his Ointments, and administering the Cordial, the Patient gave up the Ghost, to the great confusion of Signior *Cavallo*, and the great Joy of *Bull* and his Friends. Signior flung away out of the House in great disorder, and swore there was foul Play, for he was sure his Medicines were infallible. Mrs. *Bull* having dy'd[25] without any Signs of Repentence or Devotion, the Clergy would hardly allow her Christian Burial. The Relations had once resolved to sue *John* for the Murder, but considering better of it, and that such a Trial would rip up old Sores, and discover things not so much to the Reputation of the Deceased, they drop'd their Design. She left no Will, only there was found in her strong Box the following Words wrote on a scrip of Paper, *My Curse on* John Bull, *and all my Posterity, if ever they come to any Composition with my Lord* Strutt. There were many Epitaphs writ upon her, one was as follows;

> *Here lies* John's *Wife,*
> *Plague of his Life;*
> *She spent his Wealth,*
> *She wrong'd his Health,*
> *And left him Daughters three*
> *As bad as she.*

The Daughters Names were *Polemia, Discordia,* and *Usuria.*[26]

CHAPTER X
OF *JOHN BULL*'S SECOND WIFE AND THE GOOD ADVICE THAT SHE GAVE HIM.

John quickly got the better of his Grief, and seeing that neither his Constitution nor the Affairs of his Family could permit him to live in an unmarried State, he resolved to get him another Wife;[27] a Cousin of his last Wife's was proposed, but *John* would have no more of the Breed: in short, he wedded a sober Country Gentlewoman, of a good Family, and a plentiful Fortune, the reverse of the other in her Temper; not but that she loved Mony, for she was of a saving Temper, and apply'd her Fortune to pay *John*'s clamorous Debts, that

---

[25] Parliament was dissolved on September 21, 1710.
[26] War, Faction and Usury.
[27] The Harley-led, Tory-dominated ministry of 1710-14, which was resolved to bring the war to an end, despite the resistance of the Whigs.

the unfrugal Methods of his last Wife, and this ruinous Law Suit, had brought him into. One day, as she had got her Husband in a good Humour, she talk'd to him after the following manner: 'My Dear, since I have been your Wife, I have observed great Abuses and Disorders in your Family;[28] your Servants are mutinous and quarrelsome, and cheat you most abominably; your Cook-Maid is in a Combination with your Butcher, Poulterer, and Fishmonger; your Butler purloins your Liquor, and the Brewer sells you Hogwash; your Baker cheats both in Weight and in Tale;[29] even your Milkwoman and your Nursery-Maid have a Fellow-feeling; your Taylor, instead of Shreds, cabages[30] whole Yards of Cloath besides leaving such long Scores, and not going to Market with ready Mony, forces us to take bad Ware of the Tradesmen, at their own Price.[31] You have not posted your Books these Ten Years; how is it possible for a Man of Business to keep his Affairs even in the World at this rate? Pray God this *Hocus* be honest; would to God you would look over his Bills, and see how matters stand between *Frog* and you; prodigious Sums are spent in this Law Suit, and more must be borrowed of Scriveners and Usurers at heavy Interest. Besides, my Dear, let me beg of you to lay aside that wild Project of leaving your Business to turn Lawyer, for which, let me tell you, Nature never design'd you. Believe me, these Rogues do but flatter that they may pick your Pocket.' *John* heard her all this while with patience, till she prick'd his Maggot,[32] and touch'd him in the tender point; then he broke out into a violent Passion, 'What, I not fit for a Lawyer![33] let me tell you, my Clodpated Relations spoil'd the greatest Genius in the World, when they bred

---

[28] The financial malpractices of the fallen Whig ministry.

[29] 'An unequivocal allusion to Marlborough's peculation. Sir Solomon Medina informed the Committee established to investigate accounts that he had paid £63,000 to the Duke between 1702 and 1711 in 'commissions' on bread contracts' (Bower and Erickson, p. 146 - see also Trevelyan, iii, p. 200).

[30] 'Pilfers surreptitiously' (*OED*).

[31] As remarked above, much of this prodigality, waste and corruption was laid at Marlborough's door.

[32] 'A whimsical or perverse fancy' (*OED*).

[33] John's enthusiasm for the war suggests its continuing popularity with the people. Arbuthnot's tale continues with 'the accounts' being brought up-to-date, however. After studying them, John 'discovered that, besides the Extravagance of every Article, he had been egregiously cheated; that he had paid for Counsel that were never feed, for Writs that were never drawn, for Dinners that were never dressed, and Journeys that were never made: in short, that the Tradesmen [the Allies], Lawyers and *Frog* had agreed to throw the Burden of the Law Suit upon his Shoulders.' John is thus persuaded to seek to bring the 'lawsuit' to an end. How this is to be brought about is the subject of the subsequent pamphlets.

me a Mechanick. Lord *Strutt*, and his old Rogue of a Grandsire, have found to their Cost, that I can manage a Law Suit as well as another.' 'I don't deny what you say,' says Mrs. *Bull*, 'nor do I call in question your Parts; but I say it does not suit with your Circumstances: you and your Predecessors have liv'd in good Reputation among your Neighbours by this same Cloathing Trade, and it were madness to leave it off. Besides, there are few that know all the Tricks and Cheats of these Lawyers; does not your own Experience teach you how they have drawn you on from one Term to another, and how you have danc'd the Round of all the Courts, still flattering you with a final Issue, and, for ought I can see, your Cause is not a bit clearer than it was seven Years ago.' 'I will be damned,' says *John*, 'if I accept of any Composition from *Strutt* or his grandfather; I'll rather wheel about the Streets an Engine to grind Knives and Scissors; however, I'll take your Advice, and look over my Accounts.'[34]

---

[34] That Arbuthnot's pamphlets scored a palpable hit is testified by the (hostile) *British Journal*, in 1727. The initial provocation was the publication of two volumes of Pope-Swift *Miscellanies*, and the assertion in the Preface that the writings therein were 'innocent Diversions' and 'Amusements'. 'Political inflammatory pamphlets', spluttered the *British Journal:* 'But Opinions which are only *Amusements*, may be easily shifted; therefore *John Bull* is written: And is not this an innocent Pamphlet? Yes truly, for it only put the Nation into as great a Ferment as Dr. *Sacheverell's Sermon*.' (This item from the *British Journal* is included in Jonathan Smedley's splenetic collection of malice, *Gulliveriana*, London, 1728, pp. 296-7.)

A FULL AND TRUE ACCOUNT OF
A HORRID AND BARBAROUS REVENGE[1]
BY POISON,
ON THE BODY OF
MR. EDMUND CURLL,
BOOKSELLER;
WITH A FAITHFUL COPY OF
HIS LAST WILL AND TESTAMENT.
PUBLISH'D BY AN EYE WITNESS.

So when Curll's Stomach the strong Drench o'ercame,
(Infus'd in Vengeance of insulted Fame)
Th' Avenger sees, with a delighted Eye,
His long Jaws open, and his Colour fly;
And while his Guts the keen Emeticks urge,
Smiles on the Vomit, and enjoys the Purge.[2]

History furnishes us with Examples of many Satyrical Authors who have fallen Sacrifices to Revenge, but not of any Booksellers that I know of, except the unfortunate Subject of the following Papers; I mean Mr. *Edmund Curll,* at the *Bible*

---

[1] Edmund Curll's name is synonymous with Grub Street; he was a man of apparently boundless energy, forever on the look-out for a good deal, a quick profit. Curll was the publishing equivalent of Blackbeard the pirate: nobody's work was safe from his clutches. He was more or less permanently at war with Pope and his friends, whose writings (names, even), less protected by copyright than today, were amongst those Curll exploited without scruple. What occasioned Pope's 'revenge' was Curll's publication of *Court Poems* in 1716, attributed by Curll to Pope, Gay or 'a Lady of Quality' (suggesting Lady Mary Wortley Montague, then a close friend of Pope). This was the last of a series of irritations; Pope's response was to administer an emetic, and to follow it up with a highly-coloured account of the incident in two pamphlets. (The text is taken from the original pamphlets of 1716, re-printed in *Selected Prose of Alexander Pope*, ed. Paul Hammond (Cambridge University Press, 1987). For a further account of the practices of Edmund Curll, Bookseller, see the Introduction, above.

[2] These verses appear on the title-page of the pamphlet, and are, it is to be assumed, by Pope. Both pamphlets were published anonymously.

and *Dial* in *Fleetstreet*,[3] who was Yesterday poison'd by Mr. *Pope*, after having liv'd many Years an Instance of the mild Temper of the *British* Nation.

Every Body knows that the said Mr. *Edmund Curll*, on Monday the 26th Instant, publish'd a Satyrical Piece, entituled *Court Poems*, in the Preface whereof they were attributed to a *Lady of Quality*, Mr. *Pope*, or Mr. *Gay;* by which indiscreet Method, though he had escaped one Revenge, there were still two behind in reserve. Now on the Wednesday ensuing, between the Hours of 10 and 11, Mr. *Lintott*,[4] a neighb'ring Bookseller, desir'd a Conference with Mr. *Curll* about settling the *Title Page* of *Wiquefort's Ambassador*, inviting him at the same Time to take a Whet together. Mr. *Pope*, (who is not the only Instance how Persons of bright Parts may be carry'd away by the Instigations of the Devil) found Means to convey himself into the same Room, under pretence of Business with Mr. *Lintott*, who it seems is the Printer of his *Homer*. This Gentleman with a seeming Coolness, reprimanded Mr. *Curll* for wrongfully ascribing to him the aforesaid Poems: He excused himself, by declaring that one of his Authors (Mr. *Oldmixon*[5] by Name) gave the Copies to the Press, and wrote the *Preface*. Upon this Mr. *Pope* (being to all appearance reconcil'd) very civilly drank a Glass of Sack to Mr. *Curll*, which he as civilly pledged; and tho' the Liquor in Colour and Taste differ'd not from common Sack, yet was it plain by the Pangs this unhappy Stationer felt soon after, that some poisonous Drug had been secretly infused therein.

About Eleven a Clock he went home, where his Wife observing his Colour chang'd, said, *Are you not Sick, my Dear?* He reply'd, *Bloody Sick*; and incontinently fell a vomiting and straining in an uncommon and unnatural Manner, the Contents of his vomiting being as Green as Grass. His Wife had been just

---

[3] Curll solemnly rebuts Pope's use of the Dial and Bible to denote his shop - in *The Curliad* (published in 1729 by Curll, who else?). *The Curliad* is a rag-bag of comments, complaints and denials, loosely associated with *The Dunciad Variorum*, also published in 1729. Modestly, Curll declares that his name is his fame; he has no need of a sign, and he boldly says it in verse:
> *How little is it from the Grave we claim,*
> Lintot a *Sign preserves, and* Curll *a Name;*
> *For He desires no other Sign than Fame* (*The Curliad*, p. 23).

[4] Bernard Lintot (1675-1736), publisher of Pope's translations of Homer, and Dunce in *The Dunciad* (he takes part in the heroic games in Book II, q.v.).

[5] John Oldmixon (1673-1742), Whig propagandist; another of Pope's heroes in *The Dunciad* (see Introduction).

reading a Book of her Husband's printing, concerning *Jane Wenham,*[6] the famous Witch of *Hartford,* and her Mind misgave her that he was bewitch'd; but he soon let her know that he suspected *Poison,* and recounted to her, between the Intervals of his Yawnings and Reachings, every Circumstance of his Interview with Mr. *Pope.*

Mr. *Lintott* in the mean Time coming in, was extremely afrighted at the sudden Alteration he observed in him: *Brother Curll, says* he, *I fear you have got the vomiting Distemper, which (I have heard) kills in half an Hour. This comes from your not following my Advice, to drink old Hock as I do, and abstain from Sack.* Mr. *Curll* reply'd, in a moving Tone, *Your Author's Sack I fear has done my Business. Z—ds, says* Mr. *Lintott, My Author! — Why did not you drink old Hock?* Notwithstanding which rough Remonstrance, he did in the most friendly Manner press him to take warm Water; but Mr. Curll did with great Obstinacy refuse it; which made Mr. *Lintott* infer, that he chose to die, as thinking to recover greater Damages.

All this Time the Symptoms encreas'd violently, with acute Pains in the lower Belly. *Brother* Lintott, says he, *I perceive my last Hour approaching, do me the friendly Office to call my Partner, Mr.* Pemberton, *that we may settle our Worldly Affairs.* Mr. *Lintott,* like a kind Neighbour, was hastening out of the Room, while Mr. Curll rav'd aloud in this Manner, *If I survive this, I will be revenged on* Tonson,[7] *it was he first detected me as the Printer of these Poems, and I will reprint these very Poems in his Name.* His Wife admonish'd him not to think of Revenge, but to take care of his Stock and his Soul: And in the same Instant, Mr. *Lintott* (whose Goodness can never be enough applauded) return'd with Mr. *Pemberton.* After some Tears jointly shed by these Humane Booksellers, Mr. Curll, being (as he said) in his perfect Senses though in great bodily Pain, immediately proceeded to make a verbal Will (Mrs. *Curll* having first put on his Night Cap) in the following Manner.

---

[6] Jane Wenham (died 1730), was tried and condemned to death for witchcraft in 1712, but was pardoned by the Queen. Curll published two pamphlets in rapid succession immediately afterwards: *A Full and Impartial Account of the Discovery of Sorcery and Witchcraft, Practis'd by Jane Wenham....*The second, advertised as *Witchcraft further display'd,* was entitled *A Defence of the Proceedings against Jane Wenham.*

[7] Jacob Tonson (1656-1736), publisher of Dryden and Pope ('genial Jacob' in Book I of *The Dunciad - Poems,* p. 723).

Gentlemen, in the first Place, I do sincerely pray Forgiveness for those indirect Methods I have pursued in inventing new Titles to old Books, putting Authors Names to Things they never saw, publishing private Quarrels for publick Entertainment;[8] all which, I hope will be pardoned, as being done to get an honest livelihood.

I do also heartily beg Pardon of all Persons of Honour, Lords Spiritual and Temporal, Gentry, Burgesses, and Commonalty, to whose Abuse I have any, or every way, contributed by my Publications. Particularly, I hope it will be considered, that if I have vilify'd his Grace the Duke of *M[arlborou]gh*, I have likewise aspers'd the late Duke of *O[rmon]d;* if I have abused the honourable Mr. *W[alpo]le,* I have also libell'd the late Lord *B[olingbro]ke;*[9] so that I have preserv'd that Equality and Impartiality which becomes an honest Man in Times of Faction and Division.

I call my Conscience to Witness, that many of these Things which may seem malicious, were done out of Charity; I having made it wholly my Business to print for poor disconsolate Authors, whom all other Booksellers refuse: Only God bless *Sir Richard Bl[ackmo]re;*[10] you know he takes no Copy Money.

The Book of the *Conduct* of the *Earl of N[ottingha]m,*[11] is yet unpublished; as you are to have the Profit of it, Mr. *Pemberton,* you are to run the Risque of the Resentments of all that Noble Family. Indeed I caused the Author to assert several

---

[8] All tried and tested business practices of the master publisher.

[9] These are leading figures from both and every side of the political divide. Pope is unsubtly suggesting a cynical political balance; it's not unlike Byron's characterisation of Robert Southey in *The Vision of Judgement* (1822):

> He had written praises of a regicide;
>   He had written praises of all kings whatever;
> He had written for republics far and wide,
>   And then against them bitterer than ever...
> Then grew a hearty anti-jacobin -
> Had turn'd his coat - and would have turn'd his skin.

Pope's charge is the familiar one of base prostitution; many of the Grub Street fraternity, on the other hand, were motivated by genuine political allegiances. To suggest, as Pope was wont to do, that they were driven by mercenary motives only, was a convenient but highly partial (and not very honest!) line of attack. Curll, on the other hand, was Curll (see Introduction).

[10] Sir Richard Blackmore (1650-1729), the 'everlasting' Blackmore, whose mighty epics in verse (e.g. *Arthur*) indeed go on for ever. See *The Dunciad,* Book II, for his heroic contribution to a boredom-creating contest.

[11] In 1713, Curll printed George Sewell's *Remarks upon my Lord Nottingham's Observations on the State of the Nation.* Nottingham was a Tory extremist, the enemy of Harley and St John, and much lampooned by Swift.

A Horrid and Barbarous Revenge 85

Things in it as Facts, which are only idle Stories of the Town; because I thought it would make the Book sell. Do you pay the Author for Copy Money, and the Printer and Publisher. I heartily beg God's, and my L[or]d N[ottingha]m's Pardon; but all Trades must live.

The second Collection of Poems, which I groundlesly called Mr. *Prior's*,[12] will sell for Nothing, and hath not yet paid the Charge of the Advertisements, which I was obliged to publish against him: Therefore you may as well suppress the Edition, and beg that Gentleman's Pardon in the Name of a dying Christian.

The *French Cato*,[13] with the Criticism, showing how superior it is to Mr. *Addison*'s, (which I wickedly inscribed to Madam *Dacier*) may be suppress'd at a reasonable Rate, being damnably translated.

I protest I have no Animosity to Mr. *Rowe*, having printed Part of his *Callipaedia*, and an incorrect Edition of his Poems without his Leave, in Quarto. Mr. *Gildon's Rehearsal;* or *Bays the Younger*, did more harm to me than to Mr. *Rowe*; though upon the Faith of an honest Man, I paid him double for abusing both him and Mr. *Pope*.[14]

Heaven pardon me for publishing the *Trials of Sodomy*[15] in an *Elzevir* Letter; but I humbly hope, my printing Sir *Richard Bl[ackmo]re's* Essays will attone for them. I beg that you will take what remains of these last, which is near the whole Impression, (Presents excepted) and let my poor Widow have in Exchange the sole Propriety of the Copy of Madam *Mascranny*.

Here Mr. Pemberton *interrupted, and would by no Means consent to this Article, about which some Dispute might have arisen, unbecoming a dying Person, if Mr.* Lintott *had not interposed, and Mr.* Curll *vomited.*

---

[12] '*A Second Collection of Poems on Several Occasions* was fathered on Prior by Curll in 1716' (Paul Hammond's note, *Selected Prose of Alexander Pope*, p. 310).

[13] 'Des Champs, *Cato of Utica*, translated by John Ozell, published by Curll in May 1716' (Hammond, p. 310).

[14] Curll himself almost admits the truth of this complaint: 'It is said that Mr. *Gildon* drew *Pope* under the character of *Sawney Dapper* in his *New Rehearsal*' (*The Curliad*, p. 4). Pope evidently thought Curll was the publisher; in fact, it was James Roberts, frequently used by Curll as his front-man (see Ralph Straus, *The Unspeakable Curll*, p. 25).

[15] The fictional Curll might well apologise for publishing, in 1710, *The Case of Sodomy*, together with memorials of the life and times of Dr John Atherton, Bishop of Waterford. Curll advertised these masterpieces thus: 'The Case of John Atherton, Bp. of Waterford, in Ireland, who was Convicted of the Sin of Uncleanliness with a Cow and other Creatures, for which he was Hang'd at Dublin'. (See Ralph Straus, *The Unspeakable Curll*, p. 211.)

What this poor unfortunate Man spoke afterwards, was so indistinct, and in such broken Accents, (being perpetually interrupted by Vomitings) that the Reader is intreated to excuse the Confusion and Imperfection of this Account.

Dear Mr. *Pemberton*, I beg you to beware of the Indictment at *Hicks's-Hall*, for publishing *Rochester's* bawdy Poems; that Copy will otherwise be my best Legacy to my dear Wife, and helpless Child.

The *Case of Impotence*[16] was my best Support all the last long Vacation.

In this last Paragraph Mr. Curll's *Voice grew more free, for his Vomitings abated upon his Dejections, and he spoke what follows from his Close-stole.*[17]

For the Copies of Noblemen's and Bishop's *Last Wills and Testaments*, I solemnly declare I printed them not with any Purpose of Defamation; but meerly as I thought those Copies lawfully purchased from *Doctors Commons,* at *One Shilling* a Piece. Our Trade in Wills turning to small Account, we may divide them blindfold.

For Mr. *Manwaring's Life*, I ask Mrs. *Old[fiel]d's* Pardon: Neither *His*, nor my Lord *Halifax's* Lives,[18] though they were of great Service to their Country, were of any to me: But I was resolved, since I could not print their Works while they liv'd, to print their Lives after they were dead.

While he was speaking these Words, Mr. *Oldmixon* enter'd. *Ah! Mr.* Oldmixon (said poor Mr. *Curll) to what a Condition have your Works reduced me! I die a Martyr to that unlucky Preface. However, in these my last Moments, I will be just to all Men; you shall have your Third Share of the* Court Poems, *as was stipulated. When I am dead, where will you find another Bookseller? Your* Protestant Packet *might have supported you, had you writ a little less scurrilously, There is a mean in all things.*

Then turning to Mr. *Pemberton,* he told him, he had several *Taking Title Pages*[19] that only wanted Treatises to be wrote to them, and earnestly entreated, that when they were writ, his Heirs might have some Share of the Profit of them.

---

[16] *The Cases of Impotency and Divorce* were published in 1715 in 'Five neat Pocket Volumes, Price 12s 6d (advertised in *Curlicism Display'd*). Another of Curll's contributions to the gaiety, if not the cultural life, of the nation.

[17] 'A chamber utensil enclosed in a stool or box' (*OED*).

[18] Further examples of Curll's publishing genius - the art of the instant *Life*.

[19] Curll had a way with title-pages. Take, for example, the title-page to *EUNUCHISM DISPLAY'D*, which so exercised Defoe (see Introduction): After the title, the page continues:

After he had said this he fell into horrible Gripings, upon which Mr. *Lintott* advis'd him to repeat the Lord's Prayer. He desir'd his Wife to step into the Shop for a Common-Prayer-Book, and read it by the Help of a Candle, without Hesitation. He clos'd the Book, fetch'd a Groan, and recommended to Mrs. *Curll* to give Forty Shillings to the Poor of the Parish of St. *Dunstan's,* and a Week's Wages Advance to each of his Gentlemen Authors, with some small Gratuity in particular to Mrs. *Centlivre.*

The poor Man continued for some Hours with all his disconsolate Family about him in Tears, expecting his final Dissolution; when of a sudden he was surprizingly relieved by a plentiful foetid Stool, which obliged them all to retire out of the Room. Notwithstanding, it is judged by Sir *Richard Bl[ackmor]e,* that the Poyson is still latent in his Body, and will infallibly destroy him by slow Degrees, in less than a Month. It is to be hoped the other Enemies of this wretched Stationer, will not further pursue their Revenge, or shorten this small Period of his miserable Life.

'Describing all the different Sorts of / *EUNUCHS*; / THE / Esteem they have met with in the World, and how they came to be made so Wherein principally is examin'd, whether they are capable of Marriage, and if they ought to be suffer'd to enter into that State....Also a Comparison between Signior *Nicolini* and the Three celebrated EUNUCHS now at *Rome, viz Pasqualini, Pauluccio,* and *Jeronimo* [all celebrated operatic castrati]: With several Observations on Modern EUNUCHS' (Straus, p. 80). All this, we are informed on the same page, is 'Written by a Person of HONOUR'. We would expect no less.

A FURTHER
ACCOUNT[20]
OF THE MOST
DEPLORABLE CONDITION
OF
MR. *EDMUND CURLL,*
BOOKSELLER

Since his being POISON'D on the
28th of *March.*

The Publick is already acquainted with the Manner of Mr. *Curll's* Impoisonment, by a faithful, tho' unpolite, Historian of *Grubstreet*. I am but the Continuer of his History; yet I hope a due Distinction will be made, between an undignify'd Scribler of a Sheet and half, and the Author of a Three-Penny stitch Book, like my self.

Wit (saith Sir *Richard Blackmore*) *proceeds from a Concurrence of regular and exalted Ferments, and an Affluence of Animal Spirits rectify'd and refin'd to a degree of Purity.* On the contrary, when the igneous Particles rise with the vital Liquor, they produce an Abstraction of the rational Part of the Soul, which we commonly call *Madness.* The Verity of this Hypothesis, is justify'd by the Symptoms with which the unfortunate Mr. *Edmund Curll,* Bookseller, hath been afflicted ever since his swallowing the Poison at the *Swan* Tavern in *Fleetstreet.* For tho' the *Neck* of his *Retort,* which carries up the Animal Spirits to the Head, is of an extraordinary Length, yet the said Animal Spirits rise muddy, being contaminated with the inflammable Particles of this uncommon Poison.

---

[20] It is not to be expected that Curll would take his medicine quietly. Within days he had published a disclaimer (relating to *Court Poems*) via Oldmixon, in the *Flying Post* of April 3:

'Whereas Mr. *Lintot,* or Mr. *Pope,* has publish'd a false and ridiculous Libel, reflecting on several Gentlemen, particularly on myself; and it is said therein, that I was the publisher of certain Verses call'd *Court Poems,* and that I wrote the Preface; I hereby declare that I never saw a great part of those Verses, nor ever saw or heard of the Title or Preface to them till after the Poems were publish'd.

Witness, E. Curll.   J. Oldmixon.'

Curll followed this up with a mock advertisement of a 'Second Part of Mr. Pope's Popish Translation of Homer', and with the publication (piratically) on May 3 of Pope's *To the Ingenious Mr. Moore, Author of the Celebrated Worm-Powder.* Attached to this piece was the cheeky notice that 'all his Writings for the Future, except Homer, will be Printed for *E. Curll*'. There was more. Two weeks later came *Moore Worms for the learned Mr. Curll, Bookseller,* and, at the end of May, *The Catholick Poet* (by Oldmixon). This last appeared with John Dennis's piece of malice *A True Character of Mr. Pope, and his Writings.* Pope's response was *A Further Account...*

A Horrid and Barbarous Revenge

The Symptoms of his Departure from his usual Temper of Mind, were at first only *speaking civilly to his Customers,* taking a Fancy to *say his Prayers, singeing a Pig with a new purchas'd Libel,* and *refusing Two and Nine Pence for Sir* R[ichard] B[lackmore]'s *Essays.*

As the poor Man's Frenzy increas'd, he began to *void his Excrements in his Bed,* read Rochester's *bawdy Poems to his Wife,* gave *Oldmixon a slap on the Chops,* and wou'd have kiss'd Mr. *Pemberton's* A— *by Violence.*

But at last he came to such a pass, that he wou'd *dine upon nothing but Copper Plates,* took a *Clyster for a whipt Syllabub,* and eat a *Suppository* for a *Raddish* with *Bread* and *Butter.*

We leave it to every tender Wife to imagine how sorely all this afflicted poor Mrs. *Curll:* At first she privately put a *Bill* into several *Churches,* desiring the Prayers of the Congregation for a *wretched Stationer* distemper'd in Mind. But when she was sadly convinc'd that his Misfortune was publick to all the World, writ the following Letter to her good Neighbour Mr. *Lintott.*

A true Copy of Mrs. *Curll*'s Letter to Mr. *Lintott.*

Worthy Mr. Lintott,
'You, and all the Neighbours know too well, the Frenzy with which my poor Man is visited. I never perceiv'd he was out of himself, till that melancholy Day that he thought he was poison'd in a Glass of Sack; upon this, he took a strange Fancy to run a Vomiting all over the House, and in the new wash'd Dining Room. Alas! this is the greatest Adversity that ever befel my poor Man since he lost *one Testicle* at School by the bite of a black Boar. Good Lord! if he should die, where should I dispose of the Stock? unless Mr. *Pemberton* or you would help a distressed Widow; for God knows he never publish'd any Books that lasted above a Week, so that if we wanted daily *Books,* we wanted *daily Bread.* I can write no more, for I hear the Rap of Mr. *Curll's Ivory headed Cane* upon the Counter. - Pray recommend me to your *Pastry Cook,* who furnishes you yearly with Tarts in exchange for your Papers, for Mr. Curll has disoblig'd ours since his Fits came upon him; - before that, we generally liv'd upon bak'd Meats. - He is coming in, and I have but just time to put his Son out of the way for fear of Mischief: So wishing you a merry Easter, I remain your
 most humble Servant,
 C. Curll.
P.S. As to the Report of my poor Husband's stealing a *Calf* it is really groundless, for he always binds in *Sheep.*'

But return we to Mr. Curll, who all *Wednesday* continued outragiously Mad. On *Thursday* he had a *lucid Interval,* that enabled him to send a general Summons to all *his Authors*. There was but one Porter who cou'd perform this Office, to whom he gave the following Bill of Directions where to find 'em. This Bill, together with Mrs. *Curll's* Original Letter, lye at Mr. *Lintott's* Shop to be perus'd by the Curious.

Instructions to a Porter how to find Mr. Curll's Authors.[21]

'At a Tallow-chandlers in *Petty France*, half way under the blind Arch: Ask for the *Historian*.

'At the Bedsted and Bolster, a Musick House in *Morefields*, two Translators in a Bed together.

'At the *Hercules* and *Still* in *Vinegar-yard*, a School-Master with Carbuncles on his Nose.

'At a Blacksmiths Shop in the *Friars*, a Pindarick Writer in red Stockings.

'In the Calendar Mill Room at *Exeter* Change, a Composer of Meditations.

'At the Three *Tobacco Pipes* in *Dog* and *Bitch* Yard, one that has been a Parson, he wears a blue Camblet Coat trim'd with black: my best Writer against *reveal'd Religion*.

'At Mr. *Summers* a Thief-catchers, in *Lewkners* Lane, the Man that wrote against the Impiety of Mr. *Rowe's* Plays.

'At the Farthing Pye House in *Tooting* Fields, the young Man who is writing my new *Pastorals*.

'At the Laundresses, at the Hole in the Wall in *Cursitors* Alley, up three Pair of Stairs, the Author of my *Church History* - if his Flux be over - you may also speak to the Gentleman who lyes by him in the Flock Bed, my *Index-maker*.

---

[21] The list that follows is no doubt intended to ridicule the publications that flowed from Curll's establishment at the Dial and Bible, Fleet Street. It does that, but also, ironically, bears accurate witness to the extraordinary diversity of material to which E. Curll added his name.

'The *Cook's Wife* in *Buckingham* Court; bid her bring along with her the *Similes* that were lent her for her next new Play.

'Call at *Budge Row* for the Gentleman you use to go to in the Cock-loft; I have taken away the Ladder, but his Landlady has it in keeping.

'I don't much care if you ask at the *Mint* for the old Beetle-brow'd Critick, and the purblind Poet at the Alley over against St. *Andrews Holbourn*. But this as you have time.'

All these Gentlemen[22] appear'd at the Hour appointed, in Mr. *Curll's* Dining Room, two excepted; one of whom was the Gentleman in the Cock-loft, his Landlady being out of the way, and the *Gradus ad Parnassum*[23] taken down; the other happened to be too closely watch'd by the Bailiffs. They no sooner enter'd the Room, but all of them show'd in their Behaviour some Suspicion of each other; some turning away their Heads with an Air of Contempt; others squinting with a Leer that show'd at once Fear and Indignation, each with a haggard abstracted Mien, the lively Picture of *Scorn, Solitude,* and *short Commons*.[24] So when a Keeper feeds his hungry Charge, of Vultures, Panthers, and of *Lybian* Leopards, each eyes his Fellow with a fiery Glare: High hung, the bloody Liver tempts their Maw. Or as a Housewife stands before her Pales, surrounded by her Geese; they fight, they hiss, they gaggle, beat their Wings, and Down is scatter'd as the Winter's Snow, for a poor Grain of Oat, or Tare, or Barley. Such Looks shot thro' the Room transverse, oblique, direct; such was the stir and din, till *Curll* thus spoke, (but without rising from his Close-stool).

'*Whores* and *Authors* must be paid beforehand to put them in good Humour; therefore here is half a Crown a piece for you to drink your own Healths, and Confusion to Mr. *Addison,* and all other successful Writers.

'Ah Gentlemen! What have I not done, what have I not suffer'd, rather than the World should be depriv'd of your Lucubrations? I have taken involuntary Purges, I

---

[22] There can seldom have been collected together (outside the pages of *The Dunciad*) such a pack of unlettered, unwashed, under-nourished Grub Street scribblers.

[23] The ladder.

[24] Comfortable, wealthy Mr Pope could afford this sort of joke - we have Tom Brown's (and others') testimony, however, to the meagre existence eked out by the Grub Street tribe.

have been vomited, three Times have I been can'd, once was I hunted, twice was my Head broke by a Grenadier, twice was I toss'd in a Blanket; I have had Boxes on the Ear, Slaps on the Chops; I have been frighted, pump'd, kick'd, slander'd and beshitten.—I hope, Gentlemen, you are all convinc'd that this Author of Mr. *Lintott's* could mean nothing else but starving you by poisoning me. It remains for us to consult the best and speediest Methods of Revenge.'

He had scarce done speaking, but the *Historian* propos'd a History of his Life. The *Exeter* Exchange Gentleman was for penning Articles of his Faith. Some pretty smart *Pindarick,* (says the Red-Stocking Gentleman), would effectually do his Business. But the *Index-maker* said there was nothing like an *Index* to his *Homer.* After several Debates they came to the following Resolutions.

'Resolv'd, That every Member of this Society, according to his several Abilities, shall contribute some way or other to the Defamation of Mr. *Pope.*

'Resolv'd, That towards the Libelling of the said Mr. *Pope*, there be a Summ employ'd not exceeding Six Pounds Sixteen Shillings and Nine Pence (not including Advertisements.)

'Resolv'd, That Mr. *D[ennis]* make an Affidavit before Mr. *Justice Tully*, that in Mr. *Pope's Homer*, there are several Passages contrary to the establish'd Rules of OUR Sublime.

'Resolved, That he has on Purpose in several Passages perverted the true ancient *Heathen* Sense of *Homer*, for the more effectual Propagation of the *Popish* Religion.

'Resolv'd, That the Printing of *Homer's* Battles at this Juncture, has been the Occasion of all the Disturbances of this Kingdom.

'Ordered, That Mr. *Barnivelt* be invited to be a Member of this Society, in order to make further Discoveries.

'Resolv'd, That a number of effective *Errata's* be raised out of Mr. *Pope's Homer* (not exceeding 1746) and that every Gentleman, who shall send in one Error, for his Encouragement shall have the whole Works of this Society *Gratis.*

A Horrid and Barbarous Revenge

'Resolv'd, That a Summ not exceeding Ten Shillings and Six-pence be distributed among the Members of this Society for *Coffee* and *Tobacco,* in order to enable them the more effectually to defame him in *Coffee-Houses.*

'Resolv'd, That towards the further lessening the Character of the said Mr. *Pope,* some Persons be deputed to abuse him at Ladies *Tea Tables,* and that in Consideration our Authors are not *well dress'd* enough, Mr. *C--y* be deputed for that Service.

'Resolv'd, That a *Ballad* be made against Mr. *Pope,* and that Mr. *Oldmixon,* Mr. *Gildon* and Mrs. *Centlivre* do prepare and bring in the same.

'Resolv'd, That above all, some effectual Ways and Means be found to encrease the Joint Stock of the Reputation of this Society, which at present is exceedingly low, and to give their Works the greater Currency; whether by raising the Denomination of the said Works by counterfeit Title Pages, or mixing a greater Quantity of the fine Metal of other Authors, with the Alloy of this Society.

'Resolv'd, That no Member of this Society for the future mix *Stout* in his *Ale* in a Morning, and that Mr. *B.* remove from the *Hercules* and *Still.*

'Resolv'd, That all our Members, (except the *Cook*'s Wife) be provided with a sufficient Quantity of the *vivifying Drops,* Or *Byfield*'s *Sal Volatile.*

'Resolv'd, That Sir *R*[*ichard*] *B*[*lackmore*] be appointed to endue this Society with a large Quantity of *regular and exalted Ferments,* in order to *enliven* their *cold Sentiments* (being his true Receipt to make Wits).

These Resolutions being taken, the Assembly was ready to break up, but they took so near a-part in Mr. *Curll*'s Afflictions, that none of them could leave him without giving some Advice to re-instate him in his Health.

Mr. *Gildon* was of Opinion, That in order to drive a *Pope* out of his *Belly,* he should get the Mummy of some deceas'd Moderator of the General Assembly in *Scotland,* to be taken inwardly as an effectual Antidote against Antichrist; but Mr. *Oldmixon* did conceive, that the *Liver* of the Person who administred the Poison, boil'd in Broth, would be a more certain Cure.

While the Company were expecting the Thanks of Mr. *Curll*, for these Demonstrations of their Zeal, a whole Pile of *Essays* on a sudden fell on his Head; the Shock of which in an Instant brought back his Dilirium. He immediately rose up, over-turn'd the Close-stool, and beshit the *Essays* (which may probably occasion a *second Edition*) then without putting up his Breeches, in a most furious Tone, he thus broke out to his Books, which his distemper'd Imagination represented to him as alive, coming down from their Shelves, fluttering their Leaves, and flapping their Covers at him.

Now *G—d damn* all *Folio*'s, *Quarto*'s, *Octavo*'s and *Duodecimo*'s! ungrateful Varlets that you are, who have so long taken up my House without paying for your Lodging? - Are you not the beggarly Brood of fumbling *Journey-men;* born in *Garrets*, among *Lice* and *Cobwebs*, nurs'd upon *Grey Peas, Bullocks Liver,* and *Porter*'s *Ale*? - Was not the first Light you saw, the *Farthing* Candle I paid for? Did you not come before your Time into *dirty Sheets* of brown Paper? - And have not I cloath'd you in double *Royal*, lodg'd you handsomely on *decent Shelves*, lac'd your *Backs* with *Gold*, equipt you with splendid *Titles*, and sent you into the World with the Names of *Persons of Quality*? Must I be *always* plagu'd with you? - Why flutter ye your Leaves, and flap your Covers at me? Damn ye all, ye *Wolves* in *Sheeps Cloathing*; *Rags ye were, and to Rags ye shall return.* Why hold you forth your *Texts* to me, ye paltry *Sermons*? Why cry ye - at every Word to me, ye *bawdy Poems*? - *To* my Shop at *Tunbridge* ye shall go, by G— and thence be drawn like the rest of your Predecessors, bit by bit, to the *Passage-House:* For in this present Emotion of my Bowels, how do I compassionate those who have great need, and nothing to wipe their Breech with?

Having said this, and at the same Time recollecting that his own was yet unwiped, he abated of his Fury, and with great Gravity, apply'd to that Function the unfinish'd Sheets of the Conduct of the E[arl] of *N*[*ottingha*]*m*.

FINIS.

THE MEMOIRS OF MARTINUS SCRIBLERUS[1]

The Double Mistress

After Martin had satisfied his curiosity here, he was conducted into another Apartment. Just at the entrance of the door appear'd a Negroe Prince.[2] His habiliments bespoke him royal; his head was crown'd with the feather of an Ostrich, his sable feet and legs were interlaced with Purple and Gold, spangled with the Diamonds of Cornwall, and the precious stones of Bristol. Though his stature was of the lowest, yet he behav'd himself with such an Air of Grandeur, as gave

---

[1] This extract from *The Memoirs of the Extraordinary Life, Works, and Discoveries of Martinus Scriblerus* is taken from the edition of Charles Kerby-Miller (Oxford University Press, 1988), beginning a little way into Chapter XIV. The *Memoirs* were first published by Pope in 1741, in the second volume of a collection of miscellaneous prose works. By this time, all but Swift and Pope of the original members of the Scriblerus Club were dead; the appropriate moment for the appearance of the *Memoirs* - the height of the literary war of the 1720s - had long since passed. Pope was clearing his desk, tying up a few loose ends. Attributing responsibility for the authorship of the *Memoirs* is a complicated business, and is thoroughly examined in Charles Kerby-Miller's admirable Introduction and Notes. It seems fairly clear that Dr Arbuthnot had the largest share in the writing of the Double Mistress chapters.
  The extract included here begins at the point in the biography of Martin where his creators decided to add a little spice to the story by giving their hero an amorous adventure. There is a complication, however - the object of his attentions is one half of a pair of Siamese twins. Martin first meets his Lindamira when he visits a freak show. Before coming upon the beautiful twins, he sees a lion, a leopard, a porcupine, and a mantegar. (A handbill for one of these raree shows in 1711 describes the mantegar thus: 'A most strange and wonderful Creature, the like never seen before in *England*, it being of Seven several Colours, from the Head downwards resembling a Man, its fore parts clear, and his hinder parts all Hairy; having a long Head of Hair, and Teeth 2 or 3 Inches long; taking a Glass of Ale in his hand like a Christian, drinks it....' Quoted by Charles Kerby-Miller, p. 297.) The reader is invited to read on....
[2] An exhibit at another show, also in 1711 was 'a little *Black Man*, being but 3 Foot high, and 32 Years of Age, strait and proportionable in every way, who is distinguished by the name of the *Black Prince*' (handbill, quoted by Kerby-Miller, p. 296).

evident tokens of his Regal Birth and Education. He was mounted upon the least Palfrey[3] in the Universe; a Palfrey whose natural Beauty stood not in need of those various colour'd Ribbons which braided his Mane, and were interwoven with his Tail. Again the crystal Clarion sounded, and after several courteous speeches between the black Prince and Martin, our youthful Philosopher walk'd into the midst of the room, to bless his sight with the most beautiful Curiosity of Nature. On a sudden enter'd at another door the two Bohemian Sisters,[4] whose common parts of Generation, had so closely allied them, that Nature seem'd here to have conspired with Fortune, that their lives should run in an eternal Parallel. The Sun had twice eight times perform'd his annual course, since their Mother brought them into the world with double pangs. Lindamira's eyes were of a lively blue; Indamora's were black and piercing. Lindamira's cheeks might rival the blush of the morning; in Indamora the Lilly overcame the Rose. Lindamira's tresses were of the paler Gold, while the locks of Indamora were black and glossy as the Plumes of a Raven. How great is the power of Love in human breasts! In vain has the Wise man recourse to his Reason, when the insinuating Arrow touches his heart, and the pleasing Poison is diffused through his veins. But then how violent, how transporting must that passion prove, where not only the Fire of Youth, but the unquenchable Curiosity of a Philosopher, pitch'd upon the same object! For how much soever our Martin was enamour'd on her as a beautiful Woman, he was infinitely more ravish'd with her as a charming Monster.[5] What wonder then, if his

---

3   In the same show, 'a little *Turkey Horse*, being but 2 Foot odd Inches High' (Kerby-Miller, p. 296).
4   It will already be evident that in their creation of the Double Mistress episode, the Scriblerians relied for their material less on invention than on the exploitation of contemporary oddities. Their Siamese twins are based on those exhibited all over Europe, and brought to London in 1708. They were advertised in the usual handbill:

> 'At Mr. John Pratt's, at the Angel in Cornhil...are to be seen two Girls, who are one of the greatest Wonders in Nature that was ever seen, being Born with their Backs fastn'd to each other, and the Passages of their Bodies are both one way. These Children are very Handsome and Lusty, and Talk three different Languages; they are going into the 7th year of their Age' (Kerby-Miller, p. 295).

One of the twins suffered a slight stroke in her seventh year, but the other sister was not affected. Both died on the same day in 1723, aged 21.
5   It should be remembered that Martin is a mock-heroic figure; his admiration (and more) for Lindamira (and therefore also Indamora) reflects the passion for monsters and curiosities of contemporary scientific enquiry. Similar scientific absurdities are derided in Part III of *Gulliver's Travels* (another Scriblerian project), where Gulliver visits the grand academy of Lagado. Here he is regaled with many wonders, including a man attempting to extract sunbeams from cucumbers (primitive central heating); he finds another reducing human excrement to its original food; yet

gentle Spirit, already humaniz'd by a polite Education to receive all soft impressions, and fired by the sight of those beauties so lavishly expos'd to his view, should prove unable to resist at once so pleasing a Passion, and so amiable a Phenomenon? Martin, who felt the true emotions of Love, blush'd that the object of his flame should be so openly prostituted to vulgar eyes. And though he had been permitted to peruse her most secret charms, yet his honourable passion was so strong, that it ran into the extreme of bashfulness; so that at the first interview he made no Overtures of his Love. Pensive he return'd, and flinging himself on his Couch, pass'd away the tedious hours of the night in the utmost Inquietude. The rushy Taper afforded a glimm'ring light, by which he contemplated the tender lines of Ovid; but alas! his Remedy of Love was no cure for our unhappy Lover's Anxiety! He closed the amorous volume, sigh'd, and casting his eyes around on the Books that adorned his room, broke forth in this pathetic Apostrophe.

O ye Spirits of Antiquity, who yet live in those sacred leaves! why do I make you conscious of my shame? Yet why should I depreciate the noble Passion of Love, and call it Shame? your Heroes have felt it, your Poets and Orators have prais'd it. Were I enamour'd on some gaudy Virgin, did I doat on vulgar Perfection, the Lustre of an Eye, or the Rose of a Cheek; with reason might I blush before you, most learned Inquisitors into Nature! most reverend Pliny, Aelian, and Aldrovandus![6] Yet sure you cannot disapprove of this, which is no wanton Passion, but excited by so unparallel'd a Production; a flame, that may not only justify itself to the Severity of a Philosopher, but even to the Avarice of a Parent;

---

another great physician has devised an instrument for curing the cholic - a bellows with a 'slender muzzle of ivory...conveyed eight inches up the anus'. Air can be drawn out or pumped in by this method (*Gulliver's Travels*, ed. Harold Williams, Everyman, 1961, p. 193). Part III of the Travels has the fingerprints of Martin Scriblerus all over it; the section last quoted would appear to have been the work of Arbuthnot, the former physician to Queen Anne, and a major contributor to the *Memoirs*.

6   Pliny: Kerby-Miller notes: 'Both the personal character and the work of the elder Pliny (23-79 A.D.) come well within the scope of the Scriblerians' satire' (p. 186). Most of what is known about the Roman writer on natural history - Gaius Plinius Secundus - is derived from his nephew's *Epistles*. The younger Pliny describes a man of extraordinary energy; he filled 160 volumes of manuscript for his *Historia Naturalis*. His curiosity was his undoing; he perished when he got too close to an eruption of Vesuvius in 79 A.D. (*DNB*).

Aelian (Claudius Aelianus): Greek philosopher, 3rd century A.D., who wrote, amongst other things, *De Natura Animalium* - On the Characteristics of Animals - these are largely moral stories of animal life (*DNB*).

Aldrovandus: Ulisse Aldrovandi (1522-1605), Italian naturalist; published many handsomely illustrated books on birds, fishes and insects (*DNB*).

since she who causes it carries a most plentiful Fortune in the sole Exhibition of her person. Heavens! how I wonder at the Stupidity of mankind, who can affix the opprobrious Name of Monstrosity to what is only Variety of Beauty, and a Profusion of generous Nature? If there are charms in one face, one mouth, one body; if there are charms in two eyes, two breasts, two arms; are they not all redoubled in the Object of my Passion? What tho' she be the common Gaze of the multitude, and is follow'd about by the stupid and ignorant; does she not herein resemble the greatest Princes, and the greatest Beauties? only with this difference, that her Admirers are more numerous, and more lasting.

Thus sigh'd he away the melancholy Night; but no sooner had Aurora, with blushes in her cheeks (as conscious that she was just risen from the embraces of Tithon) advanc'd through the purple gates of the east, but Martin rose: He rose indeed, but Melancholy, the companion of his slumbers, rose and walk'd with him. This was the first day that he amused himself with the gaudy Ornaments of the body; that with secret pleasure he contemplated his Face, and the symmetry of his limbs in a looking-glass. And now forsaking his solitary apartment, he walked directly to the habitation that confin'd the Object of his desires. But as it is observ'd that the Curious never wander into the City to indulge their thirst of knowledge 'till about the hours of eleven or twelve; the Morning has ever been the season of Repose for all those Animals, who (trepann'd[7] by the frauds of Men) have been oblig'd to change their Woods and Wildernesses for Lodgings in Cities at the rate of four shillings a week. Therefore Martin at this early hour was neither saluted by the sound of the Trumpet, nor were his eyes feasted as before with the pleasing picture of his Mistress; but he walked to and fro before the door with folded arms, from the hour of five to eleven, humming in a low and melancholy tune.

The Trumpet no sooner sounded, but his heart leapt for joy, and a second sixpence gain'd him a second admittance into her apartment. Yet this day also, he only own'd his Passion in the language of his Eyes: But alas! this language is only understood by those that love, and Lindamira remain'd still ignorant of his Passion.

In the mean time it was no small cause of wonder to Mr. Randal, that this Gentleman should come every day to behold the same show. He, no less covetous

---

7 Trepan: 'a word of obscure and low origin, probably a term of thieves' slang, meaning the action of entrapping; to ensnare' (*OED*).

than the Guardian of a rich Heiress, entertain'd a suspicion that Martin had a design of stealing the Ladies. He thereupon issued out strict Orders, not to admit our Lover on any pretence whatsoever. What Torments must this occasion in the raging fever of Love? Martin had now recourse to Stratagem, and by a Bribe (which often even the Ermine and Scarlet Robe cannot resist) gain'd the Dwarf who kept the gates of the Show-room, to promote his Amour. He promis'd to convey a Letter to Lindamira the same Evening, if he would bring it him when darkness favour'd his design, at the apartment next the Monsters. Martin overjoy'd, hasted home, and after having consulted all the Authors that treat of Love, composed his Billet-doux, and at the time appointed went to entrust it to the hands of his Confident. Softly he stole up stairs, approach'd the door, and gave a gentle rap; when on a sudden a small hand was thrust through a little hole at the bottom of the door, whence issued an unintelligible squeaking voice. Martin concluding it to be the Signal, delivered his Epistle, and made his retreat unobserv'd. He was no sooner retir'd, but Mr. Randal enter'd, and (as it was his usual custom before he went to bed) took a view if all were safe in the Show-room. At his coming in, he saw his Monkey exceedingly busy in picking the Seal-wax by little bits from a Letter, which he turn'd over and over with infinite satisfaction. Mr. Randal, not thinking it a breach of honour to pry into the secrets of his own family, took the Letter from him, and read as follows.

To the most amiable LINDAMIRA.

While others, O darling of Nature, look upon thee with the eyes of Curiosity, I behold thee with those of Love. Since I have been struck with thy most astonishing Charms, how have I call'd upon Nature to make a new head, new arms, and a new body to sprout from this single Trunk of mine, and to double every member, so to render me a proper Mate for so lovely a Pair! but think to how little purpose it will be for thee to stay till Nature shall form another of thy kind! In such beauties she exhausts her whole art, and cannot afford to be prodigal. Ages must be numbred, nay perhaps some Comet may vitrify this Globe[8] on which we tread, before we

---

8 'Ever since the great comet of 1680 these celestial bodies had exercised a great effect on popular imagination, and the fear that some day a comet would destroy the earth, though laughed at by most scientists, appears to have been quite common. Some quasi-scientific grounds for this fear were provided by William Whiston, who, in February, 1714, in a work entitled *The Cause of the Deluge Demonstrated*, advanced a theory...that the comet of 1680 had brought about the great

behold a Castor and a Pollux resembling the beauteous Lindamira and Indamora. Nature forms her wonders for the Wise, and such a Master-piece she could design for none but a Philosopher. Cease then to display those beauties to the profane Vulgar, which were created to crown the desires of

        Your Passionate Admirer,
        MARTINUS SCRIBLERUS

The Dwarf enter'd as he was reading the Letter, and, perceiving his Master mov'd with passion, immediately fell on his knees and confess'd the whole affair. Mr. Randal, bent on revenge, caused him to hasten to Martin's house, with assurances that Lindamira had read his Letter with infinite satisfaction, and conjured him that he would immediately favour her escape. Martin overjoy'd at the news, flew thither on the Wings of Love. The perfidious Dwarf conducted him up stairs in the dark, gently open'd the door, and bad him enter. How happy was Martin in that instant, who thought of nothing but leaping into the four soft arms of his Mistress! when lo, on a sudden he saw at the farther end of the Room two glitt'ring balls of Fire,[9] which roll'd to and fro in a most terrible manner. Immediately his ears were invaded with horrid hissings and spittings, the balls of Fire drew nearer him, and the noise redoubled as he approach'd. Our Philosopher, bold and resolute with love, ventur'd towards it; when all at once he perceiv'd something grasp him hard by the throat, and fix as it were sharp lancets in his cheek, so that blood trickled amain down his chin. Thrice Martin essay'd to free himself, but vain were all his endeavours: till at length, to save his life, he was forced to betray his Intrigue, and alarm the house with reiterated cries of Murder. The apartment of the Bohemian Beauties being the adjoining Room, they were the first that enter'd with a light to his assistance. Martin all bloody as he was, a most fierce Cat-a-mountain hanging at his chin (which Mr. Randal had maliciously plac'd there on purpose) at the sight of Lindamira forgot his distress. Ah, my Love! (he cried) how like is thy fate to that of Thisbe![10] who staying but a moment too late, found, as she thought, her miserable

---

Deluge [Noah's]. The Scriblerians ridiculed Whiston's theory by having Martinus prepare tide tables for a comet that is to approach the earth' (Kerby-Miller's note, p.306).
9   The reader will not have forgotten the ferocious Mantegar....
10 'The most lamentable comedy, and most cruel death of Pyramus and Thisbe', is the entertainment provided at the royal wedding by the artisans in *A Midsummer Night's Dream*:

Lover torn in pieces by a Savage beast! The affrighted Damsels shriek'd aloud; Mr. Randal with all his Retinue rush'd into the room; and now every hand conspired to free his under-jaw from the sharp teeth of the enraged Monster. But the Lady, whose heart melted at the piteous Spectacle, was so zealous in this office of Humanity, that the Cat-a-mountain, provok'd at her good-natur'd diligence, leap'd furiously on her, and wounded three of her hands and her two noses, to such a barbarous degree, that she was not fit to be shown publickly for the space of three weeks. The generous Lover, more wounded at this Spectacle than by all the scratches he had himself receiv'd, charg'd the monster again with the utmost Intrepidity, and rescued his mangled Mistress. Then (having taken her by the hand, and given it a gentle grasp) he retreated with his eye fixed upon her, and just as he left the room (in a low and tender Accent) thus breath'd forth his Soul: "Behold, all this have I suffer'd for you."

Such, and so modest was the first Declaration of Love, made on this eminent occasion by our youthful Philosopher. Nor was it ungently receiv'd by the simple and innocent Lindamira; who, hitherto unus'd to the soft Protestations of adoring Slaves, had rather been wonder'd at than belov'd; and received but imperfect notions of that tender language, from the Addresses only of the black Prince or the Dwarf.

Martin, notwithstanding this unfortunate adventure, still pursued his wishes. His Letters were now no more intercepted. Lindamira read them, and behav'd like other courteous dames when they receive those amorous Testimonials; conceal'd them from her Guardian, and return'd the most engaging answers. In short, she was so far captivated as to resolve no longer to be gaz'd at like a publick Beauty in her own Assembly; but retire from the world, and become the virtuous Mistress of a Family.

But Fate had so ordain'd, that Martin was not more enamoured on Lindamira, than Indamora was on Martin. She, jealous that her Sister had the greatest share in this conquest, resented that an equal application had not been made to herself. She teiz'd Lindamira to such a degree on this subject, as made her promise to see Martin no more. But then again might Indamora be deem'd the unhappiest of Women,

---

Thisbe is the unfortunate heroine who, like Juliet, dies by her own hand after her beloved Pyramus has killed himself in the mistaken belief that Thisbe has been eaten by a lion. A sorry tale of misadventure.

whom her Passion and Imprudence had robb'd of the sight of her Lover. Yet shame caused her to conceal those anxieties from her Sister. And let the Reader judge how unhappy the Nymph must be, who was even depriv'd the universal Relief of a *Soliloquy*. However, thus she thought, without being allow'd to tell it to any Grove or purling Stream.

Wretched Indamora! if Lindamira must never more see Martin, Martin shall never again bless the eyes of Indamora. Yet why do I say wretched, since my Rival can never possess my Lover without me? The pangs that others feel in Absence, from the thought of those Joys that bless their Rivals, can never sting thy bosom; nor can they mortify thee by making thee a Witness, without giving thee at the same time a share, of their Endearments. Change then thy proceeding, Indamora; thy Jealousy must act a new and unheard-of part, and promote the interest of thy Rival, as the only way to the enjoyment of thy Lover.

From that moment she studied by all methods to advance her Sister's Amour, and in that her own. And thus there appeared in these three Lovers as extraordinary a Conjunction of Passions as of Persons: Love had reconcil'd himself to his mortal foes, to Philosophy in Martin, and to Jealousy in Indamora.

And now flourish'd the Amour of Martin; Success even prevented his wishes, the Marriage was agreed on, and the day appointed. Sunday was the time, when Mr. Randal's Absence favour'd their hopes, who never on that day omitted taking the fresh air in the fields: The key of the door he always took with him. Crambe was ready laid at a convenient distance, who accommodated them with a ladder of ropes. The ladder was thrown up, and the Signal given at the window. Lindamira hasten'd to the Alarm of Love, when behold a new Disaster! As she was getting out of the window, the weight of her body on one side, and that of Indamora's on the other, unluckily caused them to stick in the midway: Lindamira hung with her coats stript up to the navel without, and Indamora in no less immodest posture within. The Manteger, who for his gentleness was allowed to walk at large in the house, was so heightened at this sight, that he rushed upon Indamora like a barbarous Ravisher. Indamora cried aloud for help. Martin flew to revenge this insolent attempt of a Rape on his wedding-day. The lustful Monster, driven from our double Lucrece, fled into the middle of the room, pursued by the valorous and indignant Martin. Three times the hot Manteger, frighted at the furious menaces of his Antagonist, made a circle round the chamber, and three times the swift-footed Martin pursued him. He caught up the *Horn* of a *Unicorn*, which lay ready for the entertainment of the curious spectator, and brandishing it over his head in airy circles, hurled it against the hairy son of Hanniman;[11] who wrinkling his brown forehead, and gnashing his teeth in indignation, stoop'd low: The horny Lance just ras'd his left shoulder, and stuck into the tapestry hangings. Provok'd at this, the grinning Offspring of Hanniman caught up the pointed *Horn* of an *Antelope*, and aim'd a blow against his undismay'd Adversary. Our heroic Lover, who held his hat before him like a shield, receiv'd the weapon full on the Crown; it pierc'd the beaver, and gave a small rent to his breeches. Then the human Champion flung with mighty violence the hinder *foot* of an *Elk,* which hit the bestial Combatant full on the nether jaw. He reel'd, but soon recovering, and his skill in war lying rather in the close fight than in projectile weapons, he endeavour'd to close with him: Forthwith assailing him behind unawares, he clamber'd up his back, and pluck'd up by the roots a mighty grasp of hair - but Martin soon dismounted him, and kept him at a distance. Love not only inspired his breast with Courage, but gave double strength to his Sinews; he heav'd up the *hand* of a prodigious *Sea-Monster,* which when the chatt'ring Champion beheld, he no less furious, wielded the pond'rous *Thigh-bone* of a *Giant*.[12] And now they stood opposed to each other, like the dread Captain of the sevenfold Shield and the redoubted Hector.[13] The Thigh-bone miss'd its aim; but the hand of the Sea-Monster descended directly on the head of the Sylvan Ravisher. The Monster chatter'd horrible; he stretch'd his quiv'ring limbs on the floor; and eternal sleep lock'd fast his eyelids.

The lady from the window, like another Helen from the Trojan wall, was witness of the Combat caused by her own beauty. She saw with what gracefulness her Hero enter'd the Lists, admir'd his activity and courage in the combat, and was a joyful witness of his Triumph: She gave a spring from the window, and with open arms and legs embraced the neck and shoulders of her Champion. Our

---

[11] Hanniman, also spelt Hanuman, is an ape-god of India, worshipped as the personification of fertility and virility (Kerby-Miller).
[12] The hinder foot of an elk, the hand of a prodigious sea-monster, and the thigh-bone of a giant are all exhibits in Mr Randal's raree-show.
[13] The 'Captain of the sevenfold Shield' is Achilles; his encounter with Hector marked a crucial stage in the Trojan wars. Pope was still working on his translation of the *Iliad* while the Double Mistress episode was in progress.

Philosopher received her with his Face turn'd modestly from her, and in that manner convey'd her into the street. He call'd a Chair with all haste, but no chairman would take her; which obliged him to bear his extraordinary burden till he found a Coach, in which he carried her off, and was happily united to her that very evening, by a Reverend Clergyman in the Fleet,[14] in the holy Bands of Matrimony.

CHAP. XV
Of the strange and never to be parallel'd Process *at* Law[15] *upon the Marriage of* Scriblerus, *and the Pleadings of the Advocates.*

BUT Nemesis, who delights in traversing the best-laid designs of Cupid, maliciously contrived the means to make these three Lovers unhappy. No sooner had the Master of the Show received notice of their flight, but he seiz'd on the Bohemian Ladies by a *Warrant;* and not content with having recover'd the Possession of them, resolved to open all the Sluices of the *Law*[16] upon Martin. So he instantly went to Counsel to advise upon all possible methods of revenge.

---

14 Kerby-Miller points out that 'marriage in the Fleet' was a highly disreputable marriage ceremony, the resort of the very poor and couples who had eloped. The Fleet was a debtors' prison in Clerkenwell, a seedy part of London through which the Fleet Ditch ran - this is Grub Street territory. Until 1714, any clergyman who happened to be in the prison (for debt) could perform the ceremony in the prison chapel; after 1714, when marriages in the Fleet chapel were prohibited by law, marriages were performed in taverns or anywhere that was available.

15 The law was one of the Scriblerians' favourite targets. Arbuthnot's original title for his John Bull pamphlets was *Law is a Bottomless Pit.* Swift's attacks on lawyers in *Gulliver's Travels* are perhaps the most savage: the King of Brobdingnag remarks to Gulliver that his account of lawyers has revealed 'That laws are best explained, interpreted and applied by those whose interest and abilities lie in perverting, confounding and eluding them.' (*Gulliver's Travels*, ed. Harold Williams, Everyman, 1961, p. 139). Gulliver later confesses to his Houyhnhnm master that 'there was a society of men among us, bred up from their youth in the art of proving by words multiplied for the purpose, that *white* is *black* and *black* is *white*, according as they are paid' (*Gulliver's Travels*, p. 265). Gay, in his *Beggar's Opera,* and Pope (variously) are scarcely less biting.

Despite their low opinion of lawyers as a breed, the Scriblerians numbered lawyers among their friends, some one or other of whom must have provided hints for this chapter of the *Memoirs.*

16 'Much of the humour and legal reasoning in the chapter turns on the physical structure of the twins. The real twins were independent in their structure and vital functions except in the pelvic region where they were joined. Here they possessed common genital and rectal orifices situated between the two bodies in a normal relationship to each other. Since it was impossible to determine their internal anatomy exactly during their lifetime, there was some question whether they also possessed common internal genitalia. Hence the contradictory verdicts of the jury of physicians, who decide that if Martinus' wife becomes pregnant Indamora must take part in the gestation, and of the jury of matrons, who determine that the parts of generation in the two are distinct.

The first point he proceeded on was the *Property* of his Monster, and the question propounded was, (I) "Whether Slaves could marry without the consent of their Master?" To this he was answer'd in the Affirmative, but told at the same time, "That (2) the Marriage did not exempt them from Servitude."

This put him in no small hopes of having Martin added to his *Show*, and acquiring a property in his *Bodily issue* by the Ladies. But his joy was soon dash'd, when he was informed, that, since Martin was a Free Man, (3) "The Children must follow the condition of the Father: or, that indeed, if they were to follow that of their Mother, the Case would be the same, there being no slavery in England." Then his Counsel judg'd it more adviseable to plead for a *Dissolution* of the *Marriage,* upon the impossibility of Conjugal dues in the Wife. But then the *Canon Law* allow'd a *Triennial Cohabitation,* which entirely ruined this Project also. Besides it was evident by the same Law, that "Monstrosity could not incapacitate from Marriage," witness the Case of Hermaphrodites, who are allow'd *"Facultatem Conjugii,* provided they *make Election* before the *Parish Priest,* in *what sex* they will act, and take an Oath never to perform in the other Capacity."

It was next consulted whether Martin should not be permitted to *take away* his Wife? since, upon his so doing, "he might be sued for a *Rape* upon the body of her *Sister,* there being plainly the *four conditions* of a Rape." But then again they consider'd, that Martin might answer, he claim'd nothing but his own; and if another person had fix'd herself to his Wife, he must not for that cause be debarr'd the use of his Property.

Yet still, upon the same head of Martin's possessing his spouse, a Suit might be devis'd in the name of Lindamira, on this account; That a *"Wife* was not obliged to live with a *Concubine,* and such her Sister Indamora must be accounted to Martin from the common Proofs."[17] To this too it was replied, that the Law order'd the Wife to *reside* with the *Husband* if there were sufficient security given to expel the Concubine. So Martin might say he was ready to accomplish his part of the Covenant, if his wife would perform hers, and consent to the Incision. But this

---

All such questions regarding the real twins were resolved after their death in 1723. A postmortem dissection revealed that each body had its own bladder, uterus with ovaries, Fallopian tube, and a portion of vagina. These last coming together from both twins formed a common vagina with a single orifice' (Kirby-Miller, p. 309).

17 There is a footnote here from Scriblerus himself: 'Tactus, amplexus, cohabatio' (touching, embracing, cohabitation).

being an impossibility on the side of the Wife, it could no way be exacted of the Husband.

At length Mr. Randal, being vex'd to the heart, to have been so long and so quaintly disappointed, determin'd to commence a Suit against Martin for *Bigamy* and *Incest*. Meanwhile he left no Artifice or Address untried to perplex the unhappy Philosopher: He even contriv'd with infinite cunning, to alienate Indamora's affections from him; and debauch'd her into an intrigue with a Creature of his own, the black Prince; whom he secretly caus'd to marry her, while her Sister was *asleep*.

Hereupon Martin was reduc'd to turn *Plaintive,* and commenc'd a Suit in the *Spiritual Court* against the black Prince, for Cohabitation with his said wife. He was advised to insist upon a new Point, (viz.) "That Lindamira and Indamora *together* made up but *one* lawful wife."

The Monster-master, further to distress Martin, forc'd Lindamira to petition for Aliment, *lite pendente:* which was no sooner allow'd her by the Court, but he obliged her to alledge, that "it was not sufficient to maintain both herself and her Sister; and if her Sister perish'd, she could not live with the dead body about her."

Martin now began to repent that he had not executed a resolution he formerly conceived, of marrying Crambe to Indamora, as an Expedient to have made all secure. Moreover, it was insisted on, that the other also had a right to *Aliment,* "because, if Martin's Wife should prove with child, the said Sister must necessarily perform the *Offices* of a *Wife,* in contributing to the *Nutrition* and *Gestation* of the said child." A Jury of Physicians being impannel'd, declar'd, that as to Nutrition they were doubtful, whether any blood of Lindamira circulated through Indamora: But as to Gestation, it was evidently true. And upon this, Martin was order'd to allow Aliment to both, the black Prince appearing *insolvent*.

Then the Court proceeded to the Trial. And as both the Cause and the Pleadings are of an extraordinary Nature, we think fit here to insert them at length.

Dr. Penny-feather thus pleaded for Martinus Scriblerus the Plaintiff.

Dr. PENNY-FEATHER.

"I appear before your Honour in behalf of Martinus Scriblerus, Batchelor of Physick, in a Complaint against Ebn-Hai-Paw-Waw,[18] commonly call'd the black Prince of Monomotapa; Inasmuch as the said Ebn-Hai-Paw-Waw, hath maliciously, forcibly, and unlawfully seiz'd, ravish'd, and detain'd Lindamira-Indamora, the wife of the said Martin, and the body of the said Lindamira-Indamora, from time to time ever since, hath wickedly, leudly, and indecently us'd, handled, and evil entreated. And in order to make this his Villany more lasting hath presum'd to marry this Our Wife, pretending to give his wickedness the Sanction of a Law. And forasmuch as the Adulterer doth not deny the fact, but insists upon his said Marriage as lawful, we cannot open the Case more plainly to your Honour, than by answering his Reasons, which indeed, to mention, is to confute.

"He maintains no less an absurdity than this, that *One is Two*; and that Lindamira-Indamora, the individual wife of the Plaintiff, is not one, but two Persons: And that the said Ebn-Hai-Paw-Waw is not marry'd to Lindamira, the wife of the said Martin, but to his own lawful wife Indamora, another individual Person distinct from the said Lindamira, tho' join'd to her by a strong Ligament of Nature.

In answer whereunto, we shall prove three things: "First, That the said Lindamira-Indamora, now our lawful wife, makes but one individual Person.

Secondly, That if they made two individual persons, yet they constitute but one wife,

"*Thirdly,* That supposing they made two individual persons, and two wives, each lawfully married to her own husband, yet Prince Ebn-Hai-Paw-Waw hath no right to detain Lindamira our lawfully wedded wife, on pretence of being married to Indamora.

"As to the first point: It will be necessary to determine the *constituent Principle* and *Essence* of *Individuality,* which, in respect to mankind, we take to be one simple identical soul, in one simple identical body. The individuality, sameness, or identity of the body, is not determin'd (as some vainly imagine) by one head, and a

---

18 The idea of having Indamora married off to the black Prince presents more comic possibilities than does the name the Scriblerians came up with for him. It was presumably intended to suggest something exotic/North-American Indian.

certain number of arms, legs, and other members; but in one simple, single αιδοιον, or member of Generation.

"Let us search Profane History, and we shall find Geryon[19] with three heads, and Briareus[20] with an hundred hands. Let us search Sacred History, and we meet with one of the sons of the Giants with six Fingers to each Hand, and six Toes to each Foot; yet none ever accounted Geryon or Briareus more than one Person: and give us leave to say, the wife of the said Geryon would have had a good Action against any women who should have espous'd themselves to the two other heads of that Monarch. The Reason is plain; because each of these having but one simple αιδοιον, or one Member of Generation, could be look'd upon as but one single person.

"In conformity to this, when we behold this one member, we distinguish the Sex, and pronounce it a *Man,* or a *Woman*; or, as the Latins express it, *unus Vir, una Mulier, un Homme, une Femme*; *One Man, One Woman*. For the same Reason Man and Wife are said to be one Flesh, because united in that part which constitutes the Sameness and Individuality of each sex.

"And as where there is but one Member of Generation, there is but one body, so there can be but one Soul; because the said organ of Generation is the Seat of the Soul;[21] and consequently, where there is but one such Organ, there can be but one Soul. Let me here say, without Injury to truth, that no Philosopher, either of the past or present age, hath taken more pains to discover where the Soul keeps her residence, than the Plaintiff, the learned Martinus Scriblerus: And after his most diligent enquiries and experiments, he hath been verily persuaded, that the Organ of Generation is the true and only *Seat of the Soul*.[22] That this part is seated in the

---

19 Geryon (in Greek mythology) was a triple-headed monster who reigned over the western coast of Iberia. He was slain and his herd of red oxen seized by Hercules, in the course of his twelve labours.
20 Briareus (also Greek mythology) was a giant with a hundred hands and fifty heads.
21 Chapter XII of the *Memoirs* is devoted to an 'Enquiry after the Seat of the Soul'; Martin concludes that the soul is to be found in the pineal gland. As Kerby-Miller points out (p. 280), the satire here is directed at the sect of Freethinkers and the attempt to determine a material location for the soul.
22 Martin's philosophical (indeed, anatomical) quest for the seat of the soul, is the subject of Chapter XII of his *Memoirs*. Martin's meditations lead him to conclude that the soul 'resides in different parts according to different Inclinations, Sexes, Ages, and Professions. Thus in Epicures he seates her in the mouth of the Stomach, Philosophers have her in the Brain, Soldiers in their Hearts, Women in their Tongues, Fidlers in their Fingers, and Rope-dancers in their Toes. At length he grew fond of the *Glandula Pinealis*, dissecting many Subjects to find out the different

middle, and near the Centre of the whole body, is obvious to your Honour's view. From thence, like the sun in the Centre of the world, the Soul dispenses her warmth and vital influence: Let the Brain glory in the Wisdom of the aged, the Science of the learned, the Policy of the statesman, and the Invention of the witty; the accidental Amusements and Emanations of the Soul, and mortal as the Possessors of them! It is to the Organs of Generation that we owe Man himself; there the Soul is employed in works suitable to the Dignity of her Nature, and (as we may say) sits brooding over ages yet unborn.

"We need not tell your Honour, that it has been the opinion of many most learned Divines and Philosophers, that the Soul, as well as Body, is produced *ex traduce*.[23] This doctrine has been defended by arguments irrefragable, and accounts for difficulties, without it, inexplicable. All which arguments conclude with equal strength, for the Soul's being seated in the Organs of Generation. For since the whole man, both Soul and body, *is there* form'd, and since nothing can operate but where it is, it follows, that the Soul must reside in that individual place, where she exerts her generative and plastic Powers.

"This our Doctrine is confirm'd by all those Experiments, which conspire to prove the absolute Dominion which that part hath over the whole body. We see how many Women, who are deaf to the persuasions of the Eloquent, the insinuations of the Crafty, and the threats of the Imperious, are easily governed by some poor Logger-head, unfurnish'd with the least art, but that of making immediate application to this *Seat of the Soul*. The impressions made by the Ear are so distant, and transmitted thro' so many windings, that they lose their Energy: But your Honour, by immediately applying to the Organ of Generation, acts like a bold and wise Petitioner, who goes strait to the *very Throne* and *Judgment-Seat* of the Monarch.

Figure of this Gland, from which he might discover the cause of the different Tempers in mankind' (*Memoirs*, p. 137). Martin settles for the pineal gland.
23 'Dr Penny Feather does not make clear whether in using the phrase "*ex traduce*" he has specifically in mind traducianism, the doctrine that the soul of the offspring is derived by extension or division from that of the father and is transmitted during the physical act of procreation, or generationism, the non-materialistic doctrine that the soul of the child originates from that of the parent's organism. Both are opposed to creationism, according to which each soul is individually created by God' (Kerby-Miller, p. 313). The reader, having followed all that, will be aware that the Scriblerians are, of course, making fun of this theologico-legal mumbo-jumbo.

"And whereas it is objected that here are *two Wills,* and therefore *two* different *Persons;* we answer, if multiplicity of Wills implied multiplicity of Persons, there are few Husbands but what are guilty of *Polygamy,* there being in the same Woman great and notorious diversity of Wills: A Point which we shall not need to insist upon before any married person, much less of your Honour's Experience.

"Thus we have made good our first and principal Point; That if the wife of the Plaintiff, Lindamira-Indamora, hath but *one* Organ of Generation, she is but *one individual Person,* in the truest and most proper sense of Individuality. And that the matter of Fact is so, we are willing to put upon a fair Trial by a Jury of Matrons, whom your Honour shall think fit to nominate and appoint, to inspect the body of the said Lindamira-Indamora.

"*Secondly,* We are to prove, that though Lindamira-Indamora were *two* individual Persons, consisting each of a Soul and Body, yet, if they have but one Organ of Generation, they can constitute but one wife. For, from whence can the *Unity* of any thing be denominated, but from that which *constitutes* the *Essence* or principal *Use* of it? Thus, if a knife or hatchet have but one blade, though two handles, it will properly be denominated but one knife, or one hatchet; inasmuch as it hath but one of that which constitutes the Essence or principal Use[24] of a knife or hatchet. So if there were not only one, but twenty *Supposita Rationalia* with one common Organ of Generation, that one System would only make one Wife. Upon the whole, let not a few Heads, Legs, or Arms extraordinary, biass your Honour's Judgment, and deprive the Plaintiff of his legal Property: In which right our Client is so strongly fortified, that allowing both the former Propositions to be false, and that there were two Persons, two Bodies, two Rational Souls, yea, and two Organs of Generation, yet would it still be plain in the third place,

"That the Defendant, Prince Ebn-Hai-Paw-Waw, can have no Right to detain from the Plaintiff his lawfully wedded *Wife,* Lindamira. For, abstracting from the *Priority* of the marriage of our Client, by which it would seem he acquir'd a property in his Wife and *all other Matter inseparably annex'd unto her,* it is evident Prince Ebn-Hai-Paw-Waw, by his marriage to Indamora, could never acquire any Property in Lindamira; nor can produce any Cause why both of them should live

---

[24] It will not have escaped the attention of feminist readers that there is a hint of gender-orientation in this passage; the references to Martin's right to the 'use of his property' (Lindamira), will also have been noticed. And there are others to follow.

with himself, rather than with the other? Therefore, we humbly hope your Honour will order the body of Our said Wife to be restor'd to us, and due Censure past on the said Ebn-Hai-Paw-Waw."

Dr. Pennyfeather having thus ended his Pleading was thus answer'd by

DR. LEATHERHEAD

"I will not trouble your Honour with any unnecessary Preamble, or false Colours of Eloquence, which Truth hath no need of, and which would prove too thin a Veil for Falshood before the penetrating eyes of your Honour. In answer therefore to what our learned brother, Dr. Pennyfeather, hath asserted, we shall labour to demonstrate,

"*First,* That though there were but one Organ of Generation, yet are there two distinct persons.

"*Secondly,* That although there were but one Organ of Generation, so far would it be from giving the Plaintiff any right to the body of Indamora, the wife of Ebn-Hai-Paw-Waw, that it will subject the Plaintiff to the penalty of Incest, or of Bigamy.

"*Thirdly,* We doubt not to prove that the said Lindamira-Indamora hath two distinct parts of Generation.

"And, *First,* we will shew, That neither the individual Essence of mankind, nor the Seat of the Soul, doth reside in the Organ of Generation; and this first from Reason. For unreasonable indeed must it be, to make that the Seat of the Rational Soul which alone sets us on a level with beasts; or to conceive, that the Essence of Unity and Individuality should consist in that which is the Source of Discord and Division. In a word, what can be a greater absurdity, than to affirm Bestiality to be the Essence of Humanity, Darkness the Centre of Light, and Filthiness the Seat of Purity?

"We could, from the authority of the most eminent Philosophers of all ages, confirm this our Assertion; few of whom ever had the impudence to degrade this Queen, the Rational Soul, to the very lowest and vilest Apartment, or rather Sink of her whole Palace. But we shall produce still a greater Authority than these, to manifest that personal Individuality did subsist, when there was no such generative Carnality.

"It hath been strenuously maintain'd by many holy Divines (and particularly by Thomas Aquinas) that our first Parents, in the state of Innocence, did in no wise propagate their species after the present common manner of men and beasts; but that the propagation at that time must have been by Intuition, Coalition of Ideas, or some pure and spiritual manner, suitable to the dignity of their station.[25] And though the Sexes were distinguish'd in that state, yet it is plain it was not by parts, such as we have at present; since, if our First Parents had any such, they must have known it; and it is written, that they discover'd them not till after the Fall; when it is probable those parts were the immediate Excrescence of Sin, and only grew forth to render them fitter companions for those Beasts among which they were driven.

"It is a Maxim in Philosophy, that *generatio unius est corruptio alterius*;[26] whence it is apparent that the Paradisaical Generation was of a different nature from ours, free from all Corruption and Imbecillity. This is farther corroborated by the Authority of those Doctors of the Church who have asserted, that before the Fall, Adam was endow'd with a continual uninterrupted Faculty of Generation; which can be explain'd of no other than of that *Intuitive Generation* above said: Since it is well known to all, the least skill'd in Anatomy, that the present (male) part of Generation is utterly incapable of this continual Faculty.

"We come now to our *second* point, wherein the Advocate for the Plaintiff asserteth, that if there were two persons, and one Organ of Generation, this System would constitute but one Wife. This will put the Plaintiff still in a worse condition, and render him plainly guilty of Bigamy, Rape, or Incest. For if there be but one such Organ of Generation, then both the persons of Lindamira and Indamora have

---

25 An extremely prudish position. Compare Milton's view of our first parents' sexuality:
> ...into their inmost bower
> Handed they went; and eas'd the putting off
> These troublesome disguises which wee wear,
> Straight side by side were laid, nor turn'd, I ween
> Adam from his fair Spouse, nor Eve the Rites
> Mysterious of connubial Love refus'd:
> Whatever Hypocrites austerely talk
> Of purity and place and innocence,
> Defaming as impure what God declares
> Pure, and commands to some, leaves free to all (*Paradise Lost*, Book IV).

26 'The generation of one is the corruption of the other.'

an equal property in it; and what is Indamora's property cannot be dispos'd of without her consent. We therefore bring the whole to this short issue; Whether the Plaintiff *Martinus Scriblerus* had the *Consent* of Indamora, or *not?* If he hath *had* her consent, he is guilty of *Bigamy;* if *not,* he is guilty of a *Rape,* or *Incest,* or *both.*

The Defendant, Prince Ebn-Hai-Paw-Waw, having been lately baptiz'd, hath with singular modesty abstain'd from Consummation with his said Wife, until he shall be satisfied from the opinion of your Honour, his learned Judge, how far in Law and Conscience he may proceed; and therefore he cannot affirm much, nor positively, as to the structure of the Organ of Generation of this his wife Indamora. Yet make we no doubt, that it will upon inspection appear, that the said Organ is distinct from that of Lindamira: Whereupon we crave to hear the Report of the Jury of Matrons, appointed to inspect the body of the said gentlewoman.

"And if the Matter of Fact be thus, give me your Honour's permission to repeat what hath been said by the Advocate for the Plaintiff; to wit, that *Martinus Scriblerus,* Batchelor in Physick, by this his Marriage with *Lindamira,* could in no wise acquire any property in the body of Indamora, nor shew any Cause why this duplicated Wife Lindamira-Indamora, should abide with him, rather than with the Defendant, Prince Ebn-Hai-Paw-Waw of Monomotapa.

The Jury of Matrons having made their Report, and it appearing from thence that the Parts of Generation in Lindamira and Indamora were distinct, the Judge took time to deliberate, and the next Court-day he spoke to this effect.

GENTLEMEN,

"I am of opinion that Lindamira and Indamora are distinct persons, and that both the Marriages are good and valid: Therefore I order you, Martinus Scriblerus, Batchelor in Physick, and you, Ebn-Hai-Paw-Waw, Prince of Monomotapa, to cohabit with your wives, and to lie in bed each on the side of his own wife. I hope, Gentlemen, you will seriously consider, that you are under a stricter Tye than common Brothers-in law; that being, as it were, joint Proprietors of one common Tenement, you will so behave as good fellow lodgers ought to do, and with great modesty each to his respective sister-in-law, abstaining from all farther Familiarities than what Conjugal Duties do naturally oblige you to. Consider also by how small Limits the Duty and the Trespass is divided, lest, while ye discharge the duty of Matrimony, ye heedlessly slide into the sin of Adultery.

This Sentence pleas'd neither Party; and Martin appeal'd from the Consistory to the *Court of Arches*,[27] but they confirm'd the Sentence of the Consistory. It was at last brought before a *Commission of Delegates*; who, having weigh'd the Case, revers'd the Sentence of the inferior Courts, and disannull'd the marriage, upon the following Reasons; "That allowing the manner of Cohabitation enjoin'd to be practicable (though highly inconvenient) yet the *Jus petendi et reddendi Debitum conjugale*[28] being at all times equal in both husbands and both wives, and at the same time impossible in more than one; two persons could not have a Right to the entire possession of the same thing, at the same time; nor could one so enjoy his property, as to debar another from the use of his, who has an equal right. So much as to the *Debitum petendi;* and as to the *Debitum reddendi, nemo tenetur ad impossibile.*[29] Therefore the Lords, with great Wisdom, dissolv'd both Marriages, as proceeding upon a natural, as well as legal Absurdity.[30]

---

27 'The Court of Arches, which belonged to the Archbishop of Canterbury, was the chief and most ancient of the consistory courts. It derived its name from the structure of St Mary le Bow's Church in London, where it was once held' (Kerby-Miller, p. 314).
28 That is, 'the right of seeking and rendering the marital duty'.
29 As to the 'duty of rendering, no-one can be held to do that which is impossible'. Just to be quite clear: the twins could not, of course, be expected perform their marital duty with their husbands *at the same time*.
30 This is not quite the end of the *Memoirs*. Two short chapters follow, in which Martin, in grief and disappointment, sets out on his travels. A bare outline only is given of his discoveries, but they include 'the Remains of the ancient Pygmean Empire', a 'Land of Giants', and 'a whole Kingdom of *Philosophers*, who govern by the *Mathematicks*'. In his fourth voyage, Martin 'discovers a Vein of melancholy proceeding to a Disgust of his Species'. Thus Martin becomes Lemuel Gulliver. He also is given the identity of the political-economist projector of Swift's *Modest Proposal* (q.v.): 'He once went so far as to write a Persuasive to people to eat their own Children, which was so little understood as to be taken in ill part.' There is no direct evidence in the Scriblerians' correspondence to determine where the idea for *Gulliver's Travels* came from. It seems clear, however, that it was a project - like *The Beggar's Opera*, and even *The Dunciad* - that emerged from the deliberations of the Scriblerus Club.

ADVICE
TO THE
Grub-street *Verse-Writers*

Ye Poets ragged and forlorn,[1]
    Down from your Garrets haste,
Ye Rhimers, dead as soon as born,
    Not yet consign'd to Paste;

I know a Trick to make you thrive;
    O, 'tis a quaint Device:
Your still-born Poems shall revive,
    And scorn to wrap up Spice.[2]

Get all your Verses printed fair,
    Then, let them well be dry'd;
And, *Curl* must have a special Care
    To leave the margin wide.

---

[1] Swift's stereotype of the Grub Street Dunce-poet is not so very far from the truth. See Introduction and (for example), Tom Brown's lament at the meanness of his existence in 'The Poet's Condition' and 'Farewell to Poor England'. This poem is a striking example of the ability of one of the greatest writers of this (or any) period to put the boot in, with malice aforethought, when he chose. The text is from H. Williams' *Poetical Works of Jonathan Swift* (O.U.P, 1967).

[2] A fate that is at least a little less humiliating than some suggested for Grub Street (and other) fare.

Lend these to Paper-sparing *Pope*;³
  And, when he sits to write,
No letter with an *Envelope*
  Could give him more Delight.

When *Pope* has fill'd the Margins round,
  Why, then recall your Loan;
Sell them to *Curl* for Fifty Pound,
  And swear they are your own.

A Satirical Elegy on the Death of a Late Famous General⁴

His Grace! impossible! what dead!
Of old age too, and in his bed!
And could that Mighty Warrior fall?
And so inglorious, after all!
Well, since he's gone, no matter how,
The last loud trump must wake him now:
And, trust me, as the noise grows stronger,
He'd wish to sleep a little longer.
And could he be indeed so old
As by the newspapers we're told?
Threescore, I think, is pretty high;
'Twas time in conscience he should die.
This world he cumber'd long enough;
He burnt his candle to the snuff;
And that's the reason, some folk think,
He left behind *so great a stink.*

---

³ Pope was known to use any scraps of paper that came to hand.
⁴ The Duke of Marlborough died in 1722, and Swift commemorated the event with this squib. Like so much that emerged from publishers at this time, it was anonymous. (It is worth remembering that a publisher-bookseller like Curll, however unscrupulous his practices, had no such retreat available.) Swift had attacked Marlborough on previous occasions, notably in the *Examiner*, the government-backed organ Swift wrote in 1710-11.

Behold his funeral appears,
Nor widow's sighs, nor orphan's tears,
Wont at such times each heart to pierce,
Attend the progress of his herse.
But what of that, his friends may say,
He had those honours in his day.
True to his profit[5] and his pride,[6]
He made them weep before he dy'd.

Come hither, all ye empty things,
Ye Bubbles rais'd by breath of Kings;
Who float upon the tide of state,
Come hither, and behold your fate.
Let pride be taught by this rebuke,
How very mean a thing's a Duke;
From all his ill-got honours flung,
Turn'd to that dirt from whence he sprung.[7]

---

[5] Blenheim Palace, and the Duke's personal fortune stand testimony to the charge that Marlborough profited hugely from his stewardship of the army. Swift's 'Letter to Crassus', in the *Examiner* of February 8, 1711, compares Marlborough with the avaricious Roman politician (known as 'Crassus the rich'). The Duke was charged with embezzlement in December, 1711, and dismissed from all his offices. Trevelyan is of the opinion that his dismissal was a cynical but necessary manoeuvre in the Tory drive towards a peace settlement (*England Under Queen Anne*, pp. 199-201). The *Observator*, which supported the Whigs, complained at the treatment handed out to Marlborough: 'I believe it to be without precedent, that a General who has had the Approbation of so many successive Parliaments...who has been so highly applauded and rewarded by his own sovereign...should be thus insulted, and have his Reputation stab'd by the Pen of a Private Man [Swift]'. (This is part of an article by John Tutchin, another of Pope's Dunces, in the *Observator* No 91, November 25-29, 1710.)

[6] Secretary of State Henry St John hinted darkly to one of his correspondents that Marlborough had ambitions that needed watching: 'We shall send him over a subject, take care you do not put royalty into his head again' (January 12, 1711, *Correspondence During the Time He was Secretary of State to Queen Anne*, ed. Gilbert Parke, London, 1798, vol. i, p. 70).

[7] Swift maintained that he bore no personal animus towards Marlborough; that, indeed, he had even sought to protect him; 'I am of [the] opinion, that lord M. is used too hardly: I have often scratched out passages from papers and pamphlets sent me before they were printed; because I thought them too severe. But, he is certainly a vile man, and has no sort of merit beside the military' (January 25, 1712, *Correspondence*, ed H Williams, vol. i, p. 472; see also a letter written in January, 1713, op. cit. p. 597). Again, in his *Journal*, a private document, Swift claimed that the 'things that have been hardest against him were not written by me', and, he went on, 'I'm sure, now he is down, I shall not trample on him: although I love him not, I dislike his being out' (*Journal to Stella*, January 8, 1712). It is for the reader to decide the extent to which Swift's 'Satirical Elegy' might be considered to be 'trampling' on the Duke.

THE DUNCIAD (BOOK II)[1]

High on a gorgeous seat,[2] that far outshone

Henley's[3] gilt tub, or Fleckno's Irish throne,[4]

Or that where on her Curls[5] the Public pours

---

[1] *The Dunciad* was first published in 1728 in three Books; in 1729, a fuller version appeared, with the title *The Dunciad Variorum*, in which the asterisks of the first edition were replaced with actual names. Pope also added a pseudo-learned scholarly apparatus. This included a series of *Prolegomena* (by Martin Scriblerus): 'Testimonies' by various authors, a 'Dissertation' on the poem, and also a battery of notes, mostly by Pope (without ascription) or under the name of Martin Scriblerus. Sometimes this information is helpful, sometimes it is mere pedantry - part of the joke. Editors of the poem are thus undermined before they start, and themselves acquire instant duncehood. It is nevertheless hoped that the following notes will bring more enlightenment than confusion. In 1742, Pope published a revised and extended edition (Book IV was added at this point); the final, further revised version, appeared in 1743, shortly before the poet's death.

Pope's 'Argument', preceding Book II, begins: 'The king [of the Dunces] being proclaimed, the solemnity is graced with public games and sports of various kinds....'. A mock-heroic Olympiad is the central theme of Book II.

The text used here is the final, 1743 edition of the poem, based on the one-volume edition of the Twickenham text, edited by John Butt (Methuen 1963, reprinted Routledge, 1992), with some very minor simplifications of spelling or punctuation.

[2] Compare the opening lines of *Paradise Lost*, Book II:
> High on a throne of royal state, which far
> Outshone the wealth of Ormus and of Ind,
> Or where the gorgeous East with richest hand
> Showers on her Kings barbaric pearl and gold,
> Satan exalted sat....

[3] 'The pulpit of a dissenter is usually called a tub; but that of Mr. Orator Henley was covered with velvet, and adorned with gold. He also had a fair altar, and over it this extraordinary inscription, "The Primitive Eucharist"' - Pope's note.

[4] 'Richard Flecknoe was an Irish priest, but had laid aside (as himself expressed it) the mechanic part of priesthood. He printed some plays, poems, letters and travels' - Pope.

[5] Edmund Curll, the notorious bookseller, suffered a spell in the pillory at Charing Cross in 1728. His offence was the publication of the politically sensitive (but newsworthy) memoirs of a former government official. Aware of the perils of the pillory, Curll took the precaution of

All-bounteous, fragrant Grains and Golden show'rs,
Great Cibber[6] sate: The proud Parnassian sneer,
The conscious simper, and the jealous leer,
Mix on his look: all eyes direct their rays
On him, and crowds turn coxcombs as they gaze.
His Peers shine round him with reflected grace,
New edge their dulness, and new bronze their face. 10
So from the Sun's broad beam in shallow urns
Heav'ns twinkling Sparks draw light, and point their horns.

   Not with more glee, by hands Pontific crown'd,
With scarlet hats wide-waving circl'd round,
Rome in her Capitol saw Querno[7] sit,
Thron'd on sev'n hills, the Antichrist of wit.

   And now the Queen, to glad her sons, proclaims,
By herald Hawkers, high heroic Games.
They summon all her Race: an endless band
Pours forth, and leaves unpeopled half the land. 20
A motley mixture! in long wigs, in bags,
In silks, in crapes, in Garters, and in rags,
From drawing-rooms, from colleges, from garrets,
On horse, on foot, in hacks, and gilded chariots:
All who true Dunces in her cause appear'd,
And all who knew those Dunces to reward.

   Amid that area wide they took their stand,
Where the tall May-pole once o'er-look'd the Strand.
But now (so ANNE and Piety ordain)

---

printing and distributing a leaflet that cleared him of any blame. Pope naturally records the occasion, but not very accurately - only one egg was thrown in the entire hour Curll was in the stocks. The crowd treated him like a conquering hero. (See Straus, *The Unspeakable Curll*, pp. 115-122.)

6   Colley Cibber - actor, playwright, and to Pope's disgust, poet laureate. Here he is King Colley, King of the Dunces. In the first editions of the poem that honour was given to Lewis Theobald, critic and Shakespearean scholar; it was in the 1743 edition that Pope handed the laurels to Colley Cibber (see Introduction, Cibber's New-Year Odes, and elsewhere in this volume).

7   Camille Querno was a Roman poet, notorious for reciting some 20,000 lines of his *Alexias* in Rome; he was made poet laureate as a joke (*DNB*). Cibber is another joke-laureate.

  A Church collects the saints[8] of Drury Lane.   30
   With Authors, Stationers obey'd the call,
(The field of glory is a field for all).
Glory, and gain, th' industrious tribe provoke;
And gentle Dulness ever loves a joke.
A Poet's form she plac'd before their eyes,
And bade the nimblest racer seize the prize;
No meagre, muse-rid mope, adust[9] and thin,
In a dun night-gown of his own loose skin;
But such a bulk as no twelve bards could raise,
Twelve starv'ling bards of these degen'rate days.   40
All as a partridge plump, full-fed, and fair,
She form'd this image of well-body'd air;
With pert flat eyes she window'd well its head:
A brain of feathers, and a heart of lead;
And empty words she gave, and sounding strain,
But senseless, lifeless! idol void and vain !
Never was dash'd out, at one lucky hit,
A fool, so just a copy of a wit;
So like, that critics said, and courtiers swore,
A Wit it was, and called the phantom More.[10]   50
   All gaze with ardour: some a poet's name,
Others a sword-knot and lac'd suit inflame.
But lofty Lintot[11] in the circle rose:
'This prize is mine; who tempt it are my foes;
With me began this genius, and shall end.'
He spoke: and who with Lintot shall contend?
   Fear held them mute. Alone, untaught to fear,

---

8 Drury Lane was a well-known haunt of prostitutes at this time.
9 Adust: 'sallow, gloomy in features or temperament' (*OED*).
10 According to Curll (in his *Compleat Key to the Dunciad*), this was James Moore Smythe, a writer of thoroughly deserved obscurity.
11 Bernard Lintot (1675-1736), to whom Pope might have shown a little more generosity. It was Lintot who published Pope's translation of the *Iliad* (1715-20), and the *Odyssey* (1725-6).

Stood dauntless Curl;[12] 'Behold that rival here!
The race by vigour, not by vaunts is won;
So take the hindmost, Hell.'—He said, and run.   60
Swift as a bard that bailiff leaves behind,
He left huge Lintot and out-strip'd the wind.
As when a dab-chick waddles through the copse
On feet and wings, and flies, and wades, and hops:
So lab'ring on, with shoulders, hands, and head,
Wide as a wind-mill all his figure spread,
With arms expanded Bernard rows his state,
And left-legg'd Jacob[13] seems to emulate.
Full in the middle way there stood a lake
Which Curl's Corinna[14] chanc'd that morn to make: 70
(Such was her wont, at early dawn to drop
Her evening cates before her neighbour's shop,)
Here fortun'd Curl to slide; loud shout the band,
And 'Bernard! Bernard!' rings thro' all the Strand.
Obscene with filth the miscreant lies bewray'd,
Fal'n in the plash his wickedness had laid:
Then first (if Poets aught of truth declare)
The caitiff Vaticide[15] conceiv'd a pray'r.
    'Hear, Jove! whose name my bards and I adore,
As much at least as any God's, or more;   80

---

[12] 'We come now to a character of much respect, that of Mr. Edmund Curll. As a plain repetition of great actions is the best praise of them, we shall only say of this eminent man that he carried the Trade many lengths beyond what it had ever before arrived at; and that he was the envy and admiration of all his profession. He possest a command over all authors whatever; he caused them to write what he pleased; they could not call their very names their own. He was not only famous among these; he was taken notice of by the State, the Church and the Law, and received particular marks of distinction from each' - Pope.

[13] Jacob Tonson the elder (1656-1736) was Dryden's publisher from 1679 until the poet's death in 1700. 'Two left legs' is Dryden's description (*DNB*). Tonson's nephew, 'young Jacob', published works by Steele, Pope and others.

[14] Corinna - the name taken by one Mrs Thomas, who, Pope explains, delivered without his consent a number of his youthful letters into the hands of Curll. He, of course, published them in 1727.

[15] *Vates* - Latin = poet; a vaticide, then, is one who murders poets by pirating their works or by printing them inaccurately.

And him and his if more devotion warms,
Down with the Bible,[16] up with the Pope's Arms'.
    A place there is, betwixt earth, air, and seas,
Where, from Ambrosia, Jove retires for ease.
There in his seat two spacious vents appear,
On this he sits, to that he leans his ear,
And hears the various vows of fond mankind;
Some beg an eastern, some a western wind:
All vain petitions, mounting to the sky,
With reams abundant this abode supply: 90
Amus'd he reads, and then returns the bills
Sign'd with that Ichor[17] which from Gods distils.
    In office here fair Cloacina[18] stands,
And ministers to Jove with purest hands.
Forth from the heap she pick'd her Vot'ry's prayer,
And plac'd it next him, a distinction rare!
Oft had the Goddess heard her servant's call,
From her black grottos near the Temple-wall,
List'ning delighted to the jest unclean
Of link-boys vile, and watermen obscene;   100
Where as he fish'd her nether realms for Wit,
She oft had favour'd him, and favours yet.
Renew'd by ordure's sympathetic force,
As oil'd with magic juices for the course,
Vig'rous he rises; from the effluvia strong
Imbibes new life, and scours and stinks along;
Re-passes Lintot, vindicates the race,
Nor heeds the brown dishonours of his face.[19]

---

16 The Dial and Bible was the sign Curll used for his bookshop; the 'Pope's Arms' (crossed keys) was Lintot's sign.
17 Ichor - the fluid which flows in the veins of the gods.
18 Cloaca: 'An underground conduit for drainage, a common sewer' (*OED*). Cloacina is therefore the presiding priestess of the place; even Jove has basic needs.
19 Curll's prayer (see lines 79-82) has been granted: Cloacina, Jove's handmaiden of the night-closet, has heaped the 'effluvia strong' on his head, and thus inspired, Curll wins the race. It should not be difficult to find an application of this episode to Curll's publishing practices.

And now the victor stretch'd his eager hand,
Where the tall Nothing stood, or seem'd to stand;   110
A shapeless shade, it melted from his sight,
Like forms in clouds, or visions of the night.
To seize his papers, Curl, was next thy care;
His papers light fly diverse, tost in air;
Songs, sonnets, epigrams the winds uplift,
And whisk 'em back to Evans, Young, and Swift.[20]
Th' embroider'd suit at least he deem'd his prey;
That suit an unpay'd taylor snatch'd away,
No rag, no scrap, of all the beau, or wit,
That once so flutter'd, and that once so writ.   120
    Heav'n rings with laughter. Of the laughter vain
Dulness, good Queen, repeats the jest again.
Three wicked imps of her own Grubstreet choir,
She deck'd like Congreve, Addison, and Prior;
Mears, Warner, Wilkins[21] run: delusive thought!
Breval, Bond, Besaleel,[22] the varlets caught.
Curl stretches after Gay, but Gay is gone:
He grasps an empty Joseph for a John;[23]
So Proteus, hunted in a nobler shape,
Became, when seiz'd, a puppy, or an ape.   130
    To him the Goddess: 'Son! thy grief lay down,
And turn this whole illusion on the town:
As the sage dame, experienc'd in her trade,
By names of Toasts retails each batter'd jade

---

[20] It is wickedly implied that Curll would stoop to piracy - the phantom poet (the 'prize') turns out to have no substance.
[21] Booksellers, purveyors of anonymous Grub Street writings.
[22] It matters not who Bond, Breval and Besaleel were: alliterative plosives are of greater significance here!
[23] A reference to one of Curll's subtler practices: the celebrated authors in Curll's employ were J. Addison and J. Gay, i.e. *John* Addison and *Joseph* Gay. In his *Compleat Key to the Dunciad*, Curll brazenly admits: 'The first Piece that ever bore the Name of Joseph Gay for its Author was an excellent Poem in Two Books intituled, The Hoop-Petticoat, By Francis Chute Esq; and the Second was an ingenious Dramatic Performance called The Confederates By Capt. Breval, to expose that wretched farce of Gay's - *Three Hours after Marriage*.

(When hapless Monsieur much complains at Paris
Of wrongs from Duchesses and Lady Maries);[24]
Be thine, my stationer! this magic gift;
Cook shall be Prior, and Concanen, Swift:
So shall each hostile name become our own,
And we too boast our Garth and Addison.'   140
    With that she gave him (piteous of his case,
Yet smiling at his rueful length of face)
A shaggy Tap'stry, worthy to be spread
On Codrus'[25] old, or Dunton's[26] modern bed;
Instructive work! whose wry-mouth'd portraiture
Display'd the fates her confessors endure.
Earless on high stood unabash'd De Foe,
And Tutchin[27] flagrant from the scourge below.
There Ridpath, Roper,[28] cudgell'd might ye view;
The very worsted still look'd black and blue.   150
Himself among the story'd chiefs he spies,
As from the blanket[29] high in air he flies;
And 'Oh!' (he cry'd) 'what street, what lane but knows

---

24 133-140: Pope's epic (and not especially francophile) simile compares the French Madame's skill at passing off her 'battered jades' for ladies of the highest class with that of the stationer/publisher. Just as the hapless Englishman abroad can be persuaded he has had a close encounter with a 'Duchess' or a 'Lady Marie', so the innocent reading public can be conned into thinking it is buying the works of celebrated writers such as Swift and Prior, Garth and Addison.
25 Codrus was an impoverished Roman poet, satirised by Juvenal in his third *Satire*. Together with an extensive note to line 144, Pope quotes several lines from the third *Satire*, beginning with these two:
Codrus had but one bed, so short to boot,
That his short wife's short legs hung dangling out....
26 'John Dunton was a broken bookseller and abusive scribler; he wrote *Neck or Nothing*, a violent satyr on some Ministers of State' (See Note 26, below). Thus Pope, anonymously.
27 'John Tutchin, author of some vile verses, and of a weekly paper called the *Observator*: he was sentenced to be whipp'd through several towns in the west of England, upon which he petition'd King James II to be hanged. When that Prince died in exile, he wrote an invective against his memory' - Pope.
28 'Authors of the *Flying Post* and *Post-Boy*, two scandalous papers on different sides, for which they equally and alternately were cudgell'd, and deserv'd it' - Pope. So much for the freedom of the press!
29 The reference is to the punishment meted out to Curll at Westminster School in 1716 (see Introduction and also John Dunton's *Neck or Nothing: A Consolatory Letter from Mr. D-nt-n to Mr. C-rll Upon his being Tost in a Blanket*).

Our purgings,[30] pumpings, blanketings, and blows ?
In ev'ry loom our labours shall be seen,
And the fresh vomit run for ever green!'
  See in the circle next, Eliza[31] plac'd,
Two babes of love close clinging to her waist;
Fair as before her works she stands confess'd,
In flow'rs and pearls by bounteous Kirkall[32] dress'd.   160
The Goddess then: 'Who best can send on high
The salient spout,[33] far streaming to the sky;
His be yon Juno of majestic size,
With cow-like udders, and with ox-like eyes.
This China Jordan let the chief o'ercome
Replenish, not ingloriously, at home.'
Osborne[34] and Curl accept the glorious strife
(Tho' this his Son dissuades, and that his Wife).
One on his manly confidence relies,
One on his vigour and superior size.   170
First Osborne lean'd against his letter'd post;
It rose, and labour'd to a curve at most.
So Jove's bright bow displays its wat'ry round,
(Sure sign that no spectator shall be drown'd).
A second effort brought but new disgrace:
The wild Meander wash'd the Artist's face:

---

30 See Introduction and Pope's pamphlets for further details of the infamous incident of the emetic (also 1716).
31 Eliza Haywood (1693?-1756), a writer of plays and libellous memoirs; in 1744-6 she produced *The Female Spectator* (*DNB*).
32 'The name of a Graver. This Lady's Works were printed in four Volumes...with her picture thus dressed, before them' - Pope.
33 This is the second of the heroic games; after the middle-distance race, a test of nerve, strength and manly prowess. 'Shameless' Curll demonstrates that there is nothing he will not do to advertise his wares. First prize is a Juno of a poet (line 163), the second prize is a china jordan, in which the runner-up can practise at home (165-6).
34 'A bookseller in Grays-Inn, very well qualified by his impudence to act this part....This man published advertisements for a year together pretending to sell Mr. Pope's subscription books of Homer's *Iliad* at half price: of which books he had none, but cut to the size of them (which was quarto) the common books in folio, without copperplates, on a worse paper, and never half the value' - note by William Warburton, friend of Pope, and editor of the first edition of his collected poems in 1751.

Thus the small jett, which hasty hands unlock,
Spirts in the gard'ner's eyes who turns the cock.
Not so from shameless Curl; impetuous spread
The stream, and smoking flourish'd o'er his head.   180
So (fam'd like thee for turbulence and horns)
Eridanus[35] his humble fountain scorns;
Thro' half the heavens he pours the exalted urn;
His rapid waters in their passage burn.

Swift as it mounts, all follow with their eyes:
Still happy Impudence obtains the prize.
Thou triumph'st, Victor of the high-wrought day,
And the pleas'd dame, soft-smiling, lead'st away.
Osborne, through perfect modesty o'ercome,
Crown'd with the Jordan, walks contented home.   190

But now for authors nobler palms remain;
'Room for my Lord!' three jockeys in his train;
Six huntsmen with a shout precede his chair;
He grins, and looks broad nonsense with a stare.
His Honour's meaning Dulness thus exprest,
'He wins this Patron, who can tickle best.'[36]

He chinks his purse, and takes his seat of state:
With ready quills the Dedicators wait;
Now at his head the dextrous task commence,
And, instant, fancy feels th' imputed sense;   200
Now gentle touches wanton o'er his face,
He struts Adonis, and affects grimace:
Rolli[37] the feather to his ear conveys,

---

35 In Greek mythology, Eridanus was the river into which Phaeton fell, struck down by one of Zeus's thunderbolts - Phaeton attempted to take over the driving of the chariot of the sun and failed miserably, hence the thunderbolt.

36 Tickling is the third of the epic contests. The prize - for the hero who best pleases his potential patron (the Lord with the vacant stare, line 194) - is to be the great man's secretary (line 220).

37 'Paulo Antonio Rolli, an Italian Poet, and writer of many Operas....He taught Italian to some fine Gentlemen, who affected to direct the operas' - Pope's note conveys something of the lofty disdain with which he and others responded to the Italian opera, so popular in the 1720s. Gay's *The Beggar's Opera* (1728) satirises some of the excesses of the genre.

Then his nice taste directs our Operas:
Bentley[38] his mouth with classic flatt'ry opes,
And the puff'd orator bursts out in tropes.
But Welsted[39] most the Poet's healing balm
Strives to extract from his soft, giving palm;
Unlucky Welsted! thy unfeeling master,
The more thou ticklest, gripes his fist the faster. 210
    While thus each hand promotes the pleasing pain,
And quick sensations skip from vein to vein;
A youth unknown to Phoebus, in despair,
Puts his last refuge all in heav'n and pray'r.
What force have pious vows! The Queen of Love
Her sister sends, her vot'ress, from above.
As, taught by Venus, Paris learnt the art
To touch Achilles' only tender part;
Secure, through her, the noble prize to carry,
He marches off his Grace's Secretary. 220
    'Now turn to diff'rent sports,' (the Goddess cries)
'And learn, my sons, the wondrous power of Noise.
To move, to raise, to ravish ev'ry heart,
With Shakespear's nature, or with Jonson's art,
Let others aim: 'Tis yours to shake the soul
With Thunder rumbling from the mustard-bowl.
With horns and trumpets now to madness swell,
Now sink in sorrows with a tolling bell;
Such happy arts attention can command,
When fancy flags, and sense is at a stand. 230
    Improve we these. Three Cat-calls[40] be the bribe

---

38 'Not spoken of the famous Dr. Richard Bentley, but of one Thom. Bentley, a small critic, who aped his uncle in a little Horace' - Pope.

39 'Leonard Welsted, author of...a letter in verse...which was meant for a satire on Mr. Pope and his friends, about the year 1718' - Pope. See *One Epistle to Mr. Pope*, in this volume.

40 Theatrical claques - groups of people hired to shout up (or more usually down) a particular performance - were much in evidence at this time. Here, the Goddess of Dulness offers three free cat-calls (more literary riches) for the winner of the fourth contest, which is to be monkey/donkey imitations.

Of him, whose chatt'ring shames the Monkey tribe:
And his this Drum, whose hoarse heroic bass
Drowns the loud clarion of the braying Ass.'
  Now thousand tongues are heard in one loud din;
The Monkey-mimics rush discordant in;
'Twas chatt'ring, grinning, mouthing, jabb'ring all,
And Noise and Norton, Brangling and Breval,[41]
Dennis[42] and Dissonance, and captious Art,
And Snip-snap short, and Interruption smart,   240
And Demonstration thin, and Theses thick,
And Major, Minor, and Conclusion quick.
'Hold!' (cry'd the Queen) 'a cat-call each shall win:
Equal your merits! equal is your din!
But that this well-disputed game may end,
Sound forth, my Brayers, and the welkin[43] rend.'
  As when the long-ear'd milky mothers wait
At some sick miser's triple-bolted gate,
For their defrauded, absent foals they make
A moan so loud, that all the guild awake: 250
Sore sighs Sir Gilbert,[44] starting at the bray,
From dreams of millions, and three groats to pay.
So swells each wind-pipe; Ass intones to Ass
Harmonic twang! of leather, horn, and brass;
Such as from lab'ring lungs th' enthusiast blows,
High sound, attemper'd to the vocal nose;
Or such as bellow from the deep Divine;

---

41 Norton Defoe, son of Daniel, was the editor of the politically hostile *Flying Post*, Breval a very minor poet. Their names are taken in vain to give a pleasantly jarring effect.
42 John Dennis, a literary critic with a very short fuse, crossed swords with Pope on a number of occasions.
43 'The apparent arch or vault of heaven overhead; the sky, the firmament' (*OED*).
44 Sir Gilbert Heathcote (1652-1733), was one of the founders, and later the Governor, of the Bank of England; he was reputed to be the richest commoner in England, with an unmerited reputation for meanness (note by John Butt, p. 576 in the edition of Pope's *Poems* cited in Note 1, above).

There, Webster! peal'd thy voice, and Whitfield![45] thine.
But far o'er all, sonorous Blackmore's[46] strain;
Walls, steeples, skies, bray back to him again. 260
In Tot'nam fields, the brethren, with amaze,
Prick all their ears up, and forget to graze;
Long Chanc'ry-lane retentive rolls the sound,
And courts to courts return it round and round;
Thames wafts it thence to Rufus' roaring hall,[47]
And Hungerford re-echoes bawl for bawl.
All hail him victor in both gifts of song,
Who sings so loudly, and who sings so long.

   This labour passed, by Bridewell all descend,
(As morning pray'r and flagellation end)[48] 270
To where Fleet-ditch with disemboguing streams
Rolls the large tribute of dead dogs to Thames,
The King of dykes! than whom no sluice of mud
With deeper sable blots the silver flood.
'Here strip, my children! here at once leap in,
Here prove who best can dash through thick and thin,
And who the most in love of dirt excel,
Or dark dexterity of groping well.[49]

---

45 Webster and Whitfield: 'The one the writer of a newspaper called the Weekly Miscellany, the other a field preacher' - Pope.
46 'Sir Richard Blackmore, knight, who, (as Mr. Dryden expresseth it): *Writ to the rumbling of his coach's wheels,* and whose indefatigable Muse produced no less than six Epic poems: Prince and King Arthur, 20 Books...Alfred, 12...and many more. 'Tis in this sense he is styled the everlasting Blackmore' - Pope.
47 Westminster Hall, built by William Rufus, home of parliament until the nineteenth century. The sound of the dunces braying is echoed from within the palace.
48 'It is between eleven and twelve in the morning, after church service, that the criminals are whipped in Bridewell. - This is to mark punctually the time of the day' - Pope. He goes on to explain that he is following the precedent set by Homer, of observing the passing of time by means of recurring events of some moment. A similarly acid aside is to be found in *The Rape of the Lock* (1714):
    The hungry judges soon the sentence sign,
    And wretches hang that jurymen may dine (Canto III).
49 The Goddess announces the fourth of the heroic games: mud-diving, in the Fleet Ditch, a tributary of the Thames and an open sewer (see Introduction). Pope's note at this point makes explicit the significance of the event: 'The chief qualifications of Party-writers: to stick at nothing, to delight in flinging dirt, and to slander in the dark by guess.'

Who flings most filth, and wide pollutes around
The stream, be his the Weekly Journals bound; 280
A pig of lead to him who dives the best;
A peck of coals a-piece shall glad the rest.'
In naked majesty Oldmixon[50] stands,
And Milo-like surveys his arms and hands;
Then, sighing, thus, 'And am I now three-score?
Ah why, ye Gods, should two and two make four?'
He said, and clim'd a stranded lighter's height,
Shot to the black abyss, and plunged down-right.
The Senior's judgment all the crowd admire,
Who but to sink the deeper, rose the higher. 290
    Next Smedley[51] div'd, slow circles dimpl'd o'er
The quaking mud, that clos'd, and op'd no more.
All look, all sigh, and call on Smedley lost;
'Smedley' in vain resounds through all the coast.
    Then *[52] essay'd; scarce vanish'd out of sight,
He buoys up instant, and returns to light:
He bears no token of the sabler streams,
And mounts far off among the Swans of Thames.
    True to the bottom see Concanen[53] creep,
A cold, long-winded native of the deep; 300
If perseverance gain the Diver's prize,
Not everlasting Blackmore this denies;
No noise, no stir, no motion canst thou make,
Th' unconscious stream sleeps o'er thee like a lake.
    Next plung'd a feeble, but a desp'rate pack,

---

50 John Oldmixon was responsible for partisan histories of England, Scotland, Ireland and America, as well as much party-writing.
51 Jonathan Smedley was a long-standing adversary of both Swift and Pope, much given to abuse and scurrility. His collection of miscellaneous malice *Gulliveriana* appeared in 1728.
52 It is not clear who is intended by this asterisk - but evidently one not to be numbered among the Dunces: he is not seeking journalistic copy from the Fleet Ditch, nor does any of its mud stick to him.
53 'Matthew Concanen, an Irishman, bred to the law. He was author of several dull and dead scurrilities in the *British* and *London* Journals, and in a paper called the *Speculatist*' - Pope.

With each a sickly brother at his back:
Sons of a Day![54] just buoyant on the flood,
Then number'd with the puppies in the mud.
Ask ye their names? I could as soon disclose
The names of these blind puppies as of those.   310
Fast by, like Niobe,[55] (her children gone)
Sits mother Osborne, stupefy'd to stone!
And monumental brass this record bears,
'These are, — ah no! these were, the Gazetteers!'
    Not so bold Arnall;[56] with a weight of skull,
Furious he dives, precipitately dull.
Whirlpools and storms his circling arm invest
With all the might of gravitation blest.
No crab more active in the dirty dance,
Downward to climb, and backward to advance.   320
He brings up half the bottom on his head,
And loudly claims the Journals and the Lead.
    The plunging Prelate, and his pond'rous Grace,[57]
With holy envy gave one Layman place.
When lo! a burst of thunder shook the flood;
Slow rose a form, in majesty of Mud;[58]
Shaking the horrors of his sable brows,
And each ferocious feature grim with ooze.
Greater he looks, and more than mortal stares;
Then thus the wonders of the deep declares.   330

---

54 'These were daily papers, a number of which, to lessen expense, were printed one on the back of another' - Warburton.
55 In Greek mythology, Niobe was the mother of six sons and six daughters. Because she boasted she was a better mother than Apollo's, all her children but one were slain, and Niobe herself turned to stone.
56 'William Arnall, bred an attorney, was a perfect genius in this sort of work. He began under twenty with furious party-papers; then succeeded Concanen in the *British Journal*'. Pope's note continues with the claim that Arnall prevailed with him not to include him in the first edition of the poem. Arnall's subsequent abuse of Pope's friends earned him a place in the 'temple of infamy' (Pope's phrase) in later editions.
57 The prelate was Bishop Sherlock, a defender of Walpole's policies, and his 'grace' was probably the Archbishop of Canterbury, John Potter.
58 Smedley returns, victorious, and relates his adventures in the underworld.

First he relates, how sinking to the chin,
Smit with his mien the Mud-nymphs[59] suck'd him in:
How young Lutetia, softer than the down,
Nigrina black, and Merdamante brown,
Vy'd for his love in jetty bow'rs below,
As Hylas[60] fair was ravish'd long ago.
Then sung, how shown him by the Nut-brown maids
A branch of Styx here rises from the Shades,
That tinctur'd as it runs with Lethe's streams,
And wafting Vapours from the Land of dreams,   340
(As under seas Alpheus'[61] secret sluice
Bears Pisa's off'rings to his Arethuse)
Pours into Thames: and hence the mingled wave
Intoxicates the pert, and lulls the grave:
Here brisker vapours o'er the temple creep,
There, all from Paul's to Aldgate drink and sleep.

    Thence to the banks where rev'rend Bards repose,
They led him soft; each rev'rend Bard arose;
And Milbourn[62] chief, deputed by the rest,
Gave him the cassock, surcingle, and vest.   350
'Receive' (he said) 'these robes which once were mine
Dulness is sacred in a sound divine.'

    He ceas'd, and spread the robe; the crowd confess
The rev'rend Flamen[63] in his lengthen'd dress.
Around him wide a sable army stand,
A low-born, cell-bred, selfish, servile band,

---

59 Like all the great heroes of myth, Smedley has amorous encounters with the fair nymphs of the underworld (in this case, young ladies whose names suggest too close contact with their environment: 'Lutum' = clay, mud; 'Merdamante' = filth-loving).
60 Hylas was a beautiful youth who was carried away by nymphs who found his beauty irresistible.
61 One of the largest rivers in Greece. Also the river-god who fell in love with the nymph Arethusa when she bathed in his stream.
62 'Luke Milbourn...who, when he wrote against Mr. Dryden's *Virgil*, did him justice in printing at the same time his own translations of him, which were intolerable. His manner of writing has a great resemblance with that of the Gentlemen of the *Dunciad* against our author' - Pope.
63 Smedley is crowned Bard of the Grub Street Eisteddfod.

Prompt or to guard or stab, to saint or damn,
Heav'n's Swiss,[64] who fight for any God, or Man.
    Through Lud's[65] famed gates, along the well-known Fleet
Rolls the black troop, and overshades the street,   360
Till show'rs of Sermons, Characters, Essays,
In circling fleeces whiten all the ways:
So clouds, replenish'd from some bog below,
Mount in dark volumes, and descend in snow.
Here stopt the Goddess; and in pomp proclaims
A gentler exercise[66] to close the games.
    'Ye Critics! in whose heads, as equal scales,
I weigh what author's heaviness prevails;
Which most conduce to soothe the soul in slumbers,
My H-ley's periods, or my Blackmore's numbers;[67]   370
Attend the trial we propose to make:
If there be man, who o'er such works can wake,
Sleep's all-subduing charms who dares defy,
And boasts Ulysses' ear with Argus'[68] eye;
To him we grant our amplest pow'rs to sit
Judge of all present, past, and future wit;
To cavil, censure, dictate, right or wrong;
Full and eternal privilege of tongue.'
    Three College Sophs, and three pert Templars came,
The same their talents, and their tastes the same;   380
Each prompt to query, answer, and debate,
And smit with love of Poesy and Prate,

---

64 Renowned European mercenaries. Shakespeare's Claudius employs 'Switzers' as his bodyguard (*Hamlet*, IV. 5. 97).
65 A mythical king of Britain.
66 The Goddess announces the final test of the Dunces' powers. There is to be a solemn reading of the Works of the Unlearned (the actual title of one of Martin Scriblerus's ventures - q.v.). He who can withstand this barrage of boredom and remain conscious will be made 'Judge of all past and future wit' (line 376).
67 'Periods' = prose rhythms (therefore prose); 'numbers' = metrical divisions (hence verses).
68 The reference to Ulysses concerns his encounter with the Sirens on his return from the Trojan wars; Argus was the monster with a hundred eyes. To survive the coming ordeal will require (to mix the myth) Herculean resistance.

The pond'rous books two gentle readers bring;
The heroes sit, the vulgar form a ring.
The clam'rous crowd is hush'd with mugs of Mum,[69]
Till all, tun'd equal, send a gen'ral hum.
Then mount the Clerks, and in lone lazy tone
Through the long, heavy, painful page drawl on;
Soft creeping, words on words, the sense compose;
At ev'ry line they stretch, they yawn, they doze. 390
As to soft gales top-heavy pines bow low
Their heads, and lift them as they cease to blow:
Thus oft they rear, and oft the head decline,
As breathe, or pause, by fits, the airs divine.
And now to this side, now to that they nod,
As verse, or prose, infuse the drowsy God.
Thrice Budgel[70] aim'd to speak, but thrice supprest
By potent Arthur,[71] knock'd his chin and breast.
Toland and Tindal,[72] prompt at priests to jeer,
Yet silent bow'd to 'Christ No kingdom here.' 400
Who sate the nearest, by the words o'ercome,
Slept first; the distant nodded to the hum.
Then down are roll'd the books; stretch'd o'er them lies
Each gentle clerk, and mutt'ring seals his eyes.
As what a Dutchman plumps into the lakes,
One circle first, and then a second makes;
What Dulness dropt among her sons imprest
Like motion, from one circle to the rest;
So from the mid-most the nutation[73] spreads
Round and more round, o'er all the sea of heads. 410

---

69 'A kind of beer originally brewed in Brunswick' (*OED*).
70 'Famous for his speeches on many occasions about the South Sea Scheme, &c' - Pope.
71 The title of one of Sir Richard Blackmore's 'everlasting' epics.
72 'Two persons not so happy as to be obscure, who writ against the Religion of their Country' - Pope.
73 'The action of nodding the head' (*OED*).

At last Centlivre[74] felt her voice to fail;
Motteux[75] himself unfinish'd left his tale;
Boyer[76] the State, and Law[77] the Stage gave o'er;
Morgan[78] and Mandevil[79] could prate no more;
Norton,[80] from Daniel and Ostroea sprung,
Bless'd with his father's front, and mother's tongue,
Hung silent down his never-blushing head;
And all was hush'd, as Folly's self lay dead.

Thus the soft gifts of Sleep conclude the day,
And stretch'd on bulks, as usual, Poets lay.   420
Why should I sing, what bards the nightly Muse
Did slumb'ring visit, and convey to stews;[81]
Who prouder march'd, with magistrates in state,
To some fam'd round-house, ever open gate!
How Henley lay inspir'd beside a sink,[82]
And to mere mortals seem'd a priest in drink:
While others, timely, to the neighb'ring Fleet[83]
(Haunt of the Muses) made their safe retreat.

---

74 'Mrs. Susanna Centlivre, wife to Mr. Centlivre, Yeoman of the Mouth to his Majesty. She writ many plays before she was seven years old. She also writ a Ballad against Mr. Pope's *Homer* before he begun it' - Pope.
75 Peter Anthony Motteux, who published a translation of *Don Quixote* in 1700-3 (*DNB*).
76 Abel Boyer, author of the monthly *Political State of Great Britain* (1711-29), and other annals of the age.
77 William Law 'wrote with great zeal against the Stage' - Pope.
78 'A writer against religion' - Pope.
79 Bernard De Mandeville, author of *Fable of the Bees* (1705-1714).
80 Norton Defoe, son of Daniel, one of the writers of the hostile *Flying Post*.
81 Brothels. *OED* suggests the derivation is from a word meaning a 'heated room used for hot air or vapour baths', a meaning so derived from the frequent use of public hot-air bath-houses 'for immoral purposes'.
82 'A conduit, drain, or pipe for carrying away dirty water or sewage; an opening specially made for this purpose; a sewer' (*OED*).
83 'A Prison for insolvent Debtors on the bank of the Ditch' - Pope.

Apollo's *Maggot in his Cups:*[1]
OR, THE
Whimsical Creation
OF A
Little Satyrical POET

In a calm Season of the Year,
When Winds withheld their Fury,
And *Phoebus,* [2]when the Skies were clear,
Display'd his utmost Glory.

The Gods, upon a gaudy Day,

---

[1] Ned Ward (1667-1731, writer, inn-keeper) was responsible for this scatalogical epic, published anonymously, of course, in 1729. As a denizen of Grub Street (writer of the *London Spy* and other satirical stuff), he had his due place in *The Dunciad*, which he resented, and poured forth his resentment in his tedious poem *Durgen* (1729), and in copious notes attached to his *Apollo's Maggot*, the masterpiece before us. What Ward has created (if that's the word) is a jolly piece of rudery in which the gods and goddesses of Greek mythology (including the Muses) are discovered at play. Apollo, bored with endless drinking parties, decides to entertain himself and lady friends with a little human sculpturing. His method is somewhat rough and ready; this is not a piece for the squeamish or delicate of stomach! The reader will probably recognise the familiar imagery of pygmy-ape-monkey: Ward's gift is not originality, and certainly not subtlety, but an exuberant energy is not to be denied.
Title: 'Maggot' has two senses: (1) grub (2) a whimsical or perverse fancy (*OED*). Cf Pope's 'Maggots half-form'd, in rhyme exactly meet,/And learn to crawl upon poetic feet' (*The Dunciad* I, 61-2).
[2] Phoebus is the sun's chariot-driver, and Bacchus, who appears a little further down, is the god of wine, of course. Apollo himself, in his role as the overlord of music and poetry, is the presiding deity.

Resolving to be Merry,
Postpon'd the cares of heav'nly Sway,
To drink and sing *Down-derry*.

Bacchus enrich'd the Bowl of Bowls
With Nectar, fit for quaffing;   10
Round which, they sat like jolly Souls,
Some jesting, others laughing.

Each plac'd a Goddess by his Side,
To aggrandize the meeting,
Who laid by all starch'd female Pride
And drank without entreating.

Hymen,³ t' exhilerate the rest
Made Mirth his sole Imployment;
And kind *Apollo* sung his best,
To heighten their Enjoyment.   20

About the Tumbler rowl'd apace,
Whilst *Jove* with Peals of Thunder,
Did e'ery round their Bumpers grace,
Till half the Gods knock'd under.⁴

Yet e'ery Female kept her place,
No Goddess prov'd a Sneaker,
But, like good Wives, unlac'd their Stays,
To make more room for Liquor:

Retiring now and then to seek
A Place to ease their Bodies;   30

---

3 The god of marriage - one might have expected him to be involved, however indirectly.
4 The table, presumably.

For Goddesses that drink must leak,[5]
As well as mortal Dowdies.[6]

Whence Nectar flow'd, at second hand,
On this low'r World in Showers,
Which fructify'd each Farmer's Land,
And fill'd the Meads with Flowers.

Made Herbs and Plants spring up apace,
Set Brooks and Dykes a flowing,
And kindly water'd e'ery Place
Poor Mortals had been Sowing.   40

Bless'd with a Bowl immensly wide,
And deeper than the Ocean,
Each God drank kindly to his Bride,
A Gallon at a Potion.

Till e'ery bright celestial Dame
Behav'd like mortal Hussies,
And, in their altitudes, cry'd shame
On their inebrious Spouses.

Thus drank the Gods, like Sots on Earth
That drown their Cares and Hardships,   50
Till Nectar and excessive Mirth
Had quite disguis'd their Lordships.

Some nodding sat, with drowzy Eyes,

---

[5] Until this point, a reasonable decorum has been maintained, though the reference in the previous stanza to goddesses loosening their corsets to make more room for liquor should have alerted the reader to the directions things were taking. Much worse is to come, however.

[6] Dowdy - 'a woman or girl shabbily or unattractively dressed, without smartness or brightness' (*OED*).

To quit their Seats unable,
Whilst others made hard shift to rise,
And stagger from the Table.

Some, now and then, pop'd out a Jest,
Some foam'd with over-speaking,
Some turn d their Backs upon the rest
To ease themselves by leaking. 60

Whilst others tott'ring to and fro,
With Hickup much tormented,
Would neither tipple, stay, nor go,
But from all rule dissented.

Some squabbling here, some jossling there,
Were neither gay nor loving,
But, to be going, teas'd the Fair,
Who were not yet for moving.

Each Goddess having right to sit;
For all celestial Powers 70
May drink as long as they think fit,
The Blessed know no Hours.

As Wine, on Earth, tempts our Elect
To tipple more than fitting,
So, Nectar had the same effect,
At this their heav'nly Meeting.

For Gods, like Gownmen at a Feast,
Reel'd Brother against Brother,
And drank so long, that e'ery Guest
Seem'd Strangers to each other. 80

The weaker to their Mansions stole,
When they could quaff no longer,
And left the last triumphant Bowl,
A Trophy for the stronger.

Which charm'd all those that would not move
To fondle one another,
Till, like the Family of Love,
Each Sister bless'd a Brother.

Thus all the Gods that staid behind,
With their immortal Spouses,   90
Kiss'd and drank on, till few could find
Their own celestial Houses.

But, in their Cups, their Mantles furl'd,
Reel'd up and down the Heavens,
And left the Care of this low'r World,
At sixes and at sevens.[7]

Apollo, in this merry Mood,
Brim full of Whims and Fancies,
Slip'd down, and on *Parnassus* stood,
To soberize his Senses.   100

As thus his Godship's Presence crown'd
The lofty barren Mountain,
He 'spy'd the Muses sporting round
The *Heleconian* Fountain.

---

[7] Thus far by way of prologue. Having set his poem in a world of aristocratic gods and goddesses, evidently at something of a loose end, Ward finds employment for idle hands. It is appropriate, of course, that Apollo should decide, on a whim, to indulge his creative instincts - what he has in mind is a little human sculpting.

Fair Ladies, quoth the God, I find
You're all at present Idle,
And seem not in the least inclin'd
To handle Pipe or Fiddle;

Therefore, Sweethearts, if you think fit
To lend assistance to it,   110
We'll form a little snarling Wit,
And call the thing a POET.

Not that we'll be so bold or vain
To give him human Stature,
But 'twixt a Monkey[8] and a Man,
Just hammer out the Creature.

What if we knead the Dirt away,
Or that he warps in baking;
He will not be the only Toy
That has been spoil'd in making.   120

If so it happens, then we'll stuff
The Pigmy with ill-nature,
And give him Pride and Wit enough,
To teaze the World with Satyr.

The Muses standing side by side,
Each dizen'd like a Slattern,
We're at your service, all reply'd,
Most wise and noble Patron.

We'll exercise our utmost Arts
In e'ery gross Material,   130

---

[8] This is the first simian hint (with Pope in mind) in the poem; there will be more.

And leave to you the nobler Parts,
That must be more Aethereal.

Fond of the Work, they took their turns,
No pains were thought fatiguing,
But run and fill'd their nectar'd Urns
With Rubbish got by digging.

And when they'd fetch'd sufficient Muck,
To raise up this new wonder;
For want of Tools, with Hands they broke
The sundry'd Clods asunder.   140

Clio,[9] the Eldest of the Nine
For Arts and Science noted,
Seem'd highly pleas'd with the design
Apollo had promoted;

And taking much delight in true
Historical Relation,
Resolv'd to minute down this new
Attempt of a Creation.

Discreet *Thalia,* who restrains,
At e'ery publick Meeting,   150
Poets, from torturing their Brains,
By drinking more than fitting,

Went soberly to Work, among
The rest, but never prated;

---

[9] There is much invoking of the Muses, as might be expected, in Ward's mock-epic. Clio, as he says, was the eldest of Zeus's nine daughters; her responsibility was for history. The rest of the cast, in order of appearance, are as follows: Thalia - comedy and pastoral poetry; Euterpe - lyric poetry; Melpomene - tragedy; Polyhymnia - sacred song; Calliope - epic poetry; Terpsichore - dancing; Erato - love-poetry; Urania - astronomy.

Because much Liquor or much Tongue,
The prudent Sister hated.

Her biggest Harp, *Euterpe* brings
Most kindly condescending,
To skreen the Dirt between the Strings
And fit the Mass for blending.   160

Melpom'ne, her assistance lent,
And so did *Polyhimny,*
Whose crabbed Name would ne'er consent
To any Rhime but *Chimny.*

Calliope, Terpsichore,
Erato and *Urania,*
All join'd and made up three times Three
To punish poor *Britannia,*

In raising up a new Tom *Thumb,*
To mortify her Poets,   170
Whose lofty Genius should become
A terror to all Low-wits:

For plaguing a contentious Age,
With Party-Lyes and Verses,
And foisting on the British Stage,
Dull Madrigals and Farces.

Apollo, in this drunken fit,
Provok'd by these Abuses,
To raise a bold reforming Wit,
Thus exercis'd the Muses.   180

Who had no sooner skreen'd the Soil
From Bodies hard and knotty,
And made it fit, by Care and Toil,
For temp'ring into Putty.

But they their Hose and Shoes pull'd off,
Tuck'd up their Coats much shorter,
First leak'd and wet, then trod the Stuff,
As Lab'rers do their Mortar.

Thus all harmoniously agreed
To work up this foul Matter,   190
And as the jumbl'd Mass had need,
To blend it with Maid's Water.

But Maidens they, alass, had none,
Each Muse had been a Mother,
Were therefore forc'd to use their own,
Which did as well as t'other.

But e'er the Jades had wrought their Starch
Into a right consistence,
The Gods beheld, from Heav'ns high Arch,
Apollo at a distance.   200

And wond'ring what the Game could be
That he was there pursuing,
Descended in a Train to see
What Bus'ness he was doing.

Jove ask'd *Apollo* what those fine
Delicious Dames were treading,
That frisk'd about, as if all nine

Were dancing at a Wedding.

Apollo, with a silent Mouth,
Stood blushing for a Moment,   210
At last pop'd out the naked Truth,
Without Excuse or Comment.

To which, Great Jove made this reply,
Affecting Godlike Passion,
Apollo, know you not that I
Am Lord of the Creation.

How durst you mimick human Shape?
Or give a Pigmy Reason?
To Coin, like Man, a little Ape,
'Gainst Heaven is High-Treason.   220

However, having some regard
For an immortal Brother,
I'll let you form one Monkey Bard,
But ne'er attempt another.

Apollo bowing, did reply,
O pardon this Transgression!
We'll never more offend you by
A counterfeit Creation.

When thus the great celestial King
The Secret had discover'd,   230
The Gods and Goddesses took Wing,
And o'er the Muckhill hover'd,

Some laughing till they drop'd their sweet

And soft perfuming *Ichor*,[10]
Which falling at the Muses Feet,
Still made their Paist the thicker.

At length, when wrought as stiff as Clay
That bungs a Brewer's Barrel,
To make it bind, instead of Straw,
They mix'd it with chop'd Laurel.   240

Then humbly squatting o'er the Mass,
They open'd both their Sluces,
Thro' which was drop'd, by e'ery Lass,
A tincture of the Muses.

When thus the Soil, both thick and thin,
Most carefully was blended,
Envy[11] arose, just piss'd therein,
And then again descended.

The jumbl'd Matter now in trim,
For their design'd formation,   250
Each took a Lump to make a Limb,
And mould it into fashion.

Some form'd an Arm, and some a Leg,
Regarding not Proportion,
Which prov'd too little or too big,
All ending in Distortion.

---

[10] Ichor - the ethereal fluid flowing in the veins of the gods.
[11] It suits Ward's purposes to sustain the notion that human emotions, especially governing passions, are seated in particular parts of the anatomy. Thus envy would appear likely to be present in the sculpting material in large quantities as a result of the Muses' energetic exercising of their 'Sluces'. Obviously, it's an essential ingredient in Ward's malicious concoction.

Like Claws the Fingers and the Toes,
The Muscles soft and flabby,
Knotted the Joints, and weak as those
Of ricketty poor Baby.   260

When these were hung to dry for use,
Upon some Crabtree Branches,
To frame the Trunk, made e'ery Muse
Scratch both her Head and Haunches.

Till Goody *Hunx*, a neighb'ring Scold,
But notable old Puzzle,
Lent 'em a Hog-Trough for a Mould,[12]
Where Swine were us'd to guzzle,

But hollow'd by some rural Lout,
The Bottom prov'd unlevel,   270
Which caus'd the Back to belly-out,
Skew-waw upon a bevel.

To this wry Trunk the Limbs they join'd
Some crooked and some straighter,
Which made the Muses blush to find
Their Workmanship no better.

The God then carefully survey'd
The poor unfinish'd Figure;
I wish, said he, it had been made
More perfect and much bigger.   280

Besides, my Dames, in this your Work,

---

[12] The mould is for the trunk; that the mould (see next lines) should be misshapen will come as no surprise - Pope's malformed body was the source of ironic comment even from those from whom, like Lady Mary Wortley Montague, one might have expected better.

There's one Neglect that vexes,
You've quite forgot the middle Mark
That should distinguish Sexes.

For what Anatomist can tell,
By this poor thingless Body,
Whether you mean it for a Male,
Or for a Female Dowdy.

'Tis strange you Mistresses of Art,
With Love so well acquainted,   290
Should quite forget that noble Part
For your delight appointed.

The Muses blush'd at this Reproof,
Being modest, young and tender,
So dab'd on just an Inch of Stuff,
Enough to shew the Gender.[13]

For Wits are very rarely blest
With an extensive Label,
The am'rous Fool is always best
Adorn'd below the Navel.   300

Besides, they proving thus unkind
To this our rhiming Brother,
Discover'd plainly they'd no mind
He should beget another.

Once more the God their Work survey'd,
With this new Emendation,

---

[13] Not just a gratuitous joke - Pope's sexuality (or supposed lack of it) was a constant source of amusement for Pope's enemies.

But shook his Tresses and his Head,
To shew disapprobation.

I hop'd, said he, I should have prais'd
A pritty little Fellow,   310
Instead of which, you've only rais'd
An aukward Punchionello.

But since you've cast, with so Much pains,
So odd a dumpling Creature,
I'll form the Head and stuff in Brains
Sufficient for a Satyr.

Then humbly stooping to the Ground,
He gave his Hands the trouble
To take a Lump, so squeez'd it round,
As Youngsters do a Snowball.   320

When modell'd to his Mind, the God
Blow'd twice or thrice upon it,
And thus inspir'd the little Clod,
With Satyr and with Sonnet.

When, with much pleasure and success,
The God had made this trial,
He dab'd the Clay against a Face
That grac'd his brazen Viol,

Which such a fine Impression made,
Well tinctur'd with the Mettle,   330
That, to this day, adorns the Head,
And shines like any Kettle.

> This done, he fix'd the Costard[14] on,
> Between two rising Shoulders,
> Then top'd it with a laurel Crown,
> To th' Joy of the Beholders.
>
> The lifeless Image thus compleat,
> Breath only now was wanting,
> To animate this unborn Wit,
> The God had been inventing,   340
>
> He therefore for old Vulcan sent,
> Who with him brought his Bellows,
> And plac'd 'em to the backward Vent,
> As modern Authors tell us,
>
> There blow'd, till the cornuted[15] Cuff,
> With Air, had fill'd each Organ,
> Which kind suppository Puff
> Gave Life to little *Durgen*;[16]
> *Ward, Ned:Durgen*
> Who skip'd as nimbly as a Flea,
> And danc'd like any Fairy,   350
> Which pleas'd *Apollo* much, to see
> His pigmy Son so airy.
>
> The God then took him to himself,
> And warm'd him in his Bosom,

---

[14] 'A kind of prominently ribbed apple, of large size, applied derisively to the head' (*OED*).

[15] Presumably a reference to the infidelity of Vulcan's wife (Venus); 'cuff' is slang, a contemptuous term for an old man (*OED*) - here a cuckolded ('cornuted') old man.

[16] This is the title of a poem by Ward (see also note 1, above) of inordinate length (fifty-six pages), and painful single-mindedness. 'Durgen' is a dialect word for an undersized person or animal, a dwarf (*OED*), to which Ward seems particularly attached. He high-mindedly attacks Pope (in *Durgen*) on the grounds that he has debased satire, which was 'design'd/Not to affront, but to reform Mankind'. Pope is also accused of being a bully, attacking poor defenceless dunces.

But found the Breath of this new Elf
Prov'd very strong and loathsome.

Come, come, said he, my little Son,
There's some defect within you,
But my approv'd Catholicon[17]
Shall gently purge and clean-you.   360

Then snatch'd him up into a Cloud,
There doctor'd him with Physick,
But left some Humours in his Blood,
That turn'd to Spleen and Phtisick.[18]

When thus the God had done his best,
To serve his little Creature,
And taught him to excel the rest
That live or starve by Meter;
Adorn'd him as a fav'rite Son,
With many quaint Devices,   370
He gently drop'd him down upon
The Banks of *Thame* and *Isis*,

Where the kind God, to shew his Love,
As with his Son he parted,
Wanting to imitate Great *Jove*,
Instead of Thunder, farted.

Then bounding from the Earth at once,
To show his Godlike Nature,
He this kind Blessing did pronounce
Upon his darling Satyr: 380

---

[17] 'An electuary (medicinal conserve) supposed to be capable of evacuating all humours; a universal remedy or prophylactic' (*OED*).
[18] 'A wasting disease of the lungs; pulmonary consumption (*OED*).

Thy Body, tho' deform'd and lean,
Yet, great shall be thy Merit,
Lofty thy Muse, sublime thy Pen,[19]
And very proud thy Spirit.

Tho' little, thou shalt sing aloud,
Be famous, tho' thou'rt homely,
Grow old and gray before thou'rt good,
And bald before thou'rt comely.

The Ladies that admire thy Strains,
When they behold the Poet,   390
Shall laugh in Scorn behind their Fans,
But thou, alass, not know it.

Thy own Defects thou shalt not see,
Yet find out Faults in others,
And shalt Flogmaster-Gen'ral be,
O'er all thy rhiming Brothers.

When thus the God of Wit had said,
Returning to the Heavens,
He left the little dough-bak'd Blade,
At sixes and at sevens.   400

Where like a River-God he sits,
Fenc'd round with Flags and Bushes,
There reigns as King of modern Wits,
Upon a Throne of Rushes.

His Royal Scepter is a Pen,

---

[19] It is worthy of note, that, even in a piece as wickedly malicious as this one, there is still an acknowledgement of Pope's standing as a poet. Not that the complimentary mode lasts very long (see the next few lines).

His Kingdom only Paper,
His Treasure a distemper'd Brain,
His Power empty Vapour.

Adore your Prince, ye scrib'ling Rakes,
As Tyrant of all Satyrs,   410
Who when he Rails, no diff'rence makes,
'Twixt Fools and Men of Letters.

But Hedge-hog like, wrapt up in Down,
As soft as that of Thistles,
He sleeps secure, and to the Town
Turns nothing but his Bristles.

Whilst other Wits, in muddy Streams,
He plunges as he pleases,
And dawbs 'em in his dirty Dreams,
That rise from his Diseases.   420

Sonif'rous Words he greatly loves,
Is gravely supercilious,
And, to his Brethren, always proves
A snarling *Terrae-filius*.

Ill-humour'd Pride and Self-conceit,
Join'd with a restless Spirit,
Prompt him t'abuse all Men of Wit,
And Women that have Merit.

No Sex or Quality escape
The fury of his Lashes,   430
And what he fears to say, the Ape

Supplies with Stars and Dashes.[20]
Pope, Alexander:Dunciad Variorum, The
Since, in foul Calumny, we own
He greatly does surpass us,
Fleet-ditch shall be his *Helicon*,
And *Bridewell*[21] his *Parnassus*.

There shall the Blue-coats flog his Back,
Till he's much better natur'd,
And dip him in the Ditch, till black
As those he has bespatter'd.   440
Pope, Alexander:Dunciad, The
Then shall the little dirty Bard,
From Pleasure-Boat and Chariot,
Be ship'd to Monkey-Land like *W---d*,[22]
And there reign Poet-Laureat.

FINIS.

---

[20] The first edition of *The Dunciad* (1728) has plenty of stars and dashes; however, the Grub Street fraternity - Ward among them - was even more upset by *The Dunciad Variorum* (1729), which removed all pretence at anonymity and named names.

[21] Bridewell was the house of correction for women. In *The Dunciad* (Book II, 269-70), Pope uses a mock-Homeric device to indicate the passing of time, punctuating the heroic games: ' This labour past, by Bridewell all descend,/(As morning-pray'r and flagellation end).' Pope himself noted that it was 'between eleven and twelve in the morning, after church service, that the criminals are whipp'd in Bridewell'. The Blue-coats, in the next line, are the beadles who would have administered the whipping.

[22] Ward probably has himself in mind here, as he's making use of a line from Book I of *The Dunciad* : 'Or shipp'd with Ward to ape and monkey lands'. Pope's note on this line, in *The Dunciad Variorum*, runs thus: 'Edward Ward, a very voluminous Poet....but best known by the *London Spy*, in Prose. He has of late Years kept a publick house in the City (but in a genteel way and with his wit, humour, and good liquor (Ale) afforded his guests a pleasureable entertainment, especially those of the High Church party....Great numbers of his works are yearly sold into the Plantations...' Ward, it seems, objected both to this summary despatch of his works to the Plantations, and to the location given to his tavern. Pope concludes his note - 'Ward in a Book called Apollo's Maggot, declar'd this account to be a great Falsity, protesting that his publick house was not in the City, but in Moorfields.'

AN
AUTHOR
To be Lett[1]

GENTLEMEN,

I AM glad to find you meddle with the dirty Works of your Brother Journalists. To be inoffensive is a puritannical Spirit and will never succeed in a free-thinking Age. What is Gold itself (says the Philosopher) but Dirt?[2] It is dug out of dirty Mines, and as a Proof it retains its Nature, we come at it easiest thro' dirty Means. Be assured, a Scavenger of Wit is a more gainful Occupation than that of a delicate, moral Writer.

BY this I mean to let you see my Ability and to proffer my Service. You must know when my Mother was pregnant of me, she once dreamt she was delivered of a Monster. It was observed also, at the Time of my Birth, that a Weezle was heard

---

[1] Nine days after the appearance of *The Dunciad Variorum* in 1729, the *Flying Post* announced the publication of *An Author to be Lett*. Its author, Richard Savage, was known to Pope, and according to some of Pope's victims in *The Dunciad*, was his chief supplier of anecdotes and gossip. (See the Introduction to the Augustan Reprint Society edition of *An Author...*, Number 84, 1960.) Savage's intention, evidently, was to present a portrait of a Grub Street hack in all his glory. His very name - Iscariot Hackney - is suggestive of base, mercenary treachery. The title-page is worth quoting in full: 'AN AUTHOR To be LETT. Being A PROPOSAL humbly address'd to the Consideration of the Knights, Esquires, Gentlemen, and other worshipful and weighty Members of the Solid and Ancient Society of the BATHOS. By their Associate and Well wisher *ISCARIOT HACKNEY*. ' Just to complete his point, Savage adds a Grub-Street motto: '*Evil be thou my Good*. SATAN'.
The text is taken from the British Library copy of the pamphlet of 1729.

[2] It is useful to be aware from the outset the nature of the persona created here. Our writer loftily proclaims himself above filthy lucre - but then he would, wouldn't he? His claim hardly squares with the title of 'his' piece: he is an author available for hire.

to shriek; and a Bat (tho' at Noon Day) flew into the Room, and settled upon the Midwife's Wrist, just as she received me. While in the Cradle, I was very froward. Early at School I discovered a promising Genius for Mischief. I carried Tales from one Boy to another to set them a fighting, and afterwards to the Master to have them whipp'd. I had always Cunning enough, when I committed a fault to lay the Blame upon another, and laugh'd to see him suffer for it. (A sure Prognostick of my future judgement in Politicks!) I was fond of tearing away the Legs and Wings of Flies, of picking out the Eyes of some little Bird, or laming some favourite Lap-Dog, merely by way of Amusement. This was only a Sign that one Time or other I should have Ill-nature enough for a *great Wit*. Now I understand to be a *great Wit* is to take a Pleasure in giving every Body Pain, and to shew no mercy to a Reputation, which is dearer to some Fools than perhaps a Limb, or an Eye. I was also given to pilfer whatever lay in my Way, a Proof only that I wou'd never scruple being a Plagiary, shou'd I turn Author. I was expert at almost every thing except learning my Book; but neither Encouragement nor Correction could bring me to any Sense of Duty. I was always very sullen after being corrected; and if my Master forgave and admonished me in a friendly Manner, I all the while ridiculed the old *Put*[3] (as I then call'd him) by making Mouths or Horns over his Shoulder. This shew'd I had always Wit enough to laugh at the common Notion of Gratitude. I hooted at any unfortunate, ill dress'd Person in the Street, if he look'd like a Gentleman, and never fail'd to mock the Infirmities of *old Age*. When at Sermon, I was very full of Play myself, and fond of interrupting the Devotions of others; so that (I thank my Stars!) in my Youth I had a fashionable Contempt for Religion. I came young into the world with little Education, less Money, and no visible Way of living: However, I qualified myself (tho' of mean Birth) for a Gentleman of Wit and Humour about Town. I have naturally a Sourness of Temper, a droll Solemnity of Countenance, and a dry Manner of joking upon such Accidents, as Fools who value themselves upon Humanity, would be apt to be compassionate. I have also a Propensity to sneer upon all Mankind, and particularly upon those who fancy they can oblige me. These elegant Qualities recommended me early to the Friendship of *Dick Morley*, Author of *Mother Wiseborn*. We met frequently at a little, snug gaming-House, never yet discovered by informing Constables. A Similitude of

---

3   '17th century slang; a stupid man, silly fellow, blockhead' (*OED*).

Circumstances and Sympathy of Souls endeared us to each other; and to him I owe the Improvements of my afore-mentioned Faculties. These he cultivated, and many others implanted in me of the like Nature.

WE commenced Authors together. At my first setting out, I was hired by a reverend Prebend to libel *Dean Swift* for Infidelity. Soon after I was employed by *Curll* to write a merry Tale, the Wit of which was its Obscenity. This we agreed to palm upon the World for a posthumous Piece of *Mr. Prior*. However, a certain Lady, celebrated for certain Liberties, had a Curiosity to see the real Author. *Curll*, on my Promise that if I had a Present, he should go Snacks,[4] sent me to her. I was admitted while her Ladyship was *shifting*; and on my Admittance, *Mrs. Abigail* was order'd to withdraw. What passed between us, a Point of Gallantry obliges me to conceal; but after some extraordinary Civilities, I was dismiss'd with a Purse of Guineas, and a Command to write a Sequel to my Tale. Upon this I turn'd out smart in my Dress, bit *Curll* of his Share, and run out most of my Money in printing my Works at my own Cost. But some Years after (just at the time of his starving poor *Pattison*,[5] the varlet was revenged. He arrested me for several Months Board, brought me back to my Garret,[6] and made me drudge on in my old, dirty Work. 'Twas in his Service that I wrote Obscenity and Profaneness, under the Names of *Pope* and *Swift*. Sometimes I was Mr. *Joseph Gay*,[7] and at others Theory *Burnet* [8] or *Addison*. I abridg'd Histories and Travels, translated from the

---

[4] 'To have a share, to divide profits' (*OED*). We should know the sort of environment we are in, with the introduction of Curll. It is a measure of his fame (or notoriety) that no reference to publishing or bookselling at this time is complete without some mention of him. Curll's methods are also universally known - the repetition, here, of the accusations of piracy, plagiarism and other sharp practice are by now familiar. Our author imagines he can put one over on Curll; he quickly discovers his error - see below.

[5] One of Curll's poets, who was responsible for *Cupid's Metamorphosis; or Love in all Shapes* (1727), a collection of poems, despite the title (a typical Curll come-on). Pope virtually accused Curll, as Savage does here, of actually starving Pattison to death. The opposite was in fact the case - Curll nursed him throughout his last illness (he died of small-pox, aged twenty-one). See Ralph Straus, *The Unspeakable Curll*, p. 41.

[6] It is an odd thing, but true, that a starving poet in his garret (or, at least, *some* starving poets), can be romanticised, sanctified, even, whereas the striving journalist, similarly impoverished, is condemned to the deeps in *The Dunciad*. Johnson's *Life of Savage* perpetuates this myth, observable in a passage in which Savage's life and Iscariot hackney's appear to blend - with one major difference: Savage was a man of 'exalted sentiments' and 'extensive views'. (*Life of Savage*, 1744, in *Johnson's Lives of the English Poets*, George Birkbeck Hill, 3 vols, ii, p. 399. See also Introduction, in which this passage is quoted.)

[7] See notes to *The Dunciad* (Book II, 126-7) in this volume, and the Introduction, above.

French, what they never wrote, and was expert at finding out new Titles for old Books. When a notorious Thief was hanged, I was the *Plutarch* to preserve his Memory; and when a great Man died, mine were his Remains, and mine the Account of his last Will and Testament. Had Mr. *Oldmixon* and Mr. *Curll* agreed, my Assistance had probably been invited into Father *Boheur's* Logick, and the critical History of *England.*

BUT before all this happened, a young Nobleman gratified me for letting some Verses of mine be handed about at Court in Manuscript under his Name. This was the first Time that I ever heard my Writings generally commended. But alas! how short-lived the Applause? They unfortunately stole into Print, lost their Reputation at once, and I am now asham'd to write any more, as a Person of Quality. I am a great Joker, and deal in Clenches,[9] Puns, Quibbles, Jibes, Conundrums, and carry Whichits. Many a good Time have I lash'd the whole Body of Clergy, and crack'd many a smart Joke upon the Trinity. One of my Books had the Honour of being presented for a Libel, by the Grand-Jury, and another was made a Burnt-Offering by the Hands of the Common Hangman. When an Author writes a Piece that has Success in his own Character, I abuse him; but if in a fictitious one, I endeavour to personate him, and write a Second Part to his Work. I am very deeply read in all Pieces of Scandal, Obscenity, and Profaneness, particularly in the Writings of Mrs. *Haywood, Henley, W-lst-d, Morley, Br-v-l, Foxton, Cooke, D'Foe, Norton, Woolston, Dennis,*[10] and the Author of the *Rival Modes.* From these I propose to compile a very grand Work, which shall not be inferior to *Utopia, Carimania, Gulliveriana,*[11] *Art of Flogging,*[12] *Daily Journal* Epigrams on the *Dunciad,* or *Oratory Transactions;* and as this is designed for the Use of young Templers, it is

---

8   Thomas Burnet (1694-1753); 'Theory' Burnet on account of his *Theory of the Earth* (1721) and *Theory of the Visible World* (1728), Parts 1 and 2 of his *Archaeologica Philosophica.* Publisher: E. Curll.

9   A play on words, pun, quibble: '[Shakespeare]is many times flat, insipid; his comic wit degenerating into clenches' - Dryden, *Essay of Dramatick Poesie (OED).*

10   Almost all, deservedly or not, have a place in *The Dunciad.*

11   *Gulliveriana* (1728) was a particularly malicious collection of satirical pieces, directed, for the most part, at Swift and Pope. Jonathan Smedley, a long-standing adversary (hero of the mock Olympiad in *The Dunciad,* q.v.), was responsible.

12   Not all these items are worth exploration - this one is. Curll, needless to say, was the man behind the publication of *The Treatise of Flogging.* It was another piece, however, that provoked the authorities into a prosecution; this was *Venus in the Cloister; or the Nun in her Smock* (1724). Curll spent five months in jail even before he was found guilty. (See Introduction for details of this episode.)

hoped they will promote my Subscription. Since private Vices have been proved to be publick Benefits, I wou'd venture to call it, *An useful Body of* IMMORALITY, and print it in a broad, pompous Folio; but such a one as may very well be bound up with Dean *Smedley's* intended *Body of Divinity.*

BY the Help of Indexes, and technical Dictionaries, I work on every Branch of Learning. I pore often over the Volumes of State Tracts, whence I collect Paragraphs which I mix with Remarks of my own, and range under several Heads.[13] Those against a discarded Minister I send to the *London* and *British Journals,* and others more virulent against a Prime One (for I naturally hate my Superiors) are for my very good Friend the *Craftsman.* Rather than stand out of Play, I have penn'd Panegyricks in *Mist* on *Rich's* Pantomimes, and *Theobald's Shakespear Restored.*[14] I am always listed by Mr. *Lun* the Harlequin, to hiss the first Night at any of the Drury Lane Performances. Sometimes I draw up Challenges for the Champions of Mr. *Figg's* Amphitheatre, and sometimes for the Disputants of Mr. *Henley's* Oratory.

I HAVE an excellent Knack at Birth-day Odes, Elogies, Acrosticks, Anagrams, Epithalamiums, Prologues, Recommendatory Poems, Rhimes for Almanack-Makers, and witty Distichs for the Signs of Country Inns and Ale-houses. When with an audible Voice I spout forth my own Verses, marvelous is their Effect! The very Bellman has been touch'd with Envy!---An Author, who like Mr. *Ralph,* has distinguish'd himself by *Night;* the Shrilness of my clamorous, dunning Landlady

---

[13] Savage evidently takes the view, in common with Pope and his friends, that these activities are tedious, anti-literature, the work of the Goddess of Dulness. Abel Boyer, for example, the chronicler of Queen Anne's reign, is pilloried in *The Dunciad.* His *Political State of Great Britain* and *Annals of Queen Anne,* however, are an invaluable collection of state papers, political commentary etc.. They were a significant step, however limited by government control, towards a thorough reporting of political activity.

[14] Savage here takes Pope's side in the controversy over the latter's edition of Shakespeare's plays, published in 1725. Lewis Theobald, in his *Shakespear Restored: Or, a Specimen of the Many Errors, As Well Committed, as Unamended, by Mr. Pope In His Late Edition of this Poet* (1726), criticised Pope's methods. (For example, Pope rejected many lines as spurious, on critical grounds - they offended him.) Dr Johnson, in the Preface to his own edition of the plays (1765), put his finger precisely on the spot: 'This was a work which Pope seems to have thought unworthy of his abilities, being not able to suppress his contempt of the 'dull duty of an editor' [Pope's remark in his Preface to the Works]....Pope's edition fell below his own expectations, and he was so much offended when he was found to have left anything to do that he passed the latter part of his life in a state of hostility with verbal criticism' (*Samuel Johnson on Shakespeare,* ed. H.R. Woodhuysen, Penguin, 1989, pp. 149-150). As a reward for pointing out some of Pope's errors and omissions, Theobald was made the hero of the first version of *The Dunciad* (1728).

has been charm'd into a still Attention! Nay, the very Bailiff, in act to rush upon me, has stop'd short to listen, and for a Minute suspended the rapacious Palm that was to fall upon my Shoulder!

I HAVE well perused the Writings of *Luke Milbourn, Shadwell, Settle, Blackmore*, and many others of our Stamp, notable for salt Wit upon *Dryden*. From these I have extracted curious Hints to assist *Welsted* in his new Satire against *Pope*, which was once (he told me) to have been christen'd *Labeo*.[15] 'Tis yet an Embrio, and there are divers Opinions about the Birth of it. Some expect it will spring from his wise Noddle, like *Minerva* from the Head of *Jupiter*, and work Wonders. Others, that it will resemble *Milton*'s Figure of *Sin* coming from the Brain of the Father of Lies.[16] Then, say they, it will damn its Parent's Reputation. But most are of Opinion, that my Brother has no Reputation to lose, and therefore the Brat will be still-born. 'Tis possible *Barnham Goode* also may miscarry of his *Mock Aesop*, tho' *James Moore Smythe*, Esq., is to officiate Man-Midwife.

WHEN a Man of Quality is distinguish'd for wit or an Encourager of it, I endeavour to strike him for a Dedication; but I have generally been so unhappy as to disgust my Patrons by praising them in the wrong Place. For want of being acquainted with polite Life, I have unwittingly complemented a Person for an illustrious Birth, who really owed his Rise entirely to his Merit. Thus have I caused his Enemies to sneer, and, perhaps, to libel him for my squab Complement; when, had I left him to his Choice, he had rather chose my Satire than my Panegyrick.

THERE is a certain Right Honourable *Didapper*[17] *Knight* of the *BATH-os*, a Man of my Namesake, *Iscariot*'s own Probity, and famous, like one of the Suitors in *Homer*'s *Odyssey*, for *dead-born Jests*. Many a Sonnet of mine, and several

---

15 Presumably Welsted's *One Epistle to Mr. Pope* (1730), q.v., in the present volume. It would appear that Savage had seen this piece in manuscript, and had forewarned Pope (as he no doubt did on other matters also - it was perhaps his value as Pope's eyes and ears that kept him out of *The Dunciad*). A reference to the *One Epistle*, using the name Savage gives it - *Labeo* - appears in *The Dunciad Variorum* (published before the *One Epistle*) - Pope had evidently been warned by Savage of the imminent appearance of this same 'Labeo' ('one who has large lips, one who is blubber-lipped' - definition from Lewis and Short, the Latin equivalent of the *OED*).
16 *Paradise Lost*, Book II, 746ff.
17 'A small diving water-fowl; dabchick' (*OED*); 'The Didappers are Authors that keep themselves long out of sight, under water, and come up now and then where you least expected them' (*Peri Bathous: Or, The Art of sinking in Poetry*, Chap. VI, Pope and the Scriblerians, 1727). Savage's hack can only be referring to Pope here - adding his mite of contumely to the mountain of abuse directed at the poet. ('Didapper' is a name, like 'Durgen' and 'Sawney', which glances derisively at Pope's stature - see, for example, *Sawney and Colley*, in the present volume.)

Bouts Rimez that were filled up by me, has he read with his usual Modesty, at *White*'s[18] and the Drawing-Room for his own; but as they were mere Slips of my Pen and could be of no Advantage to my Reputation, (low as it stands) I am contented to humour his Vanity, and forbear to claim them. To deal plainly, this little Knight is a Person whom I, even I, *Iscariot Hackney*, treat with Contempt; and furthermore, I fear no Revenge from him for publishing this Declaration, unless he should breathe upon me -- It must be confess'd, indeed, there is a strange Influence in all that issues from his *Mouth*. I assisted him in a pretty Play of Words on the Letter P, and the Advertisement of the *Lady's Writing Desk* for which our Printer underwent the Discipline of the Cane. I was really sorry for the poor Fellow's Misfortune, and cou'd have heartily wished it had fallen with more Justice and less Mercy on the little smart Knight. Soon after I chopp'd Sides, and wrote the *History of the Norfolk Dumpling,* the Verses on the *Norfolk Lanthorn* and many other popular Libels on Persons who least deserv'd them; but the reason of that was, because they were of the Ministry.

Now is the Session of Parliament, and the Poetical Quarrels must give way to the Political. Consequently the Affairs of State (as *Abel* in the Play of the *Committee* observes) will *lie heavy upon my Neck and Shoulders.* It is a Custom among great Generals to send Spies into an enemy's Camp, and among Politicians to employ 'em in foreign Courts. I have therefore (as I am determined to oppose the Ministry) settled a secret Correspondence with several Gentlemen of the Party-colour'd Cloth; Men of Dignity! such as have no less an Honour than that of holding a Plate in the Presence of some certain Knights of the Blue Ribbon. My Bribe is a Pot of Ale, and my Intelligence the Scraps of Conversation that fall at the table of great Ministers. By these I am enabled to discuss the Matters in debate at the House of Commons and the Congress of *Soissons*, to state the Debts of the Nation, to arraign the Conduct of those at Helm, and to hold the Balance *of Europe* with as much Ease as a Monkey does a Chesnut, in my own Paw.

THE Time has been when, after an Evening's hard boozing, my brother Bards (who have been what we call Seedy or Crop-sick) have bilked the publick House, and barbarously left me in pawn for the Reckoning. On this Emergency I have

---

[18] The famous Chocolate-House in London, frequented by the great and the good. Swift was to be found there from time to time.

written an Account of a *sharp and bloody Fight, a Vision in the Air*, or a *Wonderful Prophecy* to be hawk'd about Streets: And (wou'd you believe it?) even these Productions of mine have pass'd for design'd Wit, and I have silently sneered, to find the Merit of them claimed and boasted of by *Jemmy Moore*, and the abovemention'd Knight.

I HAVE sometimes taken it in my Head, that I might make a Fortune by writing for the Stage. As a Proof that I have an Excellent Taste, I always despised the Tragedies of *Shakespeare, Otway* and *Young*, referr'd with Admiration to Mr. *Rolli*'s Opera's at the *Hay-Market*. I wonder, that the Success of the Latter shou'd be applied to Mr. *Hendell*'s Musick or the Performances of *Senesino, Faustina, and Cutzoni*: the Town in this have been shamefully blind to the Merit of Mr. *Rolli*. He has followed the Antients so closely in the Propriety of his Conduct, the Unity of his Characters, the natural Variety of Passions, the Strength of Sentiment, and the Elegance of Diction, that I here invite him to join with me in an *English* Tragedy on an Opera Plan.

IF the Gentleman thinks this too arduous an Undertaking, let us venture at a lower Cast! In fine, let us make Amends for the Suppression of Mr. *Gay*'s Sequel:[19] without any Recourse to Wit, Humour, Natural Dialogue, Songs aptly introduced, or any other of those Trifles with which the *Beggar's Opera* abounds. We have one sure Comfort; that is, we cannot fall short of Mr. *Johnson*'s *Village Opera*, nor be excell'd by *R---m* and his Didapper *Knight*: *R---m* cannot excel me, unless he excels himself.

I HAVE tried all Means (but what Fools call honest ones) for a Livelihood. I offer'd my Service for a secret Spy to the State; but had not Credit enough even for that. When it was indeed very low with me, I printed Proposals for a Subscription to my Works, received Money, and gave Receipts without any Intention of delivering the Book. Tho' I have been notoriously prophane, and was never at an University, I once aim'd to be admitted into Orders; but being obliged to abscond lately from the Parish-Officers, on Account of a Bastard Child, and falling besides into an unlucky Salivation, my Character was so scandalous, that I cou'd not prevail even on the lowest of the Fleet-Prison Parsons to sign my Testimonials.

---

19 To *The Beggar's Opera, Polly*. Walpole, having taken a severe drubbing in the first play, made sure its successor (1730) was banned.

MY last Attempt was to have been a Travelling Tutor to some young Gentleman. If I am deficient in Classic Learning, I cou'd yet have instructed him in the Laws of his own Country; for tho' I never studied *Coke* upon *Littleton*,[20] yet I have conversed with Bailiffs and petty-fogging Attornies; nay, I have conn'd over the *Abridgements* of Giles Jacob. I cou'd also have read him Lectures of Politicks from Essays of my own in *Weekly Journals*. What, tho' I wanted Knowledge to make Dissertations upon the Languages, Manners, Histories, Statutes, Coins, paintings, Architecture, or any other Curiosities, ancient or modern of foreign Climes? what, tho' I cou'd not have traced out any one Country in a Map? cou'd I not have pillaged Voyage Writers, and have taken the Reports of Inn-Keepers or Postilions, to have told where there were good Wine, good Beds, buxom Girls, and tall Steeples? Few foreign Tutors understand the dead Languages; but if they play at Cards, dance, talk of Things they never saw; or, having seen, cou'd not understand; if they put on the swaggering Air of Half-pay Captains, and swear *French* military Oaths with a *bon Grace*, will they not pass for Men of Wit, Experience, and Knowledge? I shou'd have made a very fashionable Tutor, I wou'd have spirited up my Pupil to run away with a Nun; and, if he aimed at smaller Game, not scrupled being Pimp. I have studied Physick under the *Anodyne Necklace* Doctor, and wou'd have prepared, and exported a whole Cargo of *Antivenereal* Pills for his Safety. No one, I am persuaded will blame me, if I took this Opportunity of feathering my own Nest. I shou'd perhaps have made him pay Ten *per Cent*. for his own Money, when I disbursed it, and a Guinea on many Occasions for his Honour; twenty Shillings of which I might have put in my own Pocket. Who knows but I might have married some rich Widow by securing my Pupil for one of her Daughters? I wou'd have contriv'd he shou'd have stolen the young Lady to avoid paying her Fortune. If this Scheme failed, I had another, for which I am afraid I might have been a little censured; 'twas only to have set him at a gaming Table (when abroad) for about a thousand Pounds, and afterwards gone Snacks with the Sharpers. But on second Thoughts, where had been the Hurt?

---

[20] Sir Edward Coke (1552-1634) and Sir Thomas Littleton (c. 1415-1481), both celebrated lawyers. Coke's *Coke upon Littleton* was published in 1628 (*DNB*).

When return'd, and at Age, I cou'd easily have made him Amends, by negotiating a Mortgage, or the Sale of a Reversion for him with honest *Ch-rt-r-s*.[21]

THUS, tho' I had but a hundred a Year, and for no more than two, or three Years Service, I cou'd retire to *Swisserland* or *Wales*, with about Fifteen Hundred Pounds in my Pocket, and an Anuity of fifty Pounds *per Annum* for Life. In such a Retirement I shou'd have set down like my Brother *Br-v-l* to writing an *Account of My Travels*. When those were finished, by carefully extracting from Gazettes, I shou'd have been able to have left my Executors the Memoirs of my own Times, then wou'd I have indulged my Spleen against the present Ministers, for neglecting to gratify my Merit. 'Tis dangerous to anger a Poet or Historian.

I observed at the Head of this Letter, that I have a Drollery in my Countenance; Egad! 'tis as *peculiar* a One as *R--m*'s.[22] We are so alike, that before he scribled himself into Preferment, we have actually been mistaken for each other. Our Looks are so happy, as to have pass'd off many a Saying in Conversation for Wit and Humour, that, when published, has been thought flat: Nay, the same Thing has been said of me, as was utter'd by a certain *Wit* (one very different from our Rank) on him, viz. that the *R--g--'s Misfortune is, he cannot print his Face to his Joke.*

WHILE I am thus delineating my Features, permit me to own, that I wish my Portrait might shine in a *Mezitento*[23] thro' the Glass-Windows of Picture-Shops in *Fleet-Street*, and St. *Paul*'s Church-Yard; then shou'd I be gaz'd on with Admiration by Mercers 'Prentices! But I will at least indulge my Vanity in appearing on a large Sheet of Paper, in a Wooden Cut, which ingenious School-Boys may delight to colour with yellow and red *Ocker*. What a glaring Figure shall I then make in the long Piazza of *Covent Garden*! I shall be surrounded by venerable Old Ballads; and several of my Family Pieces, such as the *Sinners Coat of Arms* and the dreadful Sketches of *Death, Judgment,* and *Damnation*! Thence shall I be translated to the naked Walls of Country Ale-houses, Coblers Stalls, and Necessary Houses! --- And thou, O *R--m*, thou who art my *other self*! be this thy Glory! however different our Fortunes, however unlike the Incidents of our Lives;

---

21 'Honest Charteris' was the infamous Francis, for whom Arbuthnot wrote a devastating epitaph (q.v.).
22 Edward Roome (d.1729), mentioned earlier by 'Iscariot', was a weekly journalist. His father was an undertaker (according to Savage, in his Preface to *An Author to be Lett*) - hence the 'drollery' Roome is here said to 'bear in his face'.
23 Mezzo-tint, presumably.

yet whensoe'er the Countenance of *Iscariot Hackney* is seen, thy own *dear Phiz* will be called to Remembrance.

IN short, I am a perfect Town Author: I hate all Mankind, yet am occasionally a mighty Patriot. I am very poor, and owe my Poverty to my Merit, that is, to my writings: I am as proud as I am poor; yet, what is seemingly a Contradiction, never stick at a mean Action, when the Welfare of the Republick of Letters, or, in other Words, my own Interest is concerned. My Pen, like the Sword of a *Swiss*, or the pleading of a *Lawyer,* is generally employed for *Pay*.[24] There is one Piece of Advice, Gentlemen, which I wou'd propose to you: If any Papers of a *dead Wit* shou'd fall into the Hands of a Member of your Society, let him be sure to print them, tho' never so derrogatory to the Person's Reputation, to get himself Money; and if, among whole Heaps of indigested Papers, he finds a few with large *Corrections* and Additions by *another eminent Hand* (which he well knows) let him be sure to suppress that *Circumstance* in his Publication.

BUT to return to myself---My Pamphlets sell many more Impressions than those of celebrated Writers; the Secret of this is, I learned from *Curll* to clap a new Title-Page to the Sale of every half Hundred; so that when my Bookseller has sold Two Hundred and Fifty Copies, my Book generally enters into the *Sixth Edition.* 'Tis reckon'd a villanous Action to write a Libel, but more so to father one on a Person, who neither wrote it, nor approves it; now, I own I never scruple to do both. When a Man of Figure (perhaps an ornament of his Country) has been cruelly aspersed in his Life-time, I love to revive the Aspersion at his Death: It is Mirth to me to grieve a whole Family, by insulting his Memory before his Body is cold in the Grave. In this I imitate the Author of *Sarah the Quaker in the Shades,* to *Lothario lately deceased.* Tho' I am so ready to libel others, I am downright frighten'd if I but hear of a Satire where my Name is likely to be inserted. When a Person does me a Favour, I either suspect he has some Design on me; or think it less than my due, and that he is obliged to me, because an *Author,* for accepting it. I am very testy if I am not allow'd *Dictator* of my Company; nor had I ever a Friend, whom I did not in his Absence sacrifice to my Jest. I contemn the Few who admire me, am angry with the Multitude who despise me, and mortally hate all, who have any Ways

---

[24] The key charge levelled (neither fairly nor honestly) by the Scriblerians at the Grub-Street brethren - that they were inspired, not by the Muse of Literature, but by the need to earn a crust.

obliged me. I assure you I am very famous for several Treatises in Defence of *Ingratitude.* I never fail to illustrate them with the Examples of *Marcus Brutus* among the *Ancients,* and very eminent *Statesmen* among the *Moderns.* My private Resentment, like that of other *Great Men,* is always a publick Justice.

Now, Gentlemen, if you like me for a Correspondent, my Price is the Price of a *Journalist,* a Crown; and, in the Stile of a Love Bargain, Half Wet, Half Dry. You may find me in a Morning at my Lucubrations,[25] over a Quartern Pot in a *Geneva* Shop in *Clare-Market*; a House where I propose many learned Interviews with Orator *Henley,* who has removed his Stage to that place. I generally dine with a brother Bard at one of the little Cook's Shops near St. Martin's Church, and probably spend the Evening with him at a Night-Cellar in the Strand, where I shall be ready to enter into a Treaty with you.

Yours,

From my Chamber,
Hockley in the Hole.[26]
Hackney.

Iscariot

---

[25] 'The product of nocturnal study and meditation; hence, a literary work showing signs of careful elaboration' (*OED*).
[26] Not the fashionable end of London; it was famous for its bear-baiting garden and as one of the numerous haunts of prostitutes.

ONE
EPISTLE[1]
TO
Mr. A. POPE

If noble *B—m*,[2] in Metre known,
With Strains has grac'd thee, humble as thy own;
Who *G-l-n*'s[3] Dullness did for thine discard,

---

[1] Printed for Joseph Roberts, one of Edmund Curll's close associates, and probably acting on his behalf - Curll was having to keep out of trouble at this time (1730) after he was found guilty of publishing obscene articles (see Introduction). The author was Leonard Welsted, helped by one or two collaborators, one of whom may have been Lady Mary Wortley Montague, a former friend of Pope. This piece may be the *Labeo*, anticipated by Pope in *The Dunciad Variorum* (see Richard Savage's *An Author to be Lett*, and the notes thereto, in this volume). In Book II of *The Dunciad*, Welsted performs heroically in the mud-diving contest, winning one of the coveted prizes:
   Not Welsted so: drawn endlong by his scull,
   Furious he sinks; precipitately dull.
   Whirlpools and storms his circling arm invest,
   With all the Might of gravitation blest.
   No crab more active in the dirty dance,
   Downward to climb, and backward to advance;
   He brings up half the bottom on his head,
   And boldly claims the Journals and the lead (Book II, 293-300).
Welsted was clearly upset by this and other slighting references (in *The Dunciad*) to his literary productions. In the Preface to *One Epistle*, he refers to Pope's claim 'that he has meddled with no one, that had not before hurt him'; he, Welsted, had not 'hurt' Pope, and so did not deserve the treatment handed out to him. Charge and counter-charge of this sort are commonplace in Grub-Street quarrels; in this instance, Welsted must be forgetting his attack on *Three Hours After Marriage* (1717).

[2] 'The late Duke of *Buckingham*...has also printed a Copy of Verses in Praise of *Pope*, which were returned by another in Praise of his Grace. There is so great a Similitude in the Stile of these Writers, that the Reader, I think, need not doubt their Sincerity in admiring each other' (Welsted's own note).

[3] Charles Gildon (1665-1724), one of Pope's favourite butts.

A better Critick for as bad a Bard!
Not unregarded let this Tribute be,
Tho' humble, just; well-bred, tho' paid to Thee.
Parnassian Groves, and *Twick'nam* Fountains, say,
What Homage to the Bard shall *Britain* pay!
The Bard! that first, from *Dryden*'s thrice-glean'd Page,
Cull'd his low Efforts to Poetic Rage;   10
Nor pillag'd only that unrival'd Strain,
But raked for Couplets *Chapman*[4] and *Duck-Lane*,
Has sweat each Cent'ry's Rubbish to explore,
And plunder'd every Dunce that writ before,
Catching half Lines, till the tun'd Verse went round,
Complete, in smooth dull Unity of Sound;
Who, stealing Human, scorn'd Celestial Fire,
And strung to *Smithfield* Airs the *Hebrew* Lyre....[5]

Oh say, to him what Trophies shall be rais'd,   20
That unprovok'd will strike, and fawn unprais'd!
Each fav'rite Toast[6] who marks, or rising Wit,
To sketch a Satire, that in Time may fit;
Still hopes your Sun-set, while he views your Noon,
And still broods o'er the closely kept Lampoon;
The lurking Presents o'er the Tomb he paid,
And thus atton'd *our British Virgil*'s Shade,
A Mushroom Satire[7] in his Life conceal'd,
Since chang'd to Libel, and in Print reveal'd;

---

[4] George Chapman (1559?-1634?), known chiefly for his translation of Homer. The charge levelled at Pope is plagiarism - from both the sublime and the ridiculous (Duck-Lane, at the heart of the Grub-Street bookselling trade). See also the lines immediately following.

[5] Fourteen lines have here been omitted; they are so stuffed with references to obscure personalities (or rather irritating hints given through first and last letters with dashes) that removing them is rather an act of charity rather than of deprivation.

[6] 'Toasts' - the belles of the season - were regularly celebrated at the (male) coffee-houses.

[7] This refers to the 'Libel' on Addison ('Atticus', a minor squib) for which Pope is also chided in *The Blatant-Beast* (in this volume).

Who lets not Beauty[8] base Detraction 'scape,   30
And mocks Deformity with *Aesop*'s Shape;
Who *Cato*'s Muse with faithless Sneers belied,
The Prologue father'd, and the Play decried,
On *H—y*'s[9] learned Page, dull-sporting trod,
Betray'd his Patrons, and lampoon'd his God;
Translator, Editor, could far out-go
In *Homer Ogleby*,[10] in *Shakespeare R—*[11]
O! how burlesqu'd, great *Dryden*, is thy Strain,
When little *Alexander slays the Slain*!

On, mighty Rhimer, haste new Palms to seize,   40
Thy little, envious, angry Genius teize;
Let thy weak wilful Head, unrein'd by Art,
Obey the Dictates of thy flatt'ring Heart;
Divide a busy, fretful Life between
Smut, Libel, Sing-song, Vanity, and Spleen;
With long-brew'd Malice warm thy languid Page,
And urge delirious Nonsense into Rage;
Let bawdy Emblems, now, thy Hours beguile;
Now, Fustian[12] Epic, aping *Virgil*'s Stile;
To *Virgil* like, to *Indian* Clay as *Delf*,[13]   50
Or *Pulteney*, drawn by *Jervase*,[14] to Herself:

---

[8] Lady Mary Montague, according to Welsted.

[9] Benjamin Hoadly (1676-1761), Bishop successively of Bangor, (1715), Hereford (1721), Salisbury (1723) and Winchester (1734). He was a controversial defender of the cause of civil and religious liberty against both crown and clergy (*DNB*).

[10] John Ogilby (1600-76), author and printer, published verse translations of Homer, Virgil and Aesop's Fables (*DNB*).

[11] Nicholas Rowe (1674-1718), edited Shakespeare's plays (1709); Pope was accused of following Rowe's edition rather closely in his own edition of 1725. (See Dr Johnson's strictures on the latter in n. 14 to *An Author to be Lett* (Richard Savage), in the present volume.)

[12] 'Inflated, turgid, or inappropriately lofty language...bombast, rant' (*OED*).

[13] Welsted's unwieldy simile is no doubt intended to convey the suggestion that Pope's 'Fustian' efforts resemble Virgil's to the same degree that Indian mud is comparable with the celebrated Delf earthenware.

[14] Another mighty simile, this time glancing unfavourably on the portraits of Charles Jervas (c. 1675-1739), who painted Swift and Stella's portraits. Lady Pulteney was one of the leading beauties of the day.

Rheams heap'd on Rheams, incessant, mayst thou blot,
A lively, trifling, pert, one knows not what!
Form thy light Measures, nimbler than the Wind,
While heavy lingring Sense is left behind;
With all thy Might pursue, and all thy Will,
That unabating Thirst, to scribble still,
Giv'n at thy Birth! the Poetaster's[15] Gust,
False and unsated as the Eunuch's Lust!

 Illustrious Fops, mean time, o'er-rate thy Lays,   60
And blooming Critics, as they spell thee, praise:
Blest Coupleteer! by blooming Critics read,
At Toilets *ogled*, and with Sweetmeats fed:
See, lisping Toilets grace thy *Dunciad*'s Cause,
And scream their witty Scavenger's Applause,
While powder'd Wits, and lac'd Cabals rehearse
Thy bawdy *Cento*,[16] and thy *Bead-roll*[17] Verse;
Gay, bugled Statesmen on thy Side debate,
And libel'd Blockheads court thee, tho' they hate.
*   *   *   *   *   *   *   *   70
*   *   *   *   *   *   *   *18
Fools of all Kinds their Suffrages impart,
The Fools of Nature, and the Fools of Art.

 These in thy threadbare Farce shall Beauties show,
Shall praise thy ribald Mirth, and maudlin Woe;
Praise ev'n thy imitating *Chaucer*'s Tales,
And call that merry Temple,[19] Fame's *Versailles*:
Thy Shepherd-Song with Rapture they shall see,

---

15 'A petty or paltry poet; a writer of poor or trashy verse; a rimester' (*OED*).
16 'A composition formed by joining scraps from other authors' (Johnson's *Dictionary*).
17 'A list or string of names, a catalogue; derived from the original meaning of a list of persons to be prayed for' (*OED*).
18 Thus in the original, without explanation.
19 Pope's *The Temple of Fame* (1715).

Which rivals *Philips*,[20] as *Banks* rivals *Lee*;[21]
Thy *Guernsey* and *Barbados* Wreath shall own,   80
Where *Durfey* ne'er was read, nor *Settle*[22] known;
That Wreath, that Name, which thro' both Worlds is gone,
Which Doctor *Y—*[23] applauds, and *Prestor John*.[24]
Lo! as *Anchises*,[25] to the Goddess-born,
So I the Worthies, that thy Page adorn,
Point out to Thee.— See here * * * *
* *   *   *   *   *   *
* *   *   *   *   *   *
* *   *   *   *   *   *[26]
The Prelate! next, exil'd by cruel Fates,   90
Who plagues all Churches, and confounds all States;
With Treasons past perplex'd, and present Cares;
A Fop in Rhime, and Bungler in Affairs.
* *   *   *   *   *   *
* *   *   *   *   *   *
And here! a Groupe of Brother Quill-men see,
Co-witlings all, and Demi-bards like Thee;
Such whom the Muse shall pass with just Disdain,

---

[20] Ambrose Philips (c. 1675-1749), nick-named 'Namby-Pamby': a reading of his pastorals makes plain the reason. Pope would have found this (unfavourable) comparison more ludicrous than offensive.

[21] Nathaniel Lee (c. 1649-92) was reputed to have written a twenty-five act play during his five years in Bedlam. (See Pope's *Poems*, pp. 616-7; this is a story to be taken with a pinch of salt, one suspects.) Banks appears in Book I of the final version of *The Dunciad* as the Dunce author of failed tragedies, now no more: a literary giant indeed, if he is a mere shadow of Nathaniel Lee.

[22] Tom Durfey (1653-1723) and Elkanah Settle (1648-1724) were sitting targets for Pope, ready-made Dunces who were literary jokes, legends in their own life-times. (See Pat Rogers, 'The Criteria of Duncehood', *Grub Street*, pp. 175-218.)

[23] Edward Young (1683-1765), rector of Welwyn from 1730; remembered chiefly for *The Complaint, or Night Thoughts on Life, Death, and Immortality*, a poem in nine books published in 1742-5. Welsted suspects Young of having cast his lot with Pope, by acceding to 'the *Treaty of Twickenham*' (Welsted's note to this line of the poem).

[24] Or 'Priest John', the name given to a Christian priest and king, supposed to have reigned somewhere in the Far East, possibly Ethiopia or Abyssinia, in the Middle Ages (*DNB*).

[25] Father (with the help of the goddess Venus) of Aeneas, the hero of Virgil's epic poem.

[26] 'The Characters left out here may perhaps be inserted in some future Edition of this Poem' (Welsted's explanation of all these asterisks). The next hiatus, four lines down, is not explained.

Nor add one Trophy to thy mottly Train:
But Quack *Arb——t*[27] shall Oblivion blot,   100
That puzzling, plodding, prating, pedant *Scot*!
The grating Scribler! whose untun'd Essays
Mix the *Scotch* Thistle with the *English* Bays,
By either *Phoebus* pre-ordain'd to Ill,
The Hand prescribing, or the flattering Quill,
Who doubly plagues, and boasts two Arts to kill!

'Midst this vain Tribe, that aid thy setting Ray,
The Muse shall view, but spare ill-fated *G—y* :
Poor *G—y*, who loses most when most he wins.
And gives his Foes his Fame, and bears their Sins;   110
Who more by Fortune than by Nature curst,
Yields his best Pieces, and must own *Thy* worst.[28]

Thus prop'd, thy Head with *Grub-street* Zephyrs tainted,
By *Rich*[29] recorded, and by *J—* painted;
J— ! who so refin'd a Rake is reckon'd,
He breaks all *Sinai's* Laws, except the Second:
Thus prais'd, thus drawn, t'extend thy Projects try,
Leave the *Blue Languish*,[30] and the Crimson Sigh;

---

[27] John Arbuthnot (see Introduction and items by him in this volume).
[28] 'Mr. *Gay*, not thought to be the entire Author of the *Beggar's Opera*, and ordered to own *Three Hours After Marriage*' (Welsted).
[29] Gilbert Pickering Rich, according to Welsted, who indulges in a little irony at Rich's expense: 'A great Admirer of *P—pe*, eminent for his Translation of *Horace*, which can be equall'd by nothing but *P—pe*'s translating of *Homer*.' Welsted then quotes two lines (of Rich's Horace) worthy of inclusion in *Peri Bathous*:
   I'll bound, I'll spring, I'll strike the weaken'd Pole,
   I'll knock so hard, I'll knock it thro' a Hole.
[30] 'The Phrases distinguished here in *Italics*, are truly quoted from *P—pe*; and the others in Company with them, ought to be in no other Company' (Welsted - referring to the next ten lines or so). Welsted is attempting to avenge his inclusion in Pope's *Peri Bathous; Or, The Art of Sinking in Poetry*, in which the supposed author, Martin Scriblerus, asks, innocently: '...Flow my Numbers [verses] with the quiet thoughtlessness of Mr. *W[el]st[e]d?*' A little of this 'flowing' can be found in *The Dunciad Variorum*:
   Flow, Welsted, flow! like thine inspirer, Beer,
   Tho' stale, not ripe; tho' thin, yet never clear;

Leave the gay Epithets that Beauty crown, 130
White *Whitylinda*, and *Brownissa*[31] Brown;
Forget awhile *Belinda* and the Sun;
Forget the *Fights of Stand*, and Flights of Run:
No more let *Ombre*'s Play inspire thy Vein,
Nor strow with Captive Kings the *Velvet Plain*;
Omit awhile the Silver Peal to ring,
Nor talk dulcissant, nor mellifluous sing,
Nor *hang suspended*, nor *adherent cling*.
But haste to mount Immortal Envy's Throne,[32]
To crush all Merit, that disputes thy own; 140
For thou wert born to damp each rising Name,
And hang, like Mildews, on the Growth of Fame;
Fame's fairest Blossoms let thy Rancour blast,
Bane of the modern Laurel, like the past;
While stupid Riot stands in Humour's Place,
And bestial Filth, Humanity's Disgrace,
Low Lewdness, unexcited by Desire,
And all great *Wilmot* 's[33] Vice, without his Fire.

At length, when banish'd *Pallas*[34] shall withdraw,
And Wit's made Treason by the *Popian* Law; 150
When minor Dunces cease, at length, their strife,
And own thy Patent to be dull for Life;
By Tricks sustain'd, in Poet-craft compleat,
Retire triumphant to thy *Twick'nam* Seat;

So sweetly mawkish, and so smoothly dull;
Heady, not strong, and foaming tho' not full. (Book III, 161-5)

[31] Very feeble parody of 'Nigrina black and Merdamante brown' (*The Dunciad Variorum*, Book II, 310). Pope's names are perfect for the water-nymphs of the Fleet Ditch.

[32] It is a back-handed compliment to Pope (and *The Rape of the Lock*), that it is assumed the reader will recognise the quotations and references in this and the preceding lines.

[33] John Wilmot, second Earl of Rochester (1648-1680), notorious rake and hell-raiser.

[34] The goddess of wisdom.

That Seat! the Work of half paid drudging *Br—me*,[35]
And call'd by joking *Tritons*,[36] *Homer*'s Tomb:
There to stale, stol'n, stum[37] Crambo[38] bid adieu,
And sneer the Fops, that thought thy Crambo new;
There, like the *Grecian* Chief, on whom thy Song
Has well reveng'd unhappy *Priam*'s[39] Wrong;   160
Waste, in thy hidden Cave, the Festive Day,
With mock *Machaon*,[40] and *Patroclus G—*[41]
Sleep, Sleep in Peace[42] the Works, for *Wapping* born!
No more thy Cuckoo Note shall wake the Morn;
In Ease, and Avarice, and aukward State,
The Fool of Fortune, shalt thou hail thy Fate;
Slumbring in Quiet o'er Lampoons half writ,
Which, ripe in Malice, only wait for Wit.

So when *Vanessa* yielded up her Charms,
The blest *Cadenus*[43] languish'd in her Arms;   170

---

[35] William Broome, Pope's collaborator in the translation of Homer, frequently (as here) seen by Pope's enemies as the unsung, under-paid drudge.

[36] The Tritons were half-men, half-fish, their bodies covered with scales, their teeth sharp and their fingers armed with claws; the sons of the sea-god Poseidon (*Larousse Encyclopaedia of Mythology*).

[37] 'Unfermented or partly fermented grape-juice, must' (*OED*). See also next note.

[38] 'A game in which one player gives a word or line of verse to which each of the others has to find a rime' (*OED*). With connotations of contempt, here. 'Stum Crambo' is therefore a half-fermented (or half-baked) versifying.

[39] The last king of Troy, slain when the city fell.

[40] Machaon was the son of one of the Greek gods of health; he fought in the Trojan war, cured Menelaus of an arrow wound, and was killed before Troy (*Larousse Encyclopaedia of Mythology*). This is a scintillatingly witty mock-compliment to Dr Arbuthnot, 'the plodding, prating, pedant Scot' (see above).

[41] Patroclus, friend of Achilles. John Gay is obviously referred to here.

[42] 'These Lines are a Parody of a famous Passage in the Tragedy of *Phædra* and *Hyppolitus*.' (Authors' note; Welsted and his friends appear to be trying, perhaps too hard, to demonstrate their learning. No Grub Street Dunces they!)

[43] *Cadenus and Vanessa* (written in 1713 but not published until after Vanessa's death in 1723) is Swift's account of his complex relationship with Hesther Vanhomrigh ('Vanessa'). 'Cadenus' is a rather obvious anagram of 'Decanus' (Swift became Dean of St Patrick's, Dublin, in 1713). Much was made of this relationship at the time, and has been made since. It appears to have been largely platonic on Swift's part, but not on Vanessa's. (See David Nokes's biography *Jonathan Swift, A Hypocrite Reversed*, Oxford University Press, 1985, especially pp. 154-9, 212-18, 249-265.)

High, on a Peg, his unbrush'd Beaver hung,
His Vest unbutton'd, and his God unsung;
Raptur'd he lies; Deans, Authors are forgot,
Wood's Copper Pence,[44] and *Atterbury*'s[45] Plot;
For her he quits the Tythes of *Patrick*'s Fields,
And all the Levite to the Lover yields.

---

[44] In 1722, an English ironmonger named William Wood was granted a patent to provide copper coinage for Ireland (and the opportunity to enrich himself at the same time). Swift was not alone in seeing this as certain debasement of the Irish currency, and further impoverishment of the Irish people. His campaign against the coinage, in *The Drapier's Letters*, was highly successful, the plan was dropped and Swift became a national (Irish) hero.

[45] Francis Atterbury (1663-1732), bishop of Rochester and a friend of Pope's. He was imprisoned in the Tower in 1722 for alleged participation in a plot to restore the Stuarts; after his trial he was banished (1723). Pope was much alarmed at being called to give evidence at the trial.

A MODEST PROPOSAL[1]
FOR
Preventing the Children of poor People in Ireland, from being a Burden to their Parents or Country; and for making them beneficial to the Publick.
Written in the Year 1729

IT is a melancholly Object to those, who walk through this great Town, or travel in the Country; when they see the *Streets*, the *Roads*, and *Cabbin-doors* crowded with *Beggars* of the Female Sex, followed by three, four, or six Children, *all in Rags* and importuning every Passenger for an Alms. These *Mothers*, instead of being able to work for their honest Livelyhood, are forced to employ all their Time stroling to beg Sustenance for their *helpless Infants*; who, as they grow up, either turn *Thieves* for want of Work; or leave their *dear Native Country, to fight for the Pretender*[2] *in* Spain, or sell themselves to the *Barbadoes*.

---

[1] Swift had already proved he could mix it with the Grub-Street fraternity in his role as ministry propagandist during the last of Queen Anne's administrations (1710-14). His pamphlets (various), and the *Examiner* (1710-1711), were a formidable weapon in the government's armoury. His next major campaign was against Wood's copper coinage, in *The Drapier's Letters* (1724). *A Modest Proposal* (1729) was born of anger at the systematic exploitation of Ireland by England. In particular, it was an insensitive (and ignorant) publication by one Sir John Browne that provoked Swift's response. In his *Memorial of the poor Inhabitants...of Ireland*, Browne expressed wonder that the poor should starve in so rich a country. Swift wrote an *Answer* to the *Memorial*, followed by *A Modest Proposal*, offering a simple solution to the problem of poverty in Ireland. Swift is the master of the *persona*, a device perfected in *A Tale of a Tub*, and further exploited in *Gulliver's Travels* (1726). Here the voice is that of a hard nosed political economist, one who would be thought a philanthropist, deserving of his country's gratitude. (This text is taken from *A Tale of a Tub, and Other Satires*, ed. Kathleen Williams, Dent, 1975.)

[2] The 'Old Pretender' (James Stewart, son of James II). His son, the 'Young Pretender', or Bonnie Prince Charlie, was forced into exile, finally, after the Battle of Culloden in 1746.

I THINK it is agreed by all Parties, that this prodigious Number of Children in the Arms, or on the Backs, or at the *Heels* of their *Mothers*, and frequently *of their Fathers*, is *in the present deplorable State of the Kingdom*, a very great additional grievance; and therefore, whoever could find out a fair, cheap, and easy Method of making these Children sound and useful Members of the Commonwealth, would deserve so well of the Publick, as to have his Statue set up for a Preserver of the Nation.

BUT my Intention is very far from being confined to provide only for the Children *of professed Beggars*: It is of a much greater Extent, and shall take in the whole Number of Infants at a certain Age, who are born of Parents, in effect as little able to support them, as those who demand our Charity in the Streets.

As to my own Part, having turned my Thoughts for many Years, upon this important Subject, and maturely weighed the several *Schemes of other Projectors*, I have always found them grosly mistaken in their Computation. It is true a Child, *just dropt from its Dam*,[3] may be supported by her Milk, for a Solar year with little other Nourishment, at most not above the Value of two Shillings; which the Mother may certainly get or the Value in *Scraps*, by her lawful Occupation of *Begging*: And, it is exactly at one Year old, that I propose to provide for them in such a Manner, as, instead of being a Charge upon their *Parents* or the *Parish* or *Wanting Food and Raiment* for the rest of their Lives; they shall, on the contrary, contribute to the Feeding, and partly to the Cloathing, of many Thousands.

THERE is likewise another great Advantage in my *Scheme*, that it will prevent those *voluntary Abortions*, and that Horrid Practice of *Women murdering their Bastard Children*; alas! too frequent among us; sacrificing the *poor innocent Babes*, I doubt, more to avoid the Expence than the Shame; which would move Tears and Pity in the most Savage and inhuman Breast.

THE Number of Souls in *Ireland* being usually reckoned one Million and a half; of these I calculate there may be about Two hundred Thousand Couple whose Wives are Breeders; from which Number I subtract thirty thousand Couples, who are able to maintain their own Children; although I apprehend there cannot be so many, under *the present Distresses of the Kingdom*; but this being granted, there

---

[3] The language of animal husbandry, applied to human reproduction, should alert us to the nature of the persona of the humble proposer of this project. There is more of the same to follow, mingled with politician-speak compassion and concern.

will remain an Hundred and Seventy Thousand Breeders. I again subtract Fifty Thousand, for those Women who miscarry, or whose Children die by Accident, or Disease, within the Year. There only remain an Hundred and Twenty Thousand Children of poor Parents, annually born: The Question therefore is, How this Number shall be reared, and provided for? Which, as I have already said, under the present Situation of Affairs is utterly impossible, by all the Methods hitherto proposed: For we can *neither employ them in Handicraft* or *Agriculture*; we neither build Houses, (I mean in the Country) nor cultivate Land: They can very seldom pick up a Livelyhood *by Stealing* until they arrive at six Years old; except where they are of towardly Parts; although, I confess, they learn the Rudiments much earlier, during which Time, they can, however, be properly looked upon only as *Probationers*; as I have been informed by a principal Gentleman in the County of *Cavan*, who protested to me, that he never knew above one or two Instances under the Age of six, even in a Part of the Kingdom *so renowned for the quickest Proficiency in that Art*.

I AM assured by our Merchants, that a Boy or a Girl before twelve Years old, is no saleable Commodity; and even when they come to this Age, they will not yield above Three Pounds, or Three Pounds and half a Crown at most, on the Exchange, which cannot turn to Account either to the Parents or the Kingdom; the Charge of Nutriment and Rags, having been at least four Times that Value.

I SHALL now therefore humbly propose my own Thoughts; which I hope will not be liable to the least Objection.

I HAVE been assured by a very knowing *American* of my Acquaintance in *London;* that a young healthy Child, well nursed, is, at a Year old, a most delicious, nourishing, and wholesome Food; whether *Stewed, Roasted, Baked* or *Boiled,* and, I make no doubt, that it will equally serve in a *Fricasie,* or *Ragoust*.

I DO therefore humbly offer it to *publick Consideration,* that of the Hundred and Twenty Thousand Children, already: computed, Twenty thousand may be reserved for Breed, whereof only one Fourth Part to be Males; which is more than we allow to *Sheep, black Cattle* or *Swine*; and my Reason is, that these Children are seldom the Fruits of Marriage, a *Circumstance not much regarded by our Savages*; therefore one *Male* will be sufficient to serve *four Females*. That the remaining Hundred thousand, may, at a Year old, be offered in Sale to the *Persons of Quality* and *Fortune* throughout the Kingdom; always advising the Mother to let them suck plentifully in the last Month, so as to render them plump, and fat for a good Table. A Child will make two Dishes at an Entertainment for Friends; and when the Family dines alone, the fore or hind Quarter will make a reasonable Dish; and seasoned with a little Pepper or Salt, will be very good Boiled on the fourth Day, especially in *Winter*.

I HAVE reckoned upon a Medium, that a Child just born will weigh Twelve Pounds; and in a solar Year, if tolerably nursed, encreaseth to twenty eight Pounds.

I GRANT this Food will be somewhat dear, and therefore very *proper for Landlords*;[4] who, as they have already devoured most of the Parents, seem to have the best Title to the Children.

INFANTS Flesh will be in Season throughout the Year; but more plentiful in *March* and a little before and after: For we are told by a grave Author, an eminent *French* Physician, that *Fish being a prolifick Dyet*, there are more Children born in *Roman Catholick Countries* about Nine Months after *Lent* than at any other Season: Therefore reckoning a Year after *Lent*, the Markets will be more glutted than usual because the Number of *Popish Infants*, is, at least, three to one in this Kingdom; and therefore it will have one other Collateral Advantage, by lessening the Number of *Papists* among us.

I HAVE already computed the Charge of nursing a Beggar's Child (in which List I reckon all *Cottagers*, *Labourers*, and Four fifths of the *Farmers*) to be about two Shillings *per Annum*, Rags included; and I believe, no Gentleman would repine to give Ten Shillings for the *Carcase of a good fat Child*; which as I have said, will make four Dishes of excellent nutritive Meat, when he hath only some particular Friend, or his own Family, to dine with him. Thus the Squire will learn to be a good Landlord, and grow popular among his Tenants, the Mother will have Eight Shillings net Profit, and be fit for Work until she produceth another Child.

THOSE who are more thrifty (*as I must confess the Times require*) may flay the Carcase; the Skin of which, artificially dressed, will make admirable *Gloves for Ladies,* and *Summer Boots for fine Gentlemen.*

As to our City of *Dublin*; Shambles may be appointed for this Purpose, in the most convenient Parts of it; and Butchers we may be assured will not be wanting;

---

4 Absentee (mostly English) landowners.

A Modest Proposal

although I rather recommend buying the Children alive, and dressing them hot from the Knife, as we do *roasting Pigs*.

A VERY worthy Person, *a true Lover of his Country,* and whose Virtues I highly esteem, was lately pleased, in discoursing on this Matter, to offer a Refinement upon my Scheme. He said, that many Gentlemen of this Kingdom, having of late destroyed their Deer; he conceived, that the Want of Venison might be well supplied by the Bodies of young Lads and Maidens, not exceeding fourteen Years of Age, nor under twelve; so great a Number of both Sexes in every County being now ready to starve, for Want of Work and Service: And these to be disposed of by their Parents, if alive, or otherwise by their nearest Relations. But with due Deference to so excellent a Friend, and so deserving a Patriot, I cannot be altogether in his Sentiments. For as to the Males, my *American* Acquaintance assured me from frequent Experience, that their Flesh was generally tough and lean, like that of our School-boys, by continual Exercise, and their Taste disagreeable; and to fatten them would not answer the Charge. Then, as to the Females, it would, I think, with humble Submission, *be a Loss to the Publick,* because they soon would become Breeders themselves: And besides it is not improbable, that some scrupulous People might be apt to censure such a Practice (although indeed very unjustly) as a little bordering upon Cruelty; which, I confess, hath always been with me the strongest Objection against any Project, how well soever intended.

BUT in order to justify my Friend; he confessed, that this expedient was put into his Head by the famous *Salmanaazor*, a Native of the Island *Formosa*, who came from thence to *London,* above twenty Years ago, and in Conversation told my Friend, that in his Country, when any young Person happened to be put to Death, the Executioner sold the Carcase to *Persons of Quality,* as a prime Dainty; and that, in his Time, the Body of a plump Girl of fifteen, who was crucified for an Attempt to poison the Emperor, was sold to his Imperial *Majesty's prime Minister of State,* and other great *Mandarins* of the Court, *in Joints from the Gibbet,* at Four hundred Crowns. Neither indeed can I deny, that if the same Use were made of several plump young girls in this Town, who, without one single Groat to their Fortunes, cannot stir Abroad without a Chair, and appear at the *Play-house,* and *Assemblies* in foreign Fineries, which they never will pay for; the kingdom would not be the worse.

SOME Persons of a desponding Spirit are in great Concern about that vast Number of poor People, who are Aged, Diseased, or Maimed; and I have been desired to employ my Thoughts what Course may be taken, to ease the Nation of so grievous an Incumbrance. But I am not in the least Pain upon that Matter; because it is very well known, that they are every Day *dying*, and *rotting*, by *Cold* and *Famine*, and *Filth* and *Vermin*, as fast as can be reasonably expected. And as to the younger Labourers, they are now in almost as hopeful a Condition: They cannot get Work, and consequently pine away for Want of Nourishment, to a Degree, that if at any Time they are accidentally hired to common Labour, they have not Strength to perform it; and thus the Country, and themselves, are in a fair Way of being soon delivered from the Evils to come.

I HAVE too long digressed; and therefore shall return to my Subject. I think the Advantages by the Proposal which I have made, are obvious, and many, as well as of the highest Importance.

FOR, *First*, as I have already observed, it would greatly lessen the *Number of Papists*, with whom we are yearly overrun; being the principal Breeders of the Nation, as well as our most dangerous Enemies; and who stay at home on Purpose with a Design to *deliver the Kingdom to the Pretender*; hoping to take their Advantage by the Absence *of so many good Protestants* who have chosen rather to leave their Country, than stay at home, and pay Tithes against their Conscience, to an idolatrous *Episcopal Curate*.

SECONDLY, The poorer Tenants will have something valuable of their own, which, by Law, may be made liable to Distress, and help to pay their Landlord's Rent; their Corn and Cattle being already seized, and *Money a Thing unknown*.

THIRDLY, Whereas the Maintenance of an Hundred Thousand Children, from two Years old, and upwards, can be computed at less than ten Shillings a Piece *per Annum*, the Nation's Stock will be thereby encreased Fifty Thousand Pounds *per Annum*, besides the Profit of a new Dish, introduced to the Tables of all *Gentlemen of Fortune* in the Kingdom, who have any Refinement in Taste; and the Money will circulate among ourselves, the Goods being entirely of our own Growth and Manufacture.[5]

---

[5] In his pamphlet *A Proposal for the Universal Use of Irish Manufacture* (1720), Swift had argued that the Irish should ban imported goods. He had also attacked English exploitation of Ireland in more general terms (the last words on the title page, in bold type, are, *Utterly Rejecting*

FOURTHLY, The constant Breeders, besides the Gain of Eight Shillings *Sterling per Annum,* by the Sale of their Children will be rid of the Charge of maintaining them after the first Year.

FIFTHLY, This Food would likewise bring great *Custom to Taverns,* where the Vintners will certainly be so prudent, as to procure the best Receipts for dressing it to Perfection; and consequently, have their Houses frequented by all the *Gentlemen,* who justly value themselves upon their Knowledge in good Eating; and a skilful Cook, who understands how to oblige his Guests, will contrive to make it as expensive as they please.

SIXTHLY, This would be a great Inducement to Marriage, which all wise Nations have either encouraged by Rewards, or enforced by Laws and Penalties. It would encrease the Care and Tenderness of Mothers towards their Children, when they were sure of a Settlement for Life, to the poor Babes, provided in some Sort by the Publick, to their annual Profit instead of Expence. We should soon see an honest Emulation among the married Women, *which of them could bring the fattest Child to the Market.* Men would become *as fond* of their Wives, during the Time of their Pregnancy, as they are now of their *Mares* in Foal, their *Cows* in Calf, or *Sows* when they are ready to farrow; nor offer to beat or kick them, (as it is too *frequent* a Practice) for fear of a Miscarriage.

MANY other Advantages might be enumerated. For instance, the Addition of some Thousand Carcasses in our Exportation of barrelled Beef: The Propagation of *Swines Flesh,* and Improvement in the Art of making good *Bacon;* so much wanted among us by the great Destruction of *Pigs,* too frequent at our Tables, and are no way comparable in Taste, or Magnificence, to a well-grown fat yearling Child; which, roasted whole, will make a considerable Figure at a *Lord Mayor's Feast* or any other publick Entertainment. But this, and many others, I omit; being studious of Brevity.

SUPPOSING that one Thousand Families in this City, would be constant Customers for Infants Flesh; besides others who might have it at *merry Meetings,* particularly *Weddings* and *Christenings;* I compute that *Dublin* would take off,

---

and Renouncing ENGLAND). Such boldness could not go unrewarded: the printer was prosecuted (at the instigation of the Whig ministry) for printing a 'scandalous, seditious and factious' work. Despite the efforts of the trial judge to bring in a guilty verdict, the Grand Jury declined to oblige. (See David Nokes's account in *Jonathan Swift, A Hypocrite Reversed,* pp. 266-8.)

annually, about Twenty Thousand Carcasses; and the rest of the Kingdom (where probably they will be sold somewhat cheaper) the remaining Eighty Thousand.

I CAN think of no one Objection, that will possibly be raised against this Proposal; unless it should be urged, that the Number of People will be thereby much lessened in the Kingdom. This I freely own; and it was indeed one principal Design in offering it to the World. I desire the Reader will observe, that I calculate my Remedy *for this one individual Kingdom of* IRELAND, *and for no other that ever was, is, or I think ever can be upon Earth.* Therefore, let no man talk to me of other Expedients:[6] *Of taxing our Absentees at Five Shillings a Pound: Of using neither Cloaths nor Houshold Furniture except what is of our own Growth and Manufacture: Of utterly rejecting the Materials and Instruments that promote foreign Luxury: Of curing the Expensiveness of Pride, Vanity, Idleness, and Gaming in our Women: Of introducing a Vein of Parsimony, Prudence and Temperance: Of learning to love our Country, wherein we differ even from LAPLANDERS, and the Inhabitants of TOPINAMBOO: Of quitting our Animosities and Factions; nor act any longer like the Jews, who were murdering one another at the very Moment their City was taken: Of being a little cautious not to sell our Country and Consciences for nothing: Of teaching Landlords to have at least one Degree of Mercy towards their Tenants.* Lastly, *Of putting a Spirit of Honesty, Industry, and Skill into our Shop-keepers; who, if a Resolution could now be taken to buy only our native Goods, would immediately unite to cheat and exact upon us in the Price, the Measure, and the Goodness*; *nor could ever yet be brought to make one fair Proposal of just Dealing, though often and earnestly invited to it.*

THEREFORE I repeat, let no Man talk to me of these and the like Expedients; till he hath, at least, a Glimpse of Hope, that there will ever be some hearty and sincere Attempt to put *them in Practice.*

BUT, as to my self; having been wearied out for many Years with offering vain, idle, visionary Thoughts; and at length utterly despairing of Success, I fortunately fell upon this Proposal, which, as it is wholly new, so it hath something solid and *real*, of no Expence, and little Trouble, full in our own Power; and whereby we can incur no Danger in *disobliging* ENGLAND: For, this Kind of Commodity will not

---

[6] Here the mask is allowed to slip, though not everyone has noticed. The novelist Thackeray (in *The English Humourists of the Eighteenth Century*, Smith, Elder & Co., 1858), chose to read the *Proposal* literally; children should not be thus abused, but 'fondled and caressed' (p. 35).

bear Exportation; the Flesh being of too tender a Consistence, to admit a long Continuance in Salt; *although perhaps I could name a Country which would be glad to eat up our whole Nation without it.*

AFTER all, I am not so violently bent upon my own Opinion, as to reject any Offer proposed by wise Men, which shall be found equally innocent, cheap, easy, and effectual. But before something of that Kind shall be advanced, in Contradiction to my Scheme, and offering a better; I desire the Author, or Authors, will be pleased maturely to consider two Points. *First*, As Things now stand, how they will be able to find Food and Raiment, for a Hundred Thousand useless Mouths and Backs? And *secondly*, There being a round Million of Creatures in human Figure, throughout this Kingdom; whose whole Subsistence, put into a common Stock, would leave them in Debt two Millions of Pounds *Sterling*; adding those, who are Beggars by Profession, to the Bulk of Farmers, Cottagers, and Labourers, with their Wives and Children, who are Beggars[7] in Effect; I desire those Politicians, who dislike my Overture, and may perhaps be so bold to attempt an Answer, that they will first ask the Parents of these Mortals, Whether they would not, at this Day, think it a great Happiness to have been sold for Food at a Year old, in the Manner I prescribe; and thereby have avoided such a perpetual Scene of Misfortunes, as they have since gone through; by the *Oppression of Landlords*; the Impossibility of paying Rent, without Money or Trade; the Want of common Sustenance, with neither House nor Cloaths, to cover them from the Inclemencies of Weather; and the most inevitable Prospect of intailing the like, or greater Miseries upon their Breed for ever.

I PROFESS, in the Sincerity of my Heart, that I have not the least personal Interest, in endeavouring to promote this necessary Work; having no other Motive than the *publick Good of my Country by advancing our Trade; providing for Infants, relieving the Poor, and giving some Pleasure to the Rich*. I have no

---

[7] Swift wrote, and published, another pamphlet, in 1737, in which he proposed a compulsory badging scheme for all Dublin's beggars (*A Proposal for Giving Badges to Beggars*). Badges were to be worn at all times; any beggars who failed to do so were to be turned out of the parish. One searches in vain for irony in this piece, but there is none. It is a disturbingly callous and prejudiced attack on the poorest members of the community (*The Prose Works of Jonathan Swift*, ed. Herbert Davis *et al.*, Oxford, 1939-68, vol. xiii).

Children, by which I can propose to get a single Penny; the youngest being nine Years old, and my Wife past Child-bearing.[8]

---

[8] It also ought not to have escaped Thackeray's notice (see note 6, above) that there is no evidence to prove that Swift was ever married (to Esther Johnson - Stella), and he certainly did not have any children.

ODE *for New-Years-Day*[1]

Recitativo

Once more the ever circling Sun
Thro' the cælestial signs has run,
Again old Time inverts his glass,
And bids the annual Seasons pass:
The youthful Spring shall call for birth,
And glad with op'ning show'rs the earth:
Fair Summer load with Sheaves the Field,
And golden fruit shall Autumn yield:
Each to the Winter's want their store shall bring,
'Till warmer genial Suns recall the Spring.   10

Air

Ye grateful *Britons* bless the Year,
  That kindly yields increase,
While plenty that might feed a War,
  Enjoys the guard of peace,
Your plenty to the Skies you owe,
Peace is your Monarch's care,
  Thus bounteous *Jove* and *George* below

---

[1] 'By C. Cibber, Esq', from the *Gentleman's Magazine*, January, 1731. The reader is invited to sit in judgement on the literary merit (or otherwise) of these regular effusions from the poet laureate. Cibber was elevated to that office in 1730, on the death of the previous incumbent, Laurence Eusden. Eusden has a role in *The Dunciad*, of course, but Cibber is the leading light of the final version of the poem. (See Introduction and Book II of *The Dunciad*, in this volume.)

Divided empire share.

Recitativo

Britannia pleas'd, looks round her realms to see,
Your various causes of Felicity!   20
(To glorious War, a glorious peace succeeds;
For most we triumph when the Farmer feeds)
Then truly are we great when truth supplies
Our Blood, our Treasures drain'd by victories,
Turn happy *Britons*, to the throne your Eyes,
 And in the royal offspring see,
How amply bounteous providence supplies
 The source of your Felicity.

Air

Behold in ev'ry Face imperial Graces shine
All native to the Race of *George* and *Caroline*:   30
In each young Hero we admire
The blooming virtues of his sire;
In each maturing fair we find,
Maternal charms of softer kind.

Recitativo

In vain thro' ages past has *Phoebus* roll'd,
E're such a sight blest *Albion* could behold.
Thrice happy Mortals, if your state you knew,
Where can the Globe so blest a Nation shew?
All that of you indulgent Heav'n requires,
Is loyal Hearts, to reach your own Desires.   40
Let Faction then her self born views lay down,
And Hearts united, thus address the Throne.

Air

Hail, Royal *Caesar*, hail!
 Like this may ev'ry annual Sun
 Add brighter glories to thy Crown,
'Till Suns themselves shall fail.

Recitativo

May Heav'n thy peaceful Reign prolong,
Nor let to thy great Empires wrong,
Foreign or native Foes prevail
   Hail, &c.

Ode humbly inscrib'd to the Poet Laureat[2]

Rectitativo

Accept, O Cibber, the advent'rous lay,
Which, to your honour, dates both sing and say:
To you great Prince of Comedy and Song,
The Tributes of inferior Pens belong;
You, who by royal Favour wear the Bays,
And grateful eternize our Monarch's Praise.

Air

  Let us sing to the King,
  All about the circling Year:
  Sing a *floreat* to the *laureat*,
Ev'ry Season brings good cheer;   10
Grateful *Britons*, thank the bard,
Who by Peace does plenty guard,
Such as hungry War does need,
War, that does on plenty feed.

Recitativo

Phœbus with joy looks *Britain* round to see
The happy state of his lov'd poetry;
To *Eusden, Cibber* gloriously succeeds;
Wit triumphs most when bard like farmer feeds;
Then truly are we great when he can shew

---

[2] 'Taken from [the] Lon. Evening Post Jan. 7, as there said by Stephen Duck, Esq.'. This burlesque was printed on the same page as Cibber's *Ode*, in the *Gentleman's Magazine*, January 1731. On the next page, alongside, are two more offshoots: 'An Ode on Twelfth-Day, In Imitation of an Ode on New-Year's-Day', and 'A HYMN TO THE LAUREAT'. The former is irreverent, the latter an indignant defence of the laureate and his 'Wit unequall'd'.

The way *his own out-doings to out-do.*   20
Cast, envious Poets, on his Verse your Eyes,
Behold the offspring of his brain,
How his rich Genius constantly supplies
The source of his poetick vein!

Air

Thro'out the whole what matchless Graces shine!
Paraphonalia [3] sparkles in each Line;
  Native to *Cibber*, we admire
  The style and fancy, wit and fire;
  In each maturing Word we find
  Something soft for thought design'd.   30

Recitativo

Complain not, Sol, of fruitless ages past;
Think yourself blest in such a Son at last:
Thrice happy Poets, if you knew your state;
Britain alone can boast a *Laureat*.
For if, like him, to Grandeur you aspire,
By his Example reach your own desire.
Let criticks then their self-born views lay down,
And Bards in chorus thus sing round the town.

Air

  Hail! Matchless *Colley*, hail!
Like this may ev'ry New Year's Day   40
Add fresher Honour to the Bay,
  'Till Bay itself shall fail.

Recitativo

May Heaven preserve thy Genius clear,
For *Christmas* comes but once a Year,
  Give the Poet then some Ale.
  Ale, &c.

---

[3] Corrupt form of 'paraphernalia': personal belongings, esp. articles of adornment or attire, trappings (*OED*).

Ode *for New-Year's-Day* 1732 [4]

Recitativo

AWAKE with *joyous* Songs the *day*
  That leads *the op'ning year*,
The year advancing to prolong,
Augustus' sway *demands* our song,
  And *calls* for universal cheer.

Air

Your antient Annals, Britain, read,
  And mark the Reign you most admire;
The present shall the past exceed,
  And yield enjoyment to desire.
Or if you find the coming year[5]   10
  In blessings should transcend the last
The diff'rence only will declare
  The present sweeter than the past.

Recit.

But, ah! the sweets his *Sway* bestows,
Are greater far than Greatness knows.
With various pensive cares oppress'd,
Unseen, alas, the Royal Breast
Endures *his many a weight*,
Unfelt by swains of humble state.

Air

Thus *brooding* on her *lonely* nest,   20
  Aloft the Eagle wakes.
  Her due delights forsakes,
Tho' Monarch of the air confess'd,
Her *drooping* eyes refuse to close;
  While fearless of annoy,

---

[4] 'By *C. Cibber*, Esq., Poet Laureat', the title continues. This Ode was printed in the January issue of the *Gentleman's Magazine*, 1732.
[5] Cibber's use of italics is eccentric - random, even.

Her young belov'd enjoy
Protection, food, and sweet repose.

Recit.

What thanks, ye Britons, can repay
So mild, so just, so tender sway?

Air

Your annual aid when he desires,   30
Less the King than land requires;
All the dues to him that flow
Are still but Royal wants to you:
So the seasons lend the earth
Their kindly rains to raise her birth;
And well the mutual labours suit,
His the glory, yours the fruit.

Recit.

Assist, assist, ye splendid throng,
　Who now the Royal circle form,
With duteous wishes blend the song,   40
　And every grateful wish be warm.

CHORUS

May *Cæsar's* health his reign supply,
'Till faction shall be pleas'd, or die;
'Till loyal hearts desire his fate:
　'Till happier subjects know,
　Or foreign realms can show
A land so bless'd, a King so great![6]

---

[6] Dr Johnson had this to say about Cibber's Odes: 'Colley Cibber, Sir, was by no means a blockhead....His friends gave out that he *intended* his birth-day *Odes* should be bad: but that was not the case, Sir: for he kept them many months by him, and a few months before he died he shewed me one of them, and I made some corrections, to which he was not very willing to submit. I rememember the folowing couplet in allusion to the King and himself:
　"Perch'd on the eagle's soaring wing,
　　The lowly linnet loves to sing."' (James Boswell *Life of Johnson*, ed. George Birkbeck Hill, rev. L. F. Powell, Oxford University Press, 1953, p. 285).

The *Poet Laureat*'s Ode for New-Year's-Day burlesqu'd[7]

Awake, with *Grub-street* Odes, the Day
   That leads the op'ning Year;
The Year advancing to prolong
Great *C-bb-r*'s Fame, demands a Song,
   Inspir'd by *Gin*, or by *Small Beer*.

Your Ancient *Ballad-Makers* read,
   And mark the *Fool* you most admire;
The present shall the *past* exceed,
   And yield Enjoyment to Desire:
Or, if you find the coming Ode,   10
   In *Nonsense* should transcend the last,
The Diff'rence only will make good
   The present *duller* than the past!

But ah! the *Stuff* his *Strain* bestows
Is duller far than Dulness knows;
With various *lumpish Loads* opprest
Unseen, alas! the Laureat's Breast
Endures his many a Weight,
Unfelt by all but *Bards of State*.

Thus brooding o'er her lovely Nest,   20
   The *watchful Owl* awakes,
   Her due Delight forsakes,
Restless to give all others Rest;
Her drooping Eyes refuse to close,

---

[7] This piece was taken from the *London Evening Post* for January 7, reprinted in the *Gentleman's Magazine* for January, 1732, alongside Cibber's *Ode*; it would appear that parody, even at this early stage of Cibber's reign, had become a normal part of the laureate ritual.

Whilst, fearless of Numbers
To threaten their Slumbers,
All around her enjoy much Sleep and Repose.

What Praises can repay an *Owl*
So flat, so heavy, and so *dull*?
His *annual Odes* which he admires,   30
Less the *Dunce* than *Fool* inspires!
All the *Strains* which from him flow
Are still of *noble Use* to you;
Whilst his kindly Sheets enrich
Every Bard *to wipe his B*—
And well the *mutual Labours* suit
His the *Glory*, yours the *Fruit*.

Assist, assist, you warbling Throng,
   Who now the *Grub-street Chorus* form;
With gen'rous wishes blend the Song,   40
And ev'ry grateful Wish be warm.

May *C-bb-r*'s *Muse* his *Odes* supply,
Till *Nonsense* shall be pleas'd to die;
Till *stupid Fools* desire his *Place*;
   Till *happier Courts* shall know,
   Or Foreign Realms can show
A *Dunce* so *dull*, an *Ode* so *low*;
What *Thanks* are due to —: G— ![8]

---

[8] One of the missing words must be 'Cibber'; the other word must rhyme with 'Place' - 'Grace' or 'Guess' seem as likely as any, but are rather feeble. Whatever conclusion the reader may have come to with regard to Cibber's Odes, it has to be said that the quality of the parodies leaves something to be desired.

[Epitaph on Francis Charteris][1]

An Epitaph.

Here continueth to rot
The Body of FRANCIS CHARTRES;[2]
Who, with an INFLEXIBLE CONSTANCY,
and INIMITABLE UNIFORMITY of Life,
PERSISTED,
In spite of AGE and INFIRMITIES,
In the Practice of EVERY HUMAN VICE,
Excepting PRODIGALITY and HYPOCRISY;

---

[1] The text of this Epitaph is taken from Pope's version (included with a note to his 'Epistle III, To Bathurst', from his *Moral Essays*, in *The Poem of Alexander Pope*, ed. John Butt, Methuen & Co., 1975, re-printed by Routledge and Kegan Paul, 1992, pp. 571-2). It differs, mostly in details, from the text published in *A Miscellany of the Wits: Select Pieces By William King, John Arbuthnot, And Other Hands*, ed. K. N. Colville, Philip Allan & Co., 1920, pp. 280-1. The Epitaph first appeared in the *London Magazine* for April, 1732.

[2] The reader may wonder why a man of Arbuthnot's generosity was moved to write in such devastating and uncompromising fashion about this man. Pope's note on the Epitaph provides an explanation that is difficult to improve upon, and is worth quoting in full: 'FR. CHARTRES [1675-1732], a man infamous for all manner of vices. When he was an ensign in the army, he was drumm'd out of the regiment for a cheat; he was next banish'd Brussels, and drumm'd out of Ghent on the same account. After a hundred tricks at the gaming-tables, he took to lending of money at exorbitant interest and on great penalties, accumulating premium, interest, and capital into a new capital, and seizing to a minute when the payments came due; in a word, by a constant attention to the vices, wants and follies of mankind, he acquired an immense fortune. His house was a perpetual bawdy-house. He was twice condemn'd for rapes, and pardon'd: but the last time not without imprisonment in Newgate, and large confiscation. He died in Scotland in 1731, aged 62. The populace at his funeral rais'd a great riot, almost tore the body out of the coffin, and cast dead dogs &c. into the grave along with it' (*Poems*, p. 571).

His insatiable AVARICE exempted him from the first,

His matchless IMPUDENCE from the second.

Nor was he more singular

in the undeviating *Pravity*[3] of his *Manners*,

Than successful

in *Accumulating* WEALTH.

For, without TRADE or PROFESSION,

Without TRUST of PUBLIC MONEY,

And without BRIBE-WORTHY Service,

He acquired, or more properly created,

A MINISTERIAL ESTATE.

He was the only Person of his Time,

Who cou'd CHEAT without the Mask of HONESTY,

Retain his primeval MEANNESS

When possess'd of TEN THOUSAND A YEAR,

And having daily deserved the GIBBET for what

he *did*,[4]

Was at last condemned to it for what he *could*

not *do*.

Oh Indignant Reader!

Think not his Life useless to Mankind!

---

[3] It is indeed difficult to exaggerate the depravity of Francis Charteris. Amongst his other achievements, he was a leading member of the Hell-Fire Club (see *Lives of the Rakes*, in no fewer than 6 volumes, Philip Allan and Co., London, 1924-5). Lady Mary Wortley Montague, in March, 1724, wrote an almost approving note on this 'committee of Galantry': 'They call themselves Schemers, and meet regularly 3 times a week to consult on Galant Schemes for the advancement of that branch of Happyness which the vulgar call Whoring' (*The Complete Letters of Lady Mary Wortley Montague*, ed. Robert Halsband, 3 vols., Oxford, at the Clarendon Press, vol. ii, p. 38).

[4] John Gay, writing to Swift, on 31 March, 1730, comments on the episode Pope is presumably referring to, above: 'Does not Chartres misfortunes grieve you, for that great man is like to save his life and lose some of his money, a very hard case!' (*The Correspondence of Jonathan Swift*, ed. Harold Williams, in 5 vols., vol. iii, p. 385). That Charteris was a notorious rake is evident from a letter from another of Swift's correspondents, a Miss Kelly, writing in 1733, the year after Charteris's death: 'Indeed the cause of my complaints is of such a nature, that it cannot well be told. The unhappy life of a near relation must give one a pain in the very repeating it, that cannot be described. For surely to be the daughter of a Colonel *Chartres*, must to a rational being give the greatest anxiety; for who would have a father at seventy [sic] publickly tried for an attempt of a rape?' (*Correspondence*, vol. iv, p. 173).

> PROVIDENCE conniv'd at his execrable Designs,
> To give to after-Ages
> A conspicuous PROOF and EXAMPLE,
> Of how small Estimation is EXORBITANT WEALTH
> in the Sight of GOD,
> By his bestowing it on the most UNWORTHY of
> ALL MORTALS.[5]

---

[5] The Epitaph is interesting partly because it is by Arbuthnot, partly because it affords an insight into the world that still revolved above the inky depths of Grub Street. It is a world Pope satirises in *The Rape of the Lock*, but to which he and Gay both aspired.

EPIGRAM the Second:[1]
OF *Merit Deserted.*

P---E, who oft overflows, both with Wit and with Spleen,
Felt the Want of a Dung-Cart, to keep himself Clean:
So, he furnish'd a Priest,[2] with a Carriage, ding, dong:
And, made him his Drayman, to drive it along.

Then, as oft as the Muse's Satirical Itch,
For the Poet's Discharge,[3] he lent his Vengeance a Switch;
Hey-gee-ho was the Word - 'Take it, Parson, away' -
And the reverenc'd Excrement loaded the Dray.

Sir Gravity, charm'd with the Call, for his Freight,[4]
Betwixt Load, and Load, found it tedious to wait:
And Himself having Nothing, to keep up the Trade,

---

[1] An anonymous poem, first printed in *The Prompter*, no. cvii, 18 November, 1735 (and reprinted in *Alexander Pope; The Critical Heritage*, ed. John Bernard (Routledge and Kegan Paul, 1973).
[2] This piece has some recognisable Grub Street qualities, one of which is a tendency to appeal (or an attempt to appeal) to the lowest common denominator. So, here, there is a slur on Pope's religion; there is also an insistent play on ordure=literary production, which Pope himself deployed, with rather more subtlety, in *The Dunciad* (q.v.).
[3] One has no wish to make a meal of the metaphor; but it's useful to make the connection between writing - the product of the pen - and bodily waste, another kind of 'product'. Once this is grasped, much else follows....
[4] Sir Gravity is presumably the clerical Dung-Cart driver employed by Pope to remove his 'discharges'. Thus the Drayman-Priest becomes, in a manner of speaking, Pope's publisher.

Told his Master, with Tears, how his Custom decay'd,
'What is Once, in two Months? - Now t'would make the Wheels creak,
Wou'd you find wherewithal, to load once a Week!'

'*Stand aloof,*' answer'd P--e, 'Such a Trade as you drive,
May be needful; - but, welcome to no Man alive.
Tho' I love to dress light, I'm too neat, in my Cloaths,
To let a Tom T--dman, live under my Nose.'[5]

---

[5] As a man of some fastidiousness, Pope would not wish to live in the vicinity of, or be for long in the presence of, a Tom T--dman (our anonymous poet suggests). Similarly, though publishers provide an essential service for him, they are the sort of people he would prefer to keep at arm's length. There's a neat point here. Pope was indeed a social climber, who liked to rub shoulders with the aristocracy; publishers, like Tom T--dmen, were necessary evils.

THE
BLATANT-BEAST
A
POEM[1]

BEAUTY, the fondling Mother's earliest Pray'r,
Nature's kind Gift to sweeten worldly Care.
Beauty the greatest Extasy imparts,
Steals thro' our Eyes, and revels in our Hearts;
Adds Lustre to a Crown, gives Weight to Sense,
The Orator assists in Truth's Defence.
The very Fool our Hearts resistless warms,
And while we curse the Tongue, the Figure charms.
If Beauty be the Subject of our Praise,
A rude, mishapen Lump[2] Contempt must raise.   10

WHEN Lucifer with Angels held first Place,
Seraphic Beauty sparkled in his Face.
By Pride and Malice tempted to rebel,

---

[1] Published anonymously in December 1742 (and has remained anonymous since). *The New Dunciad* was published in March of the same year (the final version appeared in 1743), and this poem is just one of many pamphlets launched at Pope that year. *The Blatant-Beast* was not reprinted until the Augustan Reprint Society edition of 1965 (ed. Joseph V. Guerinot), from which this version has been taken, with minor changes to punctuation and orthography.

[2] Not many of Pope's (many) enemies avoided the temptation to exploit his deformity. Compare 'mishapen Lump' with 'Mountain Shoulders' (line 40, below).

Vengeance pursu'd him to the lowest Hell:
Not sulph'rous Lakes suffic'd, nor dreary Plains;
Deformity was join'd t' improve his Pains.

PAINT then the Person, and expose the Mind,
Who rails at others, to his own Faults blind.
Sly *Sancho's* Paunch, meagre *Don Quixot*'s Love,
The Satyr and the Ridicule improve. 20
So when fam'd *Butler*[3] wou'd Rebellion paint,
He lasht the Traitor and the Mimic Saint.
Sir *Hudibras* he sung; the crumpled Wight,
Contempt and Laughter ever will excite.

THE Blatant-Beast once *more has* broke his Chains,
Disperses Falshoods, and remorseless reigns.
Scornful of all thy Verses dare design,
(Where useless Epithets crowd ev'ry Line),
The Blatant-Beast shall be afresh pursu'd,
Nor cease my Labours till again subdu'd. 30

Distorted Elf! to Nature a Disgrace,
Thy Mind envenom'd pictur'd in thy Face;
Malice with Envy in thy Breast combines,
And in thy Visage grav'd those ghastly Lines.
Like Plagues, like Death thy ranc'rous Arrows fly,
At Good and Bad, at Friend and Enemy.
To thy own Breast recoils the erring Dart,
Corrupts thy Blood, and rankles in thy Heart.
There swell the Poisons which thy Breast distend,
And with the Load thy Mountain Shoulders bend. 40
Horrid to view! retire from human Sight,

---

[3] Samuel Butler (1612-1680). His *Hudibras*, a satire on Puritanism, was published in three parts between 1663 and 1678.

Nor with thy Figure pregnant Dames affright.
Crawl thro' thy childish Grot,[4] growl round thy Grove,
A Foe to Man, an Antidote to Love.
In Cursies waste thy Time instead of Pray'r,
And with thy Breath pollute the fragrant Air.
There doze o'er *Shakespear*; then thy Blunders sell
At mighty Price; this Truth let *Tonson*[5] tell.
Then frontless intimate, (oh perjur'd Bard!)   50
Thy Labours were bestow'd without Reward.
On that immortal Author wreak thy Spite,

---

[4] Pope was proud of the grotto he built on his five acres of garden at his villa in Twickenham, overlooking the Thames. He was helped by Bridgman and Kent, celebrated professional gardeners. The Grotto was formed by lining the tunnel under the nearby road with wooden spars, shells, minerals and crystals. Pope described it thus:

'I have put the last hand to...finishing the subterraneous way and grotto: I there found a spring of the clearest water, which falls in a perpetual rill, that echoes thro' the cavern day and night. From the river Thames, you see thro' my arch up a walk of the wilderness, to a kind of open Temple, wholly compos'd of shells in the rustic manner; and from that distance under the temple you look down thro' a sloping arcade of trees, and see the sails on the river passing suddenly and vanishing, as thro' a perspective glass. When you shut the doors of this grotto, it becomes on the instant, a Camera obscura; on the walls of which all the objects of the river, hills, woods, and boats, are forming a moving picture....It is finished with shells interspersed with pieces of looking-glass in angular forms; and in the ceiling is a star of the same material...The bottom is paved with simple pebble, as is also the adjoining walk up the wilderness to the temple....It wants nothing to compleat it but a good statue with an inscription....'
(Taken from a letter from Pope to Edward Blount, June 2, 1725, quoted in James Thorne's *Handbook to the Environs of London*, 1876, reprinted by Adams & Dart, 1970, p. 636.) Pope also wrote the following lines - *Verses on a Grotto by the River Thames at Twickenham*...in 1740:

Thou who shalt stop, where *Thames'* translucent Wave
Shines a broad Mirrour thro' the shadowy Cave;
Where lingering Drops from Mineral Roofs distill,
And pointed Crystals break the sparkling Rill,
Unpolish'd Gemms no Ray on Pride bestow,
And latent Metals innocently glow:
Approach. Great NATURE studiously behold!
And eye the Mine without a Wish for Gold.
Approach: But aweful! Lo th'Aegerian Grott,
Where, nobly pensive, ST. JOHN sate and thought:
Where *British* Sighs from dying WYNDHAM stole,
And the bright Flame was shot thro' MARCHMONT's Soul.
Let such, such only, tread this sacred Floor,
Who dare to love their Country, and be poor (Poems, p. 707).

[5] Jacob Tonson (the printer/publisher. He gets a brief mention in *The Dunciad* (see Book II, line 60n.), but is not blessed with Duncehood. As publisher of Nicholas Rowe's (1674-1718) edition of Shakespeare (1708), he might be in a position to tell the 'truth' about the price, if not the value, of Pope's version (1725).

And on his Monument thy Nonsense write.
Should *Theobald*[6] thy presumptuous Errors shew,
Be thou to *Theobald* an invet'rate Foe.
Cibber shall foremost in thy Satyrs stand;
His Plays succeed, and thine was justly damn'd.
But *Colley* call him, when thou would'st declame;
Great is the Jest that lies in *Colley*'s Name.

Beware all ye, whom he as Friends carest,   60
How ye entrust your Secrets to his Breast.
On Backs of Letters was his *Homer*[7] wrote,
All your Affairs disclos'd to save a Groat.
He valu'd not to whom he gave Offence;
He sav'd his Paper, tho' at your Expence.

But shall a low-born Wretch[8] the best traduce,
And call it Poetry, because Abuse?
The Heav'n-born Muse, by Truth and Justice sway'd,
To false Aspersions ne'er vouchsafes her Aid.
When unprovok'd, not vengeful Wasps molest,   70
Nor dart their Stings, when undisturb'd their Nest.
Thy Muse, by *Virgil*'s Harpies taught to write,
Scatters her Ordure in her screaming Flight;
Sacred Religion and her Priests defames,

---

[6] Lewis Theobald's criticism of Pope's edition of Shakespeare (see previous note) earned him a leading role in *The Dunciad* (for further details, see notes to Richard Savage's *An Author to be Lett*, in the present volume). In *The Dunciad Variorum* (1729), Theobald has the role of King of the Dunces, whose mantle was acquired by Colley Cibber in the final version of the poem (1743). The anonymous *Sawney and Colley*, also in this volume, makes extensive reference to the war of words between Pope and Cibber, and to the row over Pope's edition of Shakespeare.

[7] There is evidence to support this (not very damning) accusation (see Swift's poem *Advice to the Grub-street Verse-Writers* (1726), in this volume. A note attached to *The Blatant-Beast* explains, in tones of outrage: 'When he sent his *Homer* to his Acquaintance for their Emendations, it was written on the Back of the Letters of his Correspondents, whether of Business, Compliment or Secrecy. A shameful Instance of Avarice and Treachery!'

[8] Pope liked to maintain that he was 'Of gentle Blood' (*Epistle to Dr. Arbuthnot, Poems*, p. 611). See Introduction.

And against Monarchs[9] saucily exclames.
The Fathers, of our Church the surest Guides,
As a poor Pack of Punsters she derides.
But chief O *Cam*! and *Isis*! dread her Frown,
Chain'd to the Footstool of the Goddess'[10] Throne.
No Order, no Degree escapes her Rage,   80
And dull, and dull, and dull swells ev'ry Page.
Thirsty, she Poison draws from ev'ry Flow'r,
Like Satan, seeks whom next she may devour.

So have I seen a Dog distracted roam;
He bites, he snaps at all, disgorging Foam.
The frighten'd Passenger the Danger flies,
And sees the Poison flashing from his Eyes.
Till some stout Dray-man dashes out his Brains,
And his corrupted Blood the Kennel stains.[11]

Thy Notes pedantic[12] shall no more engage;   90
Arbuthnot's Wit enlivens not the Page.
Thy Muse, that Prostitute abandon'd Jade,
Now flounders in the Mire without Swift's Aid.
Thy base Invectives Men no more regard;
With just Disdain thy Scare-Crow Muse is heard.

So when the latent Seeds their Fruits display,

---

[9] It may be assumed that it was in his role as prophet of cultural doom that Pope cast aspersions on the cultural shortcomings of the first two Georges: 'Still Dunce the second rules like Dunce the first' (*The Dunciad*, Book I, line 6). He had a point, however - George II, for example, patronized the music of Handel, but nothing else (see G. M. Trevelyan, *Illustrated English Social History*, vol. iii).

[10] The Goddess of Dulness, the presiding deity of *The Dunciad*.

[11] This delightful epic simile - Pope as mad dog foaming at the mouth and transmitting rabies from his very eyes until his brains are dashed out - sits uneasily with our anonymous poet's pious expressions of distaste at Pope's satirical methods.

[12] The (deliberately pedantic) notes appended (at inordinate length) by Martin Scriblerus in *The Dunciad Variorum* and subsequent editions of *The Dunciad*.

And gain fresh Vigour from a genial Ray:
The careful Hind a monst'rous Figure frames;
From various Rags unwonted Terror streams.
The feather'd Choristers in Flocks retreat,   100
And at a Distance view the tempting Bait.
At length grown bold, they perch upon his Head,
And with their Meute[13] bedawb what late they fled.

B-ns-n[14] abuse for raising *Milton's* Bust,
And impiously molest learn'd Johnston's[15] Dust.
Religious, he the Psalms in *Latin* sung,
From hence the Malice of the Deist spring.
While with a Just Derision we survey,
Thy wretched Epitaph on poor John Gay.[16]

HAD *Peter, Charters*[17] thee with Gold supply'd,   110
Peter and *Charters* had been deify'd.
But ev'ry Lord, each gen'rous Friend implore,
And by Subscriptions meanly swell thy Store.
When to the Town by sordid Int'rest led,

---

[13] 'An obsolete form of "mew", meaning "moult"' (*OED*). The crows of this elegant little figure here 'moult' something other than feathers.

[14] William Benson, in Book III of *The Dunciad Variorum* is made 'sole Judge of Architecture'; Pope noted that Benson was George I's Surveyor of the Buildings until he reported that the House of Lords would have to be demolished - a second opinion declared the building sound (*Poems*, p. 422). In a note to Book IV of the final version of *The Dunciad*, Pope makes further reference to Benson, with this additional note: 'This man endeavoured to raise himself to Fame by erecting monuments, striking coins, setting up heads [busts], and procuring translations of Milton...' (*Poems*, p. 772).

[15] Arthur Johnston, MD (1587-1641), physician, poet and humanist (*DNB*), sufficient qualifications for inclusion in *The Dunciad*, though it is without malice towards Johnston himself. William Benson (see previous note) had a bust executed for him. He appears in Book IV alongside Benson (*Poems*, p. 772).

[16] Written in 1733 (Gay died in 1732 and was buried in Westminster Abbey). 'Wretched' is scarcely deserved (*Poems*, p. 818).

[17] Peter the Great (1672-1725), perhaps, and Francis Charteris (see John Arbuthnot's Epitaph, in the present volume). Their function here is that of villains or bogeymen: there is no limit to Pope's wickedness!

Mump[18] for a dinner, flatter for a Bed.
Then to thy Grot retire, indulge thy Spite,
And rail at those who for Subsistence write.
Summon thy Rage, invoke thy scurril Muse
With keenest Malice *Addison*[19] abuse.
Sculking, the Scandal privately disperse,   120
Then own in Prose the Baseness of thy Verse.

So e're *Arachne*[20] to her Cell repairs,
Insidiously she weaves her glewy Snares.
Sullen, she meditates on Deaths to come,
And meliorates the Poison in her Womb.
Should hapless *Clarion* thither take his Flight,
He falls her Prey, mindful of antient Spite.

With Malice swoll'n, Pride, Envy, Avarice,
Ingratitude attends this Train to Vice.
Yet one remains untold; with Lust endu'd,   130
Behold the Fribler[21] lab'ring to be lewd.
Kind *Cibber* interpos'd, forbad the Banns,
He'd peopled else this Isle with *Calibans*.

---

[18] ,To beg, to play the parasite, to 'sponge' on others, (*OED*).

[19] 'He writ a vile Lampoon on Mr. *Addison*, and then in a Preface owns, he deserves Respect from every Lover of Learning' (author's note). The 'vile lampoon' was (presumably) 'Atticus', written in 1715 and published, piratically, in 1722. It ends thus:
   Like Cato, gives his little Senate Laws,
   And sits attentive to his own Applause;
   While Fops and Templars ev'ry Sentence raise,
   And wonder with a foolish Face of Praise:
   What Pity, Heav'n! if such a Man there be?
   Who would not weep, if Addison were he? (*Poems*, p. 294)

[20] Arachne was a skilled weaver who had the temerity to challenge the goddess Athene (who considered herself without equal with needle and spindle) to a competition. Faced with defeat, Athene turned Arachne into a spider, condemned to spin eternally (*Larousse Encyclopaedia of Mythology*, Hamlyn, 1974).

[21] Fribbler - 'one who acts aimlessly or feebly, who busies himself to no purpose; a trifler' (*OED*). The reference here, and in the following line, is to the notorious incident (*alleged* incident, one has to say!) related by Cibber in his *Letter from Mr. Cibber to Mr. Pope* (see Introduction and *Sawney and Colley*, in this volume). Pope did not deny the visit to the brothel, but he did deny the rest of the story.

The noble *Timon*,[22] in thy waspish Strains,
A Proof of thy Ingratitude remains.
Courteous to all, munificent, humane,
Subject of others Praise, to thee of Pain.
Exalted far above thy groveling State,
The Object of his Pity, not his Hate.
He smiles at Scandal so unjustly thrown,   140
And at thy Malice he disdains to frown.

Thus oft we see a currish, Mungrel Crew,
A stately Mastiff eagerly pursue.
They swarm around, they yelp, they snarl, they grin,
Bold in Appearance, timerous within:
With such mean Foes he deigns not to engage,
But lifts his Leg, and pisses out their Rage.

How dar'st thou, Peasant, give thy Pen this Loose?
Becomes it thee thus madly to traduce?
The Great, the Low, the Virtuous, and the Base,
Alike are grown thy Subject of Disgrace.   150
Safe in thy Weakness, thou defi'est a Foe;
E'en *Cibber's* Cudgel[23] scorn'd to stoop so low.
The Mercy of the Law restrains thy Fears;
Coventry's Act[24] secures thy Nose and Ears.
Yet there remains, to fill thy Soul with Care,
A Blanket to curvet thee in the Air.

---

[22] In Epistle IV of his *Moral Essays* 'Of the Use of Riches', Pope attacked the extravagant bad taste of 'Timon's Villa' (*Poems*, p. 592). Although Timon was nobody in particular, it suited Pope's enemies to give him an identity (a former friend of Pope's), and so be able to accuse Pope of ingratitude towards an aristocratic patron. (See also *Sawney and Colley*, n. 29.)

[23] Colley Cibber, in his *Letter*, did not exploit Pope's physical deformity; he is applauded, here, for a restraint not shown by the author of *The Blatant-Beast*.

[24] The Coventry Act outlawed maiming, making it a capital offence. It was so named after Sir John Coventry, MP for Weymouth, who asked a question in the Commons in 1670 about Charles II's love-life. This was not much to the liking of the King's party; returning to his lodgings one night, Coventry was dragged from his coach and his nose slit to the bone.

O wretched Life consum'd in restless Pains,
Where Dread of Punishment incessant reigns!
Poor Self-Tormentor! in whose gloomy Breast
The Vulture dwells, inhospitable Guest.   160
Be to my Foe no greater Curse assign'd!
Than a malignant Heart and envious Mind.

Thrice happy he ! that's with Good Nature blest,[25]
Love of his Species rules his tender Breast;
Nor there confin'd: The Brute Creation share
His kind Beneficence and gen'rous Care.
No base malicious Thoughts his Peace annoy:
Are others happy? he partakes their Joy.
Chearful and innocent the Day he spends,
And Silver Sleep his quiet Nights attends.   170

But thou, a Stranger to this Peace of Mind,
Search where thou may'st conspicuous Merit find:
There strive to blacken with thy utmost Art,
And rail the more, the greater the Desert.

Is there a Man, an Honour to the Age,
Unsully'd by the keenest Party-rage;
By Vice untainted; who, from early Youth,
Firmly adher'd to Honour, Justice, Truth;
Whom no unruly Passions e're cou'd blind?
Nor ruffle his Serenity of Mind;   180
His Country's Good, the Patriot's noblest view,
Unbrib'd, unaw'd, does stedfastly pursue;
Polite in Manners, and rever'd his Sense,

---

[25] There's a delightfully unintended irony in the pious celebration of him 'that's with Good Nature blest', guided by principles of kindness, benevolence and 'gen'rous Care', whose day is 'chearful and innocent', and whose nights are blessed with 'Silver Sleep'. All this in *The Blatant-Beast*!

And long in Senates fam'd for Eloquence;
But if to these Endowments of the Mind,
A graceful Figure happily is join'd,
Then flows thy Gall, then raves thy half-form'd Clay,
Then frets thy putrid Carcass to Decay.
   So when the croaking Toad[26] the Ox beheld,
His envious Heart with Indignation swell'd.   190
Vainly the Reptil thought he could extend
His bloated Form, and Nature's Error mend.
He drew his Breath; he swell'd — he burst; he dy'd
A Victim to his Arrogance and Pride.

FINIS.

---

[26] Pope is first a 'mishapen Lump' and finally a 'croaking Toad'.

SAWNEY and COLLEY-
A Poetical DIALOGUE[1]

ONE Morning, in his *Twickenham Grott*,
As Little SAWNEY[2] sat a-squat;
His throbbing Head on Palm reclin'd,
And Rancour brooding in his Mind,
Unknowing whom to blacken next,
So thread-bare he had worn his Text;
Had stung so oft, his Sting was gone,
And now commenc'd a harmless Drone:
When strait dire Sounds his Heart appall'd,
Whilst thus a Villain-Hawker bawl'd   10
Here's a New-Letter, *Cibber's* Letter![3]

---

[1] *Sawney and Colley* is another of the many writings spawned by *The Dunciad*. It remains anonymous. (The version used here is reproduced more or less faithfully from the facsimile published in 1960 by the Augustan Reprint Society, University of California, Los Angeles: part of the fun of the piece is its eccentric spelling and even more idiosyncratic use of type-faces. The 'Dialogue' of the poem takes place between Colley Cibber (actor-manager, playwright and - ultimately - poet-laureate) and Sawney (one of Pope's nicknames). Whilst the 'Dialogue' makes mock of Cibber's self-importance, acting ability and so on, Pope is chiefly the target of the piece, iwhich gives 'Colley' the lion's share of the sharp ripostes, the best lines in insult and invective. Pope is, for the most part, in the pillory - a not unfamiliar position.

[2] The name is derived from Sawney Dapper, a character in Charles Gildon's *New Rehearsal* (Curll refers us to this explanation in *The Curliad*, published by himself, of course, in 1729). James Ralph also used the name in his *Sawney, An Heroic Poem occasion'd by the Dunciad* (1728). See Introduction. 'Sawney' is also colloquial for a fool, a simpleton (*OED*).

[3] *A Letter from Mr. Cibber to Mr. Pope* (1742) helps date this piece to more or less the same date, as the references to it in *Sawney and Colley* are evidently to a recent, highly significant

To *Pope:* Hark! fly, and bring *it, Setter!*
Quoth SAWNEY. Quick he run it o'er,
As Spendthrifts do their long-stood Score;
Dreading to see the whole Amount,
Well knowing they can ne'er account.
But when to the TOM-TIT[4] he came,
An instant Tempest shook his Frame;
Cold Horrors thrill'd through ev'ry Vein,
Rage rent his fretful Soul in twain;   20
His *aking* Head began to swim,
A Numbness crept o'er ev'ry Limb;
His trembling Fingers dropt the Pen,
Nay, he be-paw'd himself - and then
Wiping, in fierce tho' sh---ten Mien,
With COLLEY'S Sheets, his *Bumkin* clean,
He Silence burst - O! To my Shame,
Thou hast not lost thy cruel Aim!
This is the very *Knell* - Damnation!
Of my departed Reputation.   30
'Sdeath, that TOM-TIT! 'twill never down -
My Chariot, *John* - drive on to Town:
Oh, I'll that babbling Villain rattle!
Drive quick, I say, - what crawling Cattle!
Not COLLEY's *Pegasus*[5] is duller -
I might as well have took a *Skuller.*
At length he light at COLLEY'S Door,
And rapp'd for Entrance - but, before,
Lugg'd out, and shook his *pigmy Oar.*

---

publishing event. Cibber's *Letter* is the actor-laureate's response to what he saw (with some justice) as persecution by Pope. For a full and true account of this unseemly (and therefore fascinating) little brawl, see Introduction.

[4] In his account, in his *Letter,* of Pope's supposed encounter with a prostitute, Cibber describes Pope as 'like a terrible Tom Tit, pertly perching upon the Mount of Love' (see previous note and Introduction).

[5] Pegasus was the winged horse of Greek myth, favourite of the Muses. One of his owners attempted to fly to heaven on Pegasus's back and was punished for his temerity.

COLLEY sat snug in Elbow-Chair,   40
Wrapt round with philosophic Air;
Gnawing his Thumbs, in room of *Thinking*,
And his salubrious Scarb'rough drinking;
Before him much Waste-Paper lay,
Embrioes of many an unborn *Play;*
Doom'd never to behold the Light,
Secure to die on the first Night;
For why, the *Yahooes* of the Pit
Would always *piss* out COLLEY's Wit:
To save it from which gross Abuse,   50
He turn'd it to a fitter Use;
A daily Sacrifice, supine,
At *Cloacina's*[6] candid Shrine.

On his Right-hand stood *dutious THE*,[7]
He stood, ye Gods! with half-bent Knee;
"For Heav'ns sake! *Dad,* a Piece or two":
- No, *stap my vitals*, if I do.
On t'other side was Daughter CHARK[8]
In Day-light breech'd a bullying Spark,
But a mere *Female* in the Dark.   60
G-d d—n my Liver! cry'd She-He,
Down, Father, with your Dust, d'ye see;
I must have *Rhino,*[9] *by the D-v-l,*

---

[6] Cloacina - the goddess of the cloaca (sewer). The anonymous author of *Sawney and Colley* may well have borrowed the fair Cloacina from *The Dunciad*, where she presides over Jove's privy offices (see Book II, 93 ff.).

[7] Theophilus Cibber(1703-58), described by the author as 'a Son of Colley's remarkable for his extreme Sanctity of Morals, and singular Modesty of Behaviour'. In view of The's notorious private life (much exposed in the courts), I think we have to read this note with caution, not to say a little irony.

[8] The anonymous footnote attached to Cibber's daughter is worth including in full: 'A widowed Daughter of the same great Personage, celebrated for her Performances in the *Hay-Market Theatre,* where, in the Farce of *Pasquin,* the *Historical Register,* &c she played off her Father and Brother with surprising Humour to the high Recreation of many Audiences: and has since chose to communicate herself to the Publick by Day-light in Men's Cloaths. The *Part* she is said to excel in at present, is that of crying *Black-Puddings, Sheep's Trotters*, &c'.

[9] Slang for money. Even the *OED* has no explanation of the word's origin.

So, 'Sblood! You may as well be civil.

    Um - Children, cries the Sire serene,
No Parent e'er could better mean;
To wish you well I'm always willing,
But, *split me!* if I give a Shilling.
Hark! somebody be-pounds the Door,
It must be or a Lord, or *Whore:*   70
Which e'er it is, I'd be *alone,*
So, my dear Children! pray be gone.
They went - P--E enter'd - COLLEY rose
And, plying with *Rappee*[10] *his* Nose
- Hah, old Acquaintance, this is kind!
Come, there's no Enmity I find;
True Gladiators ne'er complain,
Since he that's *cut* shares half the Gain.
Not Boxers, tho they *weep* at Nose,
Shed Tears, when Silver salves the Blows: 80
So, Thee and I may make a Pother,
And closely press, in *Print,* each other;
The more we rail, the more bespatter,
'Twill make our *Pamphlets* sell the better;
Write *Satire,* then, for Daily-bread;
By G—d, you'll not by *Prayer* be fed.
Do you *Dunce* me, I'll *Tom-Tit you*—[11]
    SAW: Heavens! Villain! what dost say thou'lt do?
Dare but to mutter that again,
I swear by *Stix,* or worse my *Pen,*   90
The keenest Vengeance thou shalt feel—
    COL: Ah, SAWNEY, I am ribb'd with Steel:

---

[10] 'A coarse kind of snuff made form the darker and ranker tobacco leaves, and originally obtained by rasping a piece of tobacco' (*OED*).

[11] Cibber evidently thinks he and Pope can achieve a comfortable, mutually-beneficial commercial relationship. Our Grub-Street poet, moreover, appears to approve of the deal 'Colley' offers.

COLLEY'S impenetrable still!
SAW: Tis well, you'll see me draw my *Quill*.
COL: Oh! Sir, I've seen your *Quill* before,
So did your *Lord,* and eke your *Whore*;
But 'twas so *very, very small,*
I trust it holds but little Gall.
SAW: On that String yet,— d'ye know me, Elf?
COL: . Um - better than you know yourself.   100
I know you first, Sir, by your *Make*—
Dear SAWNEY, don't my Words Mistake,
A Hillock on the Breast or *Back,*
Admits, I own, of no Attack;
Unless, when hung out as a *Blind*
To hide within a *hump-back'd* Mind.[12]

I know Thee, next, a *Waspish* Thing,
Whose Bus'ness is to buzz and sting;
Replete with Malice, Spleen, and Spite,
I know that thou can'st *Libels* write;   110
From sacred Throne to Stage profane
Each spotless Character can'st stain.
But thus *thy Satire's* guiltless grown,
Who slanders all Men, slanders *none*;
As impotent in *Spite* as *Love,*[13]
Contempt alone by each you move.
 Tho' lives a *Traytor* in the Land,
He claims thy *Panegyric* Hand:
Plac'd on a Column of thy Verse,
Aloft he stands, and shews his A—se: 120
For why, *so God-like is* his Mein,

---

[12] It has taken 107 lines, but here it is - the deformity which Pope's enemies, almost without exception, exploit.
[13] Also a regular line of attack - Pope's supposed impotence. Cp. Lady Mary Wortley Montagu, in *Verses address'd to the Imitator of the First Satire...of Horace* (q.v.): 'No more for loving made, than to be lov'd'.

His *Back-parts* only must be seen.
SAW: Thou mottley Piece of Knave and Ass!
With Brain of Lead, and Front of Brass;
In *Villany* and *Foppery* learn'd,[14]
By which alone thy Bread is earn'd;
Thou, who by *fath'ring* others Sense,
Would'st cover thy own *Impotence*;
Who call'st the *Careless Husband*[15] thine,
Tho' great A—LL wrote ev'ry Line;   130
And *Love's last Shift* dost vainly own,
When well, by thee and me, 'tis known,
That modest R—R s, (COLLEY: Hey!)[16]
Who *wrote* the *Prologue,* wrote the *Play.*
Dar'st thou, low pilf'ring Villain — COL: hold,
What, pilfer all, my dear *Cock-Scold*!
SAW: O! no, I'll give the *De'il* his Due —
Love in a Riddle sprung from you;
Caesar a *Gypsie* too you made,
And barb'rously *Tartuff* betray'd;   140
The harmless *Cid* to Hell translated,
And good *King John* annihilated.[17]
The *Natal* and the *New Year's* Lay,
That *sings* the *Man* and *sings* the *Day,*

---

[14] 'Alluding to the two principal Characters wherein COLLEY excell'd on the Stage, those of a *Fop* and a *Villain* ' (anonymous footnote).

[15] Pope is here given the assertion that *The Careless Husband* - Cibber's chief claim to fame - was the work of some illustrious other (the only name in currency at the time that fits the clue given is William Arnall, one of Pope's dunces, who demonstrates his capacity for legal dirt-digging in Book II of *The Dunciad* (q.v.). Cibber himself writes lovingly of the 'favourable reception this comedy met with from the publick' (in *An Apology for his Life*, 1739, reprinted by Everyman, 1938). Even *Love's Last Shift* is here attributed to the friend who wrote the Prologue.

[16] This interjection is not made wholly clear in the original - I have attempted to punctuate the text so as to reveal that 'Sawney''s voice continues through the indignant 'Hey!' from 'Colley'.

[17] '*Love in a Riddle*, a Pastoral Opera; *Caesar in Egypt*, a Tragedy; the *Nonjuror*, a Comedy, taken principally from the *Tartuff* of Molière; and the *Heroick Daughter*, a Tragedy, translated from Racine's *Cid*, were all of Colley's Production, and all, save the *Nonjuror*, damn'd by the Town' (anonymous author's note). Cibber's production of *King John* was withdrawn to avoid similar treatment. *The Nonjuror*, says Pope, in a note to Book I of *The Dunciad*, is 'A Comedy threshed out of Molière's Tartuffe' (*Poems*, p. 732)

All the sublime and tuneful *Odes,*
Which reach our *Caesar*'s blest Abodes,
Are, as 'tis known to all the Land,
The *Cunning* of thy *own* Right-hand;
And dost thou, *Laureat-Dunce,*[18] pretend—
COL: Dear SAWNEY, let me make an End;   150
A little longer silent sit,
I han't quite done *your* Picture yet:
SAW: Thine's Sign-post Dawbing - COL: 'Faith, that's true,
It would not else resemble you.

But, to proceed — you next apply
Your Mind to Heathnish *'Losophy:*[19]
You, and your *God-A'mighty,* club
Your uncreating Pates, and dub
Poor mortal MAN *a Thing of Nought,*
Just what the *pamper'd Gander*[20] thought,   160
And bravely prove, in *Reason's Spite,*
That Right *is wrong,* and Wrong is right;
That the same Things both good and *evil,*
And pound together *God* and *Devil.*
Then *Women* felt your righteous Fury,
Hung all at once without a Jury;
And pierc'd with more *hard Words,* than P-GE[21]

---

[18] Cibber was elevated to poet-laureate in 1730.

[19] 'Colley' has Pope's *Essay on Man* in his sights here. The lines that follow make particular reference to Pope's thoroughly orthodox philosophical poem, which scarcely renders 'Poor mortal man a Thing of Nought'. When Pope declares 'Presumptuous Man! the reason wouldst thou find,/Why form'd so weak, so little, and so blind!' (*Poems*, p. 505), he is expressing no more than received opinion.

[20] There are no ganders, pamper'd or otherwise, in the *Essay on Man*. Nor does Pope suggest that Man is 'a dull or stupid person, a fool, a simpleton' (*OED*, figurative definition of 'Gander').

[21] A judge noted for his ferocity. Pope includes him in Book IV of *The Dunciad*, with this note: 'There was a Judge of this name, always ready to hang any man, of which he was suffered to give a hundred miserable examples during a long life, even to his dotage' (*Poems*, p.768, 1.30). There is another reference to Page in Pope's *Imitations of Horace*:

Slander or Poyson, dread from Delia's Rage,
Hard words or hanging, if your Judge be Page (*Poems*, p. 616, ll. 81-2).

E'er gave to Felons in his Rage:
For, *ev'ry Woman*, you are sure,
Is, in her *Heart*, a *very Whore*.²² 170

Troth, TIT-TE, I'll allow this much,
You ne'er knew *Woman* but was *such*;
For who, except a venal *Punkey*,
That car'd not whether Man or *Monkey*,
But set to Sale her *Titillation*,
For Bread, not carnal Recreation,
Would suffer Thee, *small* Friend, to come
Within ten Foot of her *Fore-bum*?

But, SAWNEY, if thy Maxim's true!
Let's see how well 'twill sit on you: 180
What think'st thou, then, of thy own *Mammy*,²³
'Bout whom thou talk'st, and talk'st so? -- Damn ye?
She had the *like at Heart*, no doubt;
If so, '*Gad, split me*! it would out;
No Woman ever wish'd *that same*,
But got, by Hook or Crook, her Aim:
So, SAWNEY, Thou'rt, perhaps, the Spawn,
Not of thy good Old *Name-sake* gone
But of some *Serpent*-JESUIT,
Or other petulant TOM-TIT. 190

SAW: Villain! profane my Mother's Name!
Hark, Sir, but touch her spotless Fame,

---

²² Our anonymous author refers us at this point to Pope's *Moral Essays*, in particular 'Of the Characters of Women'. Not even the severest of feminist critics would put such a reading on the poem.

²³ The footnote here is too good to miss: '*Vide* his *Letters*...where he is perpetually TRUMPETTING forth his *filial piety* to his *Mamma*, and the many Virtues and Excellencies of that good old Lady, whilst at the same Time he runs riot on all the rest of her Sex...for which no apter Punishment, we deem, could be inflicted, than that he should have his *Bumkin* scourged to the Bone, by a Committee of MATRONS chosen for that Purpose.'

Thou'lt find a *Trigger* I can draw—
COL: No Wrath, my *tiny Man of Straw*:
I've of your Mother said no more,
Than you had said of *mine* before.

And wherefore, Child, this Cruelty
On all the Sex? -- Um -- I guess why.
SAWNEY, I know thy *ruling Passion*
Is *Love of Women;* but the Fashion   200
Of that *warpt* Carcase, and sad Grace
Which hangs upon thy *Wezel* Face,
Could only cold Contempt procure,
And 'gainst thee barr'd the *fringed* Door:
Hence all thy Libels on the *Fair*,
Born not of *Hatred but Despair*;
So *spiteful Imps* the Heav'n prophane,
Which they can never hope to gain.
SAW: For that, Sir, I'll appeal to B— [24]
COL: . C—'s dumb, or I'd be judg'd d by C -   210
In whose good Graces thou hast ne'er been,
Since that *drole* Hour I caught thee therein,
And by the *Heels* my Hero pluck --[25]
Hiatus Magnus..
....

Ye mortified Mortals all,
Who since have ru'd the poisonous Gall,
Distill'd from his Satyric Pen,
Forgive my saving of him *then*:
I meant it well for HOMER's Sake,   220
But oft lament my dire mistake.

---

[24] Martha Blount, Pope's close friend, to whom Epistle II of the *Moral Essays* 'Of the Characters of Women' was addressed. The identity of 'C - ', in the next line is probably to be derived from the rhyme in this couplet.

[25] The gap-in-the-manuscript joke may be a way of emphasising the (continuing) indelicacy of the anecdote (see note 4, above, on 'Cibber's Letter'), and the manner of its expression.

Could HOMER from Elysium steal
O! how he'd curse both Hands and Heel.
Much Thanks to *France*, but *none* to *Greece*,
A patch'd, vamp'd, old, reviv'd new Piece.
Translation from DACIER's *Translation*,
A HOMER of his *own* Creation
Is SAWNEY's Version — SAW: Stroler,[26] how!
My HOMER all Men will allow —
COL: Yes, that 'tis Metre on *all-four*,   230
A purling Riv'let void of Oar;[27]
Not the strong Stream the *Grecian flows*,
Whose Depth with Golden Bullion glows:
In short, poor HOMER, in thy Wit,
Is dwindled to a mere TOM-TIT.
SAW: Buffoon!—COL: Ay—yet I would not change
My Mirth for thy corroding Mange.[28]
I laugh, am laugh'd at, Sir, 'tis true;
You curse all Men, and *all Men* you.
   Remember, Child, remember TASTE![29]   240

---

[26] As in 'strolling player'.

[27] Obsolete form of 'ore'.

[28] 'A cutaneous disease analogous to the itch in man, occurring among many hairy and woolly animals....Also, sometimes loosely, a dirty, scabby or scurfy condition of the skin' (OED), or, in this case, the mind. Lowering the tone somewhat?

[29] Epistle IV of Pope's *Moral Essays* ('To Lord Burlington'), is a homily on 'the use of riches', and 'taste'. Pope starts the Argument to the poem thus: 'Of the Use of Riches. The Vanity of Expence in People of Wealth and Quality. The abuse of the word Taste....That the first principle and foundation, in this, as in everything else, is Good Sense' (*Poems*, p. 586). 'Colley"s diatribe in the next few lines is based on the false assumption that Pope has a particular target in view, rather than aristocratic misuse of wealth, in his excoriation of bad taste. The following is a sample of what 'Colley' doubtless had in mind:
   At Timon's Villa let us pass the day,
   Where all cry out, 'What sums are thrown away!'
   So proud, so grand, of that stupendous air,
   Soft and Agreeable come never there.
   Greatness, with Timon, dwells in such a draught
   As brings all Brobdignag before your thought.
   To compass this, his building is a Town,
   His pond an Ocean, his parterre a Down....
   But hark! the chiming Clocks to dinner call;
   A hundred footsteps scrape the marble Hall;

There mark thy best good Friend disgrac'd:
He, at whose Table thou wer't fed,
Lampoon'd for *filling Thee with Bread;*
He, who was ne'er *thy* friend design'd
Because he's one to *all Mankind.*
  SAW: I, Sycophant! call no Man *Friend*
For any *mercenary* End;
Nor own one such whom Folly stains,
However great might be the Gains.
Fair Virtue, and her Friend are mine,[30]   250
  COL: Yes -- *virtuous* B--L--B--KE[31] is thine:
He, SAWNEY, just as much as you,
Abhors the Thoughts of *private* View;
Inspired with a diviner Flame,
The *Publick* is his godlike Aim,
Whose Welfare he had still at Heart
For whom he acted *many* a Part,
Was *In* was *Out,* did and *undid,*
And brought *to light* the Things were *hid;*
Conducted *War* as none *durst* do,   260
And made *amazing* Treaties too.
Then, as he held all K---s were *Curses,*
Instead of their dear Country's *Nurses,*
Whenever call'd into their *Aid,*
He surely *each* of them *betray'd.*[32]
  Such are thy Friends, their Virtues *such —*

    The rich Buffet well-colour'd Serpents grace,
    And gaping Tritons spew to wash your face (*Poems*, pp. 592-3).

[30] 'TO VIRTUE ONLY AND HER FRIENDS, A FRIEND' - Pope's reference to himself in *The First Satire of the Second Book of Horace Imitated* (*Poems*, p. 615). The capitals are Pope's.

[31] Henry St John, First Viscount Bolingbroke (1678-1751), so created by Queen Anne in 1712, and one of the foremost of her ministers in the last administration of her reign. He was friend to both Swift and Pope. One of his notable achievements, referred to (sarcastically) in line 261, was the negotiation of the Treaty of Utrecht with the French in 1713.

[32] When Queen Anne died in 1714, Bolingbroke fled to France, accused of treasonous correspondence with the Pretender, James Stewart, a charge Bolingbroke gave credence to by becoming, for a time, the Pretender's secretary of state (*DNB*).

SAW: Blasphemer! how, my *Idol* touch!
I'll tell thee, Knave! 'tis Slander all,
A *Stygian* Picture drawn in Gall.
That *Genius* is all-wise, all-good,   270
Sprung, sure, from *more* than mortal Blood,
Thrice better than the best of Men ---
COL: Why, so are *you*, believe your Pen;
But, mark your *Actions* and your *Heart*,
You should be flogg'd at Vice's Cart.
What! no one *mercenary* View!
Has MACKBETH *murder'd Mem'ry* too,[33]
As you did *Shakespear*? O, for Shame!
To TONSON[34] *Hackney out* your Name!
As Beggars to a *barren* Friend,   280
For sake of *Snacks*, their *Bantlings* lend!
Promote an infamous *Deception*,
Meanly to *steal* a vast *Subscription:*
Then give us nothing for the same,
Save, in the Title, *your sweet Name*![35]
Tho' this is small to what you can,
TONSON'S *an honourable Man*!
But with the *Wizard*, C--L,[36] to *juggle*,
And, *Hocus Pocus*, help him *smuggle*
Thy *Correspondence* with thy Betters,   290
Theirs, extemp're, Thine studied LETTERS,

---

[33] 'It is said in SHAKESPEAR's *Mackbeth*, - Mackbeth has *murder'd Sleep.*' The note continues with a slighting reference to Pope's own edition of Shakespeare, published in 1725.
[34] One of Pope's publishers, responsible for his edition of the plays.
[35] The insinuation is that Pope did little more with his Shakespeare than have his name added to the title-page.
[36] Inevitably, Edmund Curll gets a mention: 'Wizard' is not inappropriate. In the next few lines, it is suggested, not altogether unfairly, that, having first obtained the return of his letters to his various correspondents, Pope carefully polished them prior to publication. Further, as lines 289-290 claim, Pope was not above slipping Curll (anonymously) copies of his letters to and from his aristocratic correspondents. After publication, Pope could then, with a moral flourish, publish a 'more correct edition' of the said letters, without incurring the opprobrium of having breached any confidences or House of Lords' privilege.

Cloath'd in a stiff, pedantic Dress,
Each Line corrected for the Press;
Intending thus to let us see
They're but, at best, a *Foil* to *Thee*!
Fye, SAWNEY, fye! -- but that's not all,
In Publick 'gainst the Deed you bawl;
You C---L, and C---L you Villain, call.
So *Lawyers*, lea-gu'd *to fleece* a Freehold,
Be-Rogue each other *thick* and *threefold*:   300
Nay, more, to rivet the Deceit,
Thy *Lord* must consecrate the Cheat;
An insult on the House of *P—rs*,
For which you ought to've *lost your Ears*, [37]
Then thou and C — L, A'kin by Trade,
Had been par *nob'le Fratrum* made.
SAW: 'Sdeath! Sir, d'ye couple C--L with me?
COL: Odso, your Pardon -- let me see --
Oh, no, Friend C — L, I wrong you there,
You vow you never lost *an Ear;*   310
And tho' oft pillory'd, hast still,
Both your *Auriculars* at will.

Thus, 'Squire, I've pointed out a few
Of those rare Virtues which *indue*
Your dear-beloved Friends and you,
And many an Instance more could lug in,
Which you imagin'd to lie snug in.
You clubb'd in that damn'd *Farce* Obscene,[38]

---

[37] Libel was still punishable in this way, in addition to a spell in the pillory. Thus (metaphorically, in this case), 'Earless on high stood unabash'd De Foe', as Pope has it (see *The Dunciad*, Book II, l.147). Defoe's ears survived intact, as did Pope's, to the evident displeasure of the anonymous writer of *Sawney and Colley*.

[38] 'A Play, called *Three Hours after Marriage*, abounding with *Ribaldry* and *Obscenity*, written by SAWNEY in Conjunction with some of his friends [Gay and Arbuthnot, in 1717], and damn'd by the Town; in which were introduced two Lovers in the Shape of a *Crocodile* and a *Mummy*' (author's note). Far from being 'damn'd', the play was given seven consecutive performances, to

Which first 'gainst COLLEY whet your Spleen,
　　　And, for the Joke, still daily hum-me　　　　　320
　　　On Messieurs *Crocodile* and *Mummy*.
　　　'Twas you made DAVID[39] talk low *Smut*,
　　　And sober HORACE[40] sent to *rut*.
　　　　Now fairly view this Portrait, Elf!
　　　And swear, if can'st, 'tis not Thyself.
　　　Then, prithee, why still more severe
　　　On Vices to thyself most dear?
　　　SAWNEY, repent thee of this Evil --
　　　SAW: 'Sblews, learn Repentance from the Dev--l!
　　　'Thou Owl, Bat, Vultur, Dragon, Boar,　　　　　330
　　　Both Son and Father of a Whore!

---

large houses, by the Drury Lane company in January, 1717. This record compares favourably with that of other plays produced that season, none of which had more than six consecutive performances (though some had a few more performances in total). A more likely reason for the play being dropped, was the realisation by Cibber - actor and manager at Drury Lane - that he had been used as a satirical butt. Cibber played the central role of Plotwell (who, in the farcical climax of the play, is disguised as a Mummy confronting a crocodile). (For a detailed account of the skulduggery and chicanery that attended this production, see George Sherburn, 'The Fortunes and Misfortunes of *Three Hours After Marriage*', in *Modern Philology*, Vol. 24, 1926, pp. 91-109.)

[39] 'Alluding to an infamous, obscene Parody on the *first Psalm*, affirmed to be written by the *pious* SAWNEY' (author's note). This is 'A Roman Catholick Version of the First Psalm', written by Pope in 1716, and published, piratically, the same year (*Poems*, p. 300). It was perhaps the last two stanzas that were found so objectionable, with their reference to 'whores' and one of their haunts, Drury Lane:

　　No wicked Whores shall have such Luck
　　　Who follow their own Wills,
　　But Purg'd shall be to Skin and Bone,
　　　With *Mercury* and *Pills*.

　　For why? the Pure and Cleanly Maids
　　　Shall All, good Husbands gain:
　　But filthy and uncleanly Jades
　　　Shall Rot in *Drury-Lane*.

[40] This time it is Pope's *Sober Advice from Horace, to the Young Gentlemen about Town* (written c. 1734, published 1734, *Poems*, pp. 667-673), to which our poet takes exception. The poem is, perhaps, a little worldly-wise in sexual matters; the urbane narrator advises his 'gentlemen'-readers to beware the deceptive female exterior:

　　Could you directly to her Person go,
　　Stays will obstruct above, and Hoops below,
　　And if the Dame says yes, the Dress says no.
　　Not thus at N[ee]dh[a]m's [notorious brothel]; your judicious Eye
　　May measure there the Breast, the Hip, the Thigh!
　　And will you run to Perils, Sword and Law,
　　All for a thing you ne'er so much as *saw*?

Sawney and Colley

    Rage! Vengeance!— O! — I can no more -
-- Here SAWNEY sunk into the Chair,
When COLLEY, judging to a Hair,
Perceiving that he did not winch,[41]
(But first he took a sober *Pinch*)
Some *Assa-foetida* minister'd,
By Vulgar Quacks y'clipt, *White Dog's T---d.*
Then, *Teague-like*, laid him on his Back,
And dosing him with GEOR---'s *Sack*,   340
It made him *puke,* and brought him back:

    Struck, by his strong Convulsions, weak,
Long SAWNEY *yawn'd, but could not speak.*
At length he sputters, foams, and stares,
And, crawling, as he could, down Stairs,
To COLLEY, speechless, left the Field,
In Par'lous Wrath to *Twit' nam* wheel'd,
And, f--rti--g all the Way he went,
Ten thousand Curses *backward* sent.

---

[41] Recoil, flinch, wince.

Bibliography

Aitken, G. *The Life and Works of John Arbuthnot* (Russell and Russell, 1892)
Anon *A Compleat Collection of all the Verses, Essays, Letters and Advertisements Which Have been occasioned by the Publication of Three Volumes of Miscellanies by Pope and Company* (London, 1728)
Anon *Sawney and Colley - A Poetical Dialogue* (1742) (Augustan Reprint Society, No 83, 1960)
Anon *The Blatant-Beast* (1742) (Augustan Reprint Society, No 114, 1965)
Arbuthnot, J. (et al) *The Memoirs of the Extraordinary Life, Works, and Discoveries of Martinus Scriblerus*, ed. C. Kerby-Miller (Oxford University Press, 1988)
Arbuthnot, J. *An Epitaph* [on Francis Charteris, 1732] in *The Poems of Alexander Pope*, ed. John Butt, Methuen, 1965, reprinted Routledge and Kegan Paul, 1992)
The History of John Bull, Or Law is a Bottomless Pit, eds A. W. Bower, and R. A. Erickson (Oxford, 1976)
The Life and Works of John Arbuthnot, ed. G. Aitken (Russell and Russell, 1892)
Bernard, J. (ed.) *Pope: The Critical Heritage* (Routledge and Kegan Paul, 1973)
Bolingbroke, Henry St John, First Viscount..*Correspondence During the Time He was Secretary of State to Queen Anne*, ed. G. Parke (London, 1798)
Boswell, J. *Life of Johnson*, ed. G. Birkbeck Hill, rev. L. F. Powell (Oxford University Press, 1953)
Boulton J. T. *Selected Writings of Daniel Defoe* (Cambridge University Press, 1965)
Boyer, A. *Annals of Queen Anne* (8 vols, London, 1710-14)
Political State of Great Britain (8 vols, London 1711-14)
Brown, T. 'The Old Fumbler'; 'The Poet's Condition'; 'Farewell to Poor England' (in*Grub Street stripped bare*, ed. P. Pinkus, Constable & Co., 1968)
Cibber, C. *A Letter From Mr. Cibber to Mr. Pope* (1742) (The Augustan Reprint Society No 158, 1973)
Odes (1731-2) in *The Gentleman's Magazine*

Colville, K. N. (ed.) *A Miscellany of the Wits*: Select Pieces By William King, John Arbuthnot, And Other Hands (Philip Allan & Co., 1920)
Curll, E. *A Compleat Key to the Dunciad* (London, 1728)
Curlicism Display'd: Or, An Appeal to the Church (London, 1718)
The Curliad. A Hypercritic Upon The Dunciad Variorum (London, 1729)
Davies, G. "The Seamy Side of Marlborough's War', *Huntingdon Library Quarterly*, xv, 1952, 21-4
Defoe, D. *The Shortest-Way with the Dissenters*, in *Selected Writings of Daniel Defoe*, ed. J. T. Boulton (Cambridge University Press, 1965)
Tour Through the Whole Island of Great Britain, 1724-6 (Everyman, 2 vols, 1962)
Dennis, J. *A True Character of Mr. Pope, and His Writings* (1716) in *The Critical Works of John Dennis*, ed. E. N. Hooker (Baltimore, 2 vols, 1939)
Remarks Upon Several Passages in the Preliminaries to the Dunciad (London, 1729)
Earle, P. *The World of Defoe* (Weidenfeld and Nicholson, 1976)
Erskine-Hill, H *Pope: The Dunciad* (Edward Arnold, 1972)
Fairer, D (ed.) *Pope: New Contexts* (Harvester Wheatsheaf, 1990)
Gay, J. (et al) *Three Hours After Marriage* (Augustan Reprint Society Nos 91-2, 1961)
Gay, J. *The Beggar's Opera*, ed. B. Loughrey and T. O. Treadwell (Harmondsworth, 1986)
George, D. M. *London Life in the Eighteenth Century* (Harmondsworth, 1966)
Glanville, P. *London in Maps* (The Connoisseur, 1972)
Hammond, B. *Pope* (Harvester New Readings, The Harvester Press, 1986)
Hammond, P. *Selected Prose of Alexander Pope* (Cambridge University Press, 1986)
Hill, B. W. *The Growth of Parliamentary Parties, 1689-1742* (London, 1976)
Holmes, G. *Politics in the Age of Anne* (London, 1967)
Johnson, S. *Lives of the Poets*, ed. G. Birkbeck Hill (3 vols, Oxford, 1905)
Lives of the Rakes, Philip Allan & Co., 6 vols, 1924-5
Maynwaring, A., Oldmixon, J. *The Medley* (London, 1710-1712)
McInnes, A. *Robert Harley* (Gollanz, 1970)
Mckeon, M. *The Origins of the English Novel, 1600-1740* (The Johns Hopkins University Press, 1987)
McMinn, J. *Jonathan Swift; A Literary Life* (Macmillan, 1991)
Milton, J. *A Ready and Easy Way to establish a Free Commonwealth* (1660), in *The Good Old Cause, The English Revolution of 1640-1660*, eds C. Hill and E. Dell (Augustus M. Kelley, rev. edn, 1969)
Montague, Lady Mary Wortley..*The Complete Letters of Lady Mary Wortley Montague*, ed. R. Halsband (3 vols, Oxford, 1965-6)
Nokes, D. *Jonathan Swift: A Hypocrite Reversed* (Oxford University Press, 1985)
Raillery and Rage; A Study of Eighteenth-Century Satire (Harvester Wheatsheaf, 1987)
Nussbaum, F., Brown, L. *The New Eighteenth Century: Theory and Politics and English Literature* (Methuen, 1987)
Oldmixon, J. *Memorials of the Press, Historical and Political, For Thirty Years past, from 1710 to 1740* (London, 1742)
Paulson, R. *Theme and Structure in Swift's Tale of a Tub* (Princeton, 1960)
Pinkus, P. *Grub Street stripped bare* (Constable & Co., 1968)

Pope, A. *The Poems of Alexander Pope* (the Twickenham edition in one volume) ed. John Butt, Methuen, 1963, reprinted by Routledge and Kegan Paul, 1992) *Selected Prose of Alexander Pope*, ed. P. Hammond (Cambridge University Press, 1986)
Prior, J. *Life of Edmund Malone...with Selections from his MSS Anecdotes* (London, 1860)
Rogers, P. *Literature and Popular Culture in Eighteenth-Century England* (The Harvester Press, 1985)
Eighteenth-Century Encounters (The Harvester Press, 1985)
Grub Street: Studies in a Subculture (Methuen & Co., Ltd, 1972)
Rogers, P. (ed.) *The Eighteenth Century* (Methuen & Co., Ltd, 1978)
Ross, A. & Woolley, D. (eds) *Swift: A Tale of a Tub and Other Satires* (Oxford University Press, 1986)
Savage, R. *An Author To be Lett* (London, 1729)
Sherburn, G. The Fortunes and Misfortunes of Three Hours After Marriage' (*Modern Philology*, vol. 24, 1926, pp. 91-109)
Smedley, J. *Gulliveriana* (London, 1728)
Straus, R. *The Unspeakable Curll* (Chapman and Hall, 1927, reprinted by Augustus M. Kelley, 1970)
Sutherland, J. *Defoe* (Longman, 1970)
Swift, J. *A Modest Proposal* (1729), in *A Tale of a Tub and Other Satires*, ed. K. Williams (Dent, 1975)
A Proposal for the Universal Use of Irish Manufacture (1720), in *Prose Writings of Jonathan Swift*, ed. H. Davis, Oxford, 1941-57)
A Tale of A Tub, eds A. Ross and D. Woolley, (World's Classics, 1986)
Correspondence of Jonathan Swift, ed. H. Williams (5 vols, Oxford, 1963-65)
Journal to Stella, ed. H. Williams (2 vols, Oxford, 1948)
Poetical Works, ed. H. Davis (Oxford, 1967)
The Drapier's Letters, ed. H. Davis (Oxford, 1935, rev. edn 1965)
The Examiner, in *Prose Writings of Jonathan Swift*, ed. H. Davis, Oxford, 1941-57)
A Proposal for Giving Badges to Beggars (1737), (*Prose Writings of Jonathan Swift*, ed. H. Davis, Oxford, 1941-57)
Gulliver's Travels (*Prose Writings of Jonathan Swift*, ed. H. Davis, Oxford, 1941-57)
Thackeray, W. *The English Humourists of the Eighteenth Century* (Smith, Elder & Co., 1858)
Thompson, E. P. *Whigs and Hunters* (Harmondsworth, rev. edn, 1977)
Thorne, J. *Handbook to the Environs of London, 1876* (reprinted by Adams and Dart, 1970)
Trevelyan, G.M. *England Under Queen Anne* (Longman, 3 vols, 1930)
Tutchin, J. (et al) *The Observator* (London, 1711)
Ward, E. *A Frolick to Horn-Fair*, (1699) (in *Grub Street stripped bare*, ed. P. Pinkus, Constable & Co., 1968)
Apollo's Maggot in his Cups:OR, The Whimsical Creation of a Little Satyrical Poet (London, 1729)
Durgen, Or, A Plain Satyr Upon a Pompous Satyrist (London, 1729)
Welsted, L. *One Epistle to Mr. Pope* (London, 1730)
Wheatley, H. B. *London, Past and Present* (John Murray, 3 vols, 1891)

Wood, N. *Swift* (Harvester New Readings, The Harvester Press, 1986)
Woodhuysen, H. R. (ed.) *Samuel Johnson on Shakespeare* (Harmondsworth, 1989)

INDEX

Addison, John 19, 124
Addison, Joseph 9, 85, 91, 124, 159, 170n, 209
Aesop 38
Amalakites, The 47
Anne, Queen of England 8, 9, 43, 45, 69n, 120, 224
Anon
   Blatant-Beast, The 203ff
   Epigram the Second 201
   Sawney and Colley - A Poetical Dialogue 209n, 213ff
Apollo's Maggot in His Cups 137ff
Arbuthnot, John 5, 9, 13, 17, 18, 174, 174
   Epitaph on Francis Charteris 197
   Law is a Bottomless Pit 69ff
   Memoirs of Martinus Scriblerus, The 95ff
Arnall, William 132
Atterbury, Francis 177
Author to be Lett, An 4
Bedlam (Bethlehem Hospital) 3, 59
Bentley, Dr Richard 128
Bentley, Thomas 128
Blackmore, Sir Richard 24, 84, 85, 87, 88, 89, 93, 130, 134
   Arthur 135
Blount, Martha 221
Bolingbroke, Henry St John, 1st Viscount 5, 8, 69, 117n, 223
Boyer, Abel 136
   Annals of Queen Anne 161

   Political State of Great Britain 161
Bridewell 155
British Journal, The 79
Broome, William
   Pope's Homer 176
Brown, Tom, 9, 94n
Browne, Sir John
   Memorial of the Poor Inhabitants of Ireland 179
Charles I, King of England 39, 40, 44
Charles II, King of England 41
Charteris, Francis 166
   Epitaph on 197
   Reputation, 198n
Church of England
   'In danger' 45
   Satirised by Defoe 38, 40
Cibber, Chark 215
Cibber, Colley 2, 22-24, 120, 206, 213ff
   Butt of *Three Hours After Marriage* 226
   Letter from Mr. Cibber to Mr. Pope, A 22, 209, 210, 214
   Ode for New Year's Day (1731) 189
   Ode for New-Year's Day (1732) 193
Cibber, Theobald 215
Compleat Key to The Dunciad, A (See Curll) 11, 13, 24
Concanen, John 24

Congreve, William 124
Coventry, John, MP for Weymouth 210
Cuckold's Point 30, 32
Curlicism 11
Curll, Edmund 7, 11-15, 19, 24, 81, 119, 122, 124, 126, 159, 160, 167, 169, 225
  Curliad, The 24, 82n
  Ebriatatis Encomium (In Praise of Drunkenness) 12
  Eunuchism Display'd. Describing all the different Sorts of Eunuchs 12
  Popiad, The 24
  Pope's emetic 11-15, 81-94
  Treatise of Flogging, The 12, 160
  Trials of Sodomy 85
  Venus in the Cloister; or, The Nun in her Smock 12-13
Curll, Henry 13
Davis, Herbert 188n
Defoe, Daniel 9 11, 19-20, 26, 35n, 53n, 125, 136, 160, 225
  Complete English Tradesman, The 41n
  Review, The 19, 20
  Shortest-Way with the Dissenters, The 19, 37ff
  Tour Through the Whole Island of Great Britain 27
Defoe, Norton 129, 136, 160
Dennis, John 20, 129, 160
Drury Lane 22
Dryden, John 170, 171
Dunton, John 125
Eridanus, River 127
Eugene of Savoy, Prince 71
Examiner, The 9, 42n, 69, 179
Fell, Dr 49n
Female Dunciad, The 24
Fleet Prison, The 104
Fleet Ditch 1, 6, 104, 131, 136
Flying Post, The 6, 9, 157
Gay, John 6, 8, 9, 13, 17, 124
  Beggar's Opera, The 6, 17, 114n, 164
  Charteris, Francis 198n
  Polly 164
  Scriblerus Club 95

Three Hours After Marriage 17, 22, 169, 173, 226
Gay, Joseph 13, 124, 163
Gentleman's Magazine, The 189, 193, 195
George I, King of England 7, 207
George II, King of England 7, 189, 207
Gildon, Charles 169, 213
Greenwich 29
Grub Street 1-26, 55, 81, 104n, 119-136, 157, 167, 169, 179, 201, 216n
Hammond, Brean 8, 21, 24, 26
Hammond, Paul 26, 81
Hanoverian Succession, The 9
Henley 160
Henri IV, King of France 56
History of John Bull, The 18, 69ff
Hockley-in-the-Hole 25, 29, 168
Horn-Fair 27, 32
James II, King of England 19, 39, 40, 41
Jervas, Charles 172
John, King of England 30
Johnson, Esther (Stella), 18, 188n
Johnson, Samuel 2
  Dictionary 4
  Edition of Shakespeare 161
  On Cibber's Odes 194
Juvenal 125
L'Estrange, Sir Roger 37
Lintot, Bernard 7, 13, 82, 87, 89, 121, 122, 123
London Evening Post, The 189
London Magazine, The 197
Louis XIV, King of France 58, 69, 70
Mandeville, Bernard De 136
Marlborough, John Churchill, 1st Duke of 18, 84, 116
  Blenheim Palace 117n
  War of the Spanish Succession 71n
Marlborough, Sarah Jennings, Duchess of 72n
Marvell, Andrew 5
McKeon, Michael 26
Medley, The 3, 6, 9

Index   235

*Memoirs of the Extraordinary Life,
   Works, and Discoveries of
   Martinus Scriblerus* 17, 95-114
Mercator, The 20
Milton, John
   Good Old Cause, The 52
Monmouth, Duke of, 19, 45
   Rebellion 41
Montague, Lady Mary Wortley 13,
   173, 175n, 198n, 217
   Court Poems 81n
Moses 48
Mother Shipton 33
Nokes, David 185n
Oates, Titus 53
Observator, The 9, 42
Occasional Conformity 19
Oldmixon, John 4, 24, 86, 131, 160
Oxford, Robert Harley, 1st Earl of 5,
   6, 8, 20
Page, Judge 220
Parnell, Thomas 17
Political State of Great Britain, The
   9
Pope, Alexander
   *A Full and True Account of a
      Horrid and Barbarous
      Revenge*...10, 81
   *A Further Account of the Most
      Deplorable Condition of Mr.
      Edmund Curll*...10, 88
   Apollo's Maggot in His Cups,
      attacked in 137ff
   Art of Sinking in Poetry, The 17,
      26
   Deformity 21, 148, 203, 217
   Dunciad Variorum, The 3, 24,
      155, 162n, 169, 207n, 208
   Dunciad, The (Book II) 119ff,
      169
   Dunciad, The 1-4, 6-8, 15-17,
      20, 24, 26, 114, 155, 157, 189,
      201, 207
   Epigram the Second, attacked in
      201
   Epistle to Dr. Arbuthnot, An 22
   Epitaph on Francis Charteris
      197n
   Essay on Criticism 21
   Essay on Man 219

   Grotto 205
   Iliad, The Translation 103
   Miscellanies 26
   Moral Essays 224, 222n
   New Dunciad, The 203
   Peri Bathous 170n, 174
   Plagiarism, accused of 170
   Rape of the Lock, The 199n
   *Roman Catholick Version of the
      First Psalm, A* 226
   Sawney and Colley, attacked in
      213ff
   Scriblerus Club 8, 9, 17, 95,
      114n, 167
   Shakespeare, Edition of 161,
      224n
   Sober Advice from Horace 225
   Temple of Fame, The 173
   Trial of Francis Atterbury 177
Popiad, The 24
Post-Boy, The 6, 9
Pretender, The 9, 179
Prior, Matthew 85, 124
Purcell, Henry 49
Raree shows 95
Rebellion of 1715 9
Regicides 41
Review, The 19, 20
Ridpath, George 125
Rogers, Pat 2, 25, 201n
Rolli, Paulo Antonio 127, 164
Roper, Abel 9, 125
Rowe, Nicholas
   Edition of Shakespeare 171
Rufus, William II, King Of England
   130
Sacheverell, Dr Henry 20, 75n, 79
Savage, Richard 3, 4
   Author To be Lett , An 157-168
   169
Sawney and Colley 21, 213ff
Scriblerus Club 8, 9, 17, 114n, 167
Scriblerus, Martin 17, 134n, 170n,
   207
Shakespeare,William
   Troilus and Cressida 51n
   Pope's edition of 161, 224n
*Shortest-Way with the Dissenters,
   The* 19, 37ff
Slave-trade 33n

Smedley, Jonathan 24, 131
  Body of Divinity 161
  Gulliveriana 79n, 160
Steele, Richard 9
Stewart Dynasty, The 16
Straus, Ralph 7n, 11n, 13n, 14n, 85n, 159n
Swift, Jonathan 4, 5, 6, 8, 9, 13, 15, 17-18, 24, 26, 124, 159, 207
  Advice to the Grub-street Verse-Writers 115ff, 206n
  Cadenus and Vanessa 176
  Conduct of the Allies, The 69, 70n
  Drapier's Letters, The 177, 179
  Examiner, The 9, 42n, 69, 179
  Gulliver's Travels 17, 104n, 114
  Journal to Stella 117n
  Modest Proposal, A 114n, 179ff
  Proposal for Giving Badges to Beggars, A 188n
  Proposal for the Universal Use of Irish Manufacture, A 184n
  Satirical Elegy on the Death of a Late famous General, A 116
  Scriblerus Club 95
  Tale of a Tub, A 15, 46n, 179
Thackeray, William 186, 188
Theobald, Lewis 20, 206
  Shakespear Restored 161
Thisbe 100
Three Hours after Marriage 17, 22, 169, 173, 226
Tonson, Jacob 83, 122, 205, 224
Treatise of Flogging, The 12, 160
Trevelyan, G.M. 30, 69n, 70n, 71n, 75n, 117n, 207
Trinity House 34
Tutchin, John 125
Venus in the Cloister; or, The Nun in her Smock 12
Walpole, Robert 6, 7, 8, 84, 160
War of the Spanish Succession 69
Ward, Ned
  Durgen 137
  in *The Dunciad* 137
  London Spy, The 137
Weekly Journal 11
Welsted, Leonard 128, 160
  In *The Dunciad* 169
  Labeo 162, 169
  One Epistle to Mr. Pope 169ff
Wenham, Jane 83
What D'Ye Call It, The 17
White's Coffee House 25, 163
William III, King of England 19
Wilmot, John, 2nd Earl of Rochester 175
Windsor-Forest, 16
Wood, William
  Coinage 177, 179